Computer Science and Technology

Computer Science and Technology

Manoj Kumar Meena
&
Shweta Meena

RANDOM

RANDOM PUBLICATIONS
NEW DELHI (INDIA)

Computer Science and Technology

ISBN 978-93-5111-398-0

Published in 2014 in India by

RANDOM PUBLICATIONS

4376-A/4B, Gali Murari Lal, Ansari Road
New Delhi-110 002
Phone : +91-11-43580356, +91-11-23289044
e-mail: randomexports@gmail.com, sales@randompublications.com, info@randompublications.com

Type Setting by : Keystoneprintads, Delhi-110051
Printed at Thomson Press (India) Ltd

Preface

Computer science is the scientific and practical approach to computation and its applications. It is the systematic study of the feasibility, structure, expression, and mechanization of the methodical processes. The history of computer development is often referred to in reference to the different generations of computing devices A generation refers to the state of improvement in the development of a product. This term is also used in the different advancements of computer technology. With each new generation, the circuitry has gotten smaller and more advanced than the previous generation before it.

Computer science is a discipline that spans theory and practice. It requires thinking both in abstract terms and in concrete terms. The practical side of computing can be seen everywhere. Nowadays, practically everyone is a computer user, and many people are even computer programmers. Getting computers to do what you want them to do requires intensive hands-on experience. But computer science can be seen on a higher level, as a science of problem solving. Computer scientists must be adept at modeling and analyzing problems. They must also be able to design solutions and verify that they are correct. Problem solving requires precision, creativity, and careful reasoning.

Computer science also has strong connections to other disciplines. Many problems in science, engineering, health care, business, and other areas can be solved effectively with computers, but finding a solution requires both computer science expertise and knowledge of the particular application domain. Thus, computer scientists often become proficient in other subjects. Finally, computer science has a wide range of specialties. These include computer architecture, software systems, graphics, artifical intelligence, computational science, and software engineering. Drawing from a common core of computer science knowledge, each specialty area focuses on particular challenges. Computer technology refers to designing, constructing and programming the computers. Some of the things involved in it include, the software, hardware, peripherals and networking. It is one of the career courses with the largest demand because of technology development. This book will be a useful asset for the students, researchers and teachers who want to have basic knowledge and other useful information in the area of Computer Science and Technology.

I thank all members of my team who have helped in the preparation of the book. My special thanks go to "Random Publications" who have published the book.

– Manoj Kumar Meena and Shweta Meena

Contents

1

Concept of Computer Science

BEGINING OF COMPUTER SCIENCE

Computer Concepts has been trading since 1980-quite an old company among various software houses. During this time the company has grown from a two-man operation selling utilities for the Acorn Atom into a multi million pound company specializing in innovation and research in both hardware and software. Computer Concepts is one of two companies in the Xara Group; visit the home page of the other company, Xara Limited, which produces graphics software for Windows, including a version of *ArtWorks* called *Xara X*.

HISTORY OF COMPUTER DEVELOPMENT AND GENERATION OF COMPUTERS

The history of computer development is often referred to in reference to the different generations of computing devices A generation refers to the state of improvement in the development of a product. This term is also used in the different advancements of computer technology. With each new generation, the circuitry has gotten smaller and more advanced than the previous generation before it.

FIRST GENERATION-1940-1956: VACUUM TUBES

The first computers used vacuum tubes for circuitry and magnetic drums for memory, and were often enormous, taking up entire rooms. A magnetic drum, also referred to as drum, is a metal cylinder coated with magnetic iron-oxide material on which data and programmes can be stored. Magnetic drums were once used as a primary storage device but have since been implemented as auxiliary storage devices. The tracks on a magnetic drum are assigned to channels located around the circumference of the drum, forming adjacent circular bands that wind around the drum. Single drum can have up to 200 tracks. As the drum rotates at a speed of up to 3,000 rpm, the device's read/write heads deposit magnetized spots on the drum during the write operation and sense these spots during a read operation. This action is similar to that of a magnetic tape or disk drive. Programs written in high-level languages retranslated into assembly language or machine language by a compiler. Assembly language programs retranslated into machine language by a program called an assembler. Every CPU has its own unique machine language. Programs must be rewritten or recompiled, therefore, to run on different types of computers. Input was based on punched cards and paper tape, and output was displayed on printouts.

SECOND GENERATION-1956-1963: TRANSISTORS

Transistors replaced vacuum tubes and ushered in the second generation of computers. Transistor is a device composed of semiconductor material that amplifies a signal or opens or closes a circuit. Invented in 1947at Bell Labs, transistors have become the key ingredient of all digital circuits, including computers. Today's microprocessors contains tens of millions of microscopic transistors. Prior to the invention of transistors, digital circuits were composed of vacuum tubes, which had many disadvantages. They were much larger, required more energy, dissipated more heat, and were more prone to failures. It's safe to say that without the invention of transistors, computing, as we know it today would not be possible. The transistor was invented in 1947 but did not see widespread use in computers until the late 50s. The transistor was far superior to the vacuum tube, allowing computers to become smaller, faster, cheaper, more energy-efficient and more reliable than their first-generation predecessors.

THIRD GENERATION-1964-1971: INTEGRATED CIRCUITS

The development of the integrated circuit was the hallmark of the third generation of computers. Transistors were miniaturized and placed on siliconchips, called semiconductors, which drastically increased the speed and efficiency of computers. Silicon is the basic material used to make computer chips, transistors, silicon diodes and other electronic circuits and switching devices because its atomic structure makes the element an ideal semiconductor. Silicon is commonly doped, or mixed, with other elements, such as boron, phosphorous and arsenic, to alter its conductive properties. A chip is a small piece of semi conducting material(usually silicon) on which an integrated circuit is embedded. A typical chip is less than ¼-square inches and can contain millions of electronic components(transistors). Computers consist of many chips placed on electronic boards called printed circuit boards. There are different types of chips. For example, CPU chips (also called microprocessors) contain an entire processing unit, whereas memory chips contain blank memory.

FOURTH GENERATION-1971-PRESENT: MICROPROCESSORS

The microprocessor brought the fourth generation of computers, as thousands of integrated circuits were built onto a single silicon chip. A silicon chip that contains a CPU. In the world of personal computers, the terms microprocessor and CPU are used interchangeably. At the heart of all personal computers and most workstations sits a microprocessor. Microprocessors also control the logic of almost all digital devices, from clock radios to fuel-injection systems for automobiles.

Three basic characteristics differentiate microprocessors:

- *Instruction Set*: The set of instructions that the microprocessor can execute.
- *Bandwidth*: The number of bits processed in a single instruction.
- *Clock Speed*: Given in megahertz (MHz), the clock speed determines how many instructions per second the processor can execute.

In both cases, the higher the value, the more powerful the CPU. For example, a 32-bit microprocessor that runs at 50MHz is more powerful than a 16-bitmicroprocessor that runs at 25MHz. Abbreviation of central processing unit, and pronounced as separate letters. The CPU is the brains of the computer. Sometimes referred to simply as the processor or central processor, the CPU is where most calculations take place. In terms of computing power, the CPU is the most important element of a computer system.

FIFTH GENERATION-PRESENT AND BEYOND: ARTIFICIAL INTELLIGENCE

Fifth generation computing devices, based on artificial intelligence, are still in development, though there are some applications, such as voice recognition, that are being used today. Artificial Intelligence is the branch of computer science concerned with making computers behave like humans. Artificial intelligence includes coined the term in 1956:

- *Games Playing*: programming computers to play games such as chess and checkers
- *Expert Systems*: programming computers to make decisions in real-life situations (for example, some expert systems help doctors diagnose diseases based on symptoms)
- *Natural Language*: programming computers to understand natural human languages
- *Neural Networks*: Systems that simulate intelligence by attempting to reproduce the types of physical connections that occur in animal brains

VOICE RECOGNITION

The field of computer science that deals with designing computer systems that can recognize spoken words. Note that voice recognition implies only that the computer can take dictation, not that it understands what is being said. Comprehending human languages falls under a different field of computer science called natural language processing. A number of voice recognition systems are available on the market. The most powerful can recognize thousands of words. However, they generally require an extended training session during which the computer system becomes accustomed to a particular voice and accent. Such systems are said to be speaker dependent.

Many systems also require that the speaker speak slowly and distinctly and separate each word with a short pause. These systems are called discrete speech systems.

Most computers have just one CPU, but some models have several. There are even computers with thousands of CPUs. With single-CPU computers, it is possible to perform parallel processing by connecting the computers in a network. However, this type of parallel processing requires very sophisticated software called distributed processing software.

AN OPERATING SYSTEM

An operating system or OS, is a software program that enables the computer hardware to communicate and operate with the computer software. Without a computer operating system, a computer and software programs would be useless.

An operating system (sometimes abbreviated as "OS") is the program that, after being initially loaded into the computer by a boot program, manages all the other programs in a computer. The other programs are called *applications* or application programs. The application programs make use of the operating system by making requests for services through a defined application program interface (API). In addition, users can interact directly with the operating system through a user interface such as a command language or a graphical user interface (GUI).

An operating system performs these services for applications:

- In a multitasking operating system where multiple programs can be running at the same time, the operating system determines which applications should run in what order and how much time should be allowed for each application before giving another application a turn.
- It manages the sharing of internal memory among multiple applications.
- It handles input and output to and from attached hardware devices, such as hard disks, printers, and dial-up ports.
- It sends messages to each application or interactive user (or to a system operator) about the status of operation and any errors that may have occurred.

- It can offload the management of what are called *batch* jobs (for example, printing) so that the initiating application is freed from this work.
- On computers that can provide parallel processing, an operating system can manage how to divide the program so that it runs on more than one processor at a time.

All major computer platforms (hardware and software) require and sometimes include an operating system. Linux, Windows 2000, VMS,OS/400, AIX, and z/OS are all examples of operating systems.

FUNCTIONS OF OPERATING SYSTEM

The operating system provides several other functions which includes:

- System tools (programs) used to monitor computer performance, debug problems, or maintain parts of the system.
- A set of libraries or functions which programs may use to perform specific tasks especially relating to interfacing with computer system components.

The operating system makes these interfacing functions along with its other functions operate smoothly and these functions are mostly transparent to the user.

DESCRIPTION OF OPERATING SYSTEM

For a computer to be able to operate a computer program (sometimes known as application or software), the machine must be able to perform a certain number of preparatory operations to ensure exchange between the processor, the memory and the physical resources (peripherals).

The operating system (sometimes referred to by its abbreviation OS), is responsible for creating the link between the material resources, the user and the applications (word processor, video game, etc.). When a programme wants to access a material resource, it does not need to send specific information to the peripheral device but it simply sends the information to the operating system, which conveys it to the relevant peripheral via its driver. If there are no drivers, each programme has to recognise and take into account the communication with each type of peripheral!

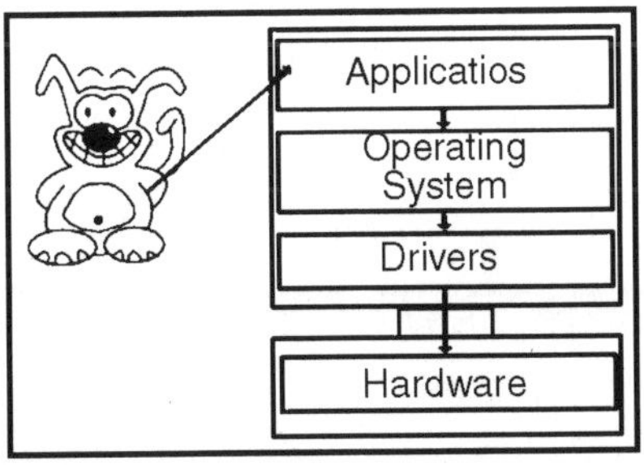

The operating system thus allows the "dissociation" of programmes and hardware, mainly to simplify resource management and offer the user a simplified Man-machine interface (MMI) to overcome the complexity of the actual machine.

ROLES OF OPERATING SYSTEM

The operating system has various roles:

- *Management of the processor*: The operating system is responsible for managing allocation of the processor between the different programmes using ascheduling algorithm. The type of scheduler is totally dependent on the operating system, according to the desired objective.
- *Management of the random access memory*: The operating system is responsible for managing the memory space allocated to each application and, where relevant, to each user. If there is insufficient physical memory, the operating system can create a memory zone on the hard drive, known as "virtual memory". The virtual memory lets you run applications requiring more memory than there is available RAM on the system. However, this memory is a great deal slower.
- *Management of input/output*: The operating system allows unification and control of access of programmes to material resources via drivers (also known as peripheral administrators or input/output administrators).
- *Management of execution of applications*: The operating system is responsible for smooth execution of applications by allocating the resources required for them to operate. This means an application that is not responding correctly can be "killed".

COMPONENTS OF OPERATING SYSTEM

The operating system comprises a set of software packages that can be used to manage interactions with the hardware.

The following elements are generally included in this set of software:

- The kernel, which represents the operating system's basic functions such as management of memory, processes, files, main inputs/ outputs and communi-cation functionalities.
- The shell, allowing communication with the operating system via a control language, letting the user control the peripherals without knowing the characteristics of the hardware used, management of physical addresses, etc.
- The file system, allowing files to be recorded in a tree structure.

OPERATING SYSTEM AS MULTI-THREADED

An operating system is known as multi-threaded when several "tasks" (also known as processes*) may be run at the same time.* The applications consist of a sequence of instructions known as "threads". These threads will be alternately active, on standby, suspended or destroyed, according to the priority accorded to them or may be run simultaneously. A system is known as pre-emptive when it has a scheduler (also called planner), which, according to priority criteria, allocates the machine time between the various processes requesting it. The system is called a shared time system when a time quota is allocated to each process by the scheduler. This is the case of multi-user systems which allow several users to use different or similar applications on the same machine at the same time. the system is then referred to as a "transactional system". To do this, the system allocates a period of time to each user.

OPERATING SYSTEM AS MULTI-PROCESSOR SYSTEMS

Multi-processing is a technique that involves operating several processors in parallel to obtain a higher calculation power than that obtained using a high-end processor or to increase the availability of the system (in the event of processor breakdown). The term SMP (Symmetric Multiprocessing or Symmetric Multiprocessor) refers to an architecture in which all processors access the same shared memory. A multiprocessor system must be able to manage memory sharing between several processors but also to distribute the work load.

OPERATING SYSTEM AS EMBEDDED SYSTEMS

Embedded systems are operating systems designed to operate on small machines, such as PDAs (personal digital assistants) or autonomous electronic devices (spatial probes, robot, on-board vehicle computer, etc.) with reduced autonomy. Thus an essential feature of embedded systems is their advanced energy management and ability to operate with limited resources.

The main "general use" embedded systems for PDAs are as follows:

- Palm OS
- Windows CE/Windows Mobile/Window Smartphone

REAL TIME SYSTEMS

Real time systems, used mainly in industry, are systems designed to operate in a time-constrained environment. A real time system must also operate reliably according to specific time constraints; in other words, it must be able to properly process information received at clearly-defined intervals (regular or otherwise).

Here are some examples of real time operating systems:

- OS-9;
- RTLinux (RealTime Linux);
- QNX;
- VxWorks.

TYPES OF OPERATING SYSTEM

There are many types of operating systems.

Real-time Operating System

It is a multitasking operating system that aims at executing real-time applications. Real-time operating systems often use specialized scheduling algorithms so that they can achieve a deterministic nature of behaviour. The main object of real-time operating systems is their quick and predictable response to events. They either have an event-driven or a time-sharing design. An event-driven system switches between tasks based of their priorities while time-sharing operating systems switch tasks based on clock interrupts.

Multi-user and Single-user Operating Systems

The operating systems of this type allow a multiple users to access a computer system concurrently. Time-sharing system can be classified as multi-user systems as they enable a multiple user access to a computer through the sharing of time. Single-user operating systems, as opposed to a multi-user operating system, are usable by a single user at a time. Being able to have multiple accounts on a Windows operating system does not make it a multi-user system. Rather, only the network administrator is the real user. But for a Unix-like operating system, it is possible for two users to login at a time and this capability of the OS makes it a multi-user operating system.

Multi-tasking and Single-tasking Operating Systems

When a single program is allowed to run at a time, the system is grouped under a single-tasking system, while in case the operating system allows the execution of multiple tasks at one time, it is classified as a multi-tasking operating system. Multi-tasking can be of two types namely, pre-emptive or co-operative. In pre-emptive multitasking, the operating system slices the CPU time and dedicates one slot to each of the programs. Unix-like operating systems such as Solaris and Linux support pre-emptive multitasking. Cooperative multitasking is achieved by relying on each process to give time to the other processes in a defined manner. MS Windows prior to Windows 95 used to support cooperative multitasking.

Distributed Operating System

An operating system that manages a group of independent computers and makes them appear to be a single computer is known as a distributed operating system. The development of networked computers that could be linked and communicate with each other, gave rise to distributed computing. Distributed computations are carried out on more than one machine. When computers in a group work in cooperation, they make a distributed system.

Embedded System

The operating systems designed for being used in embedded computer systems are known as embedded operating systems. They are designed to operate on small machines like PDAs with less autonomy. They are able to operate with a limited number of resources. They are very compact and extremely efficient by design. Windows CE, FreeBSD and Minix 3 are some examples of embedded operating systems. The most common is the Microsoft suite of operating systems.

They include from most recent to the oldest:

- *Windows XP Professional Edition*: A version used by many businesses on workstations. It has the ability to become a member of a corporate domain.
- *Windows XP Home Edition*: A lower cost version of Windows XP which is for home use only and should not be used at a business.
- *Windows* 2000: A better version of the Windows NT operating system which works well both at home and as a workstation at a business. It includes technologies which allow hardware to be automatically detected and other enhancements over Windows NT.
- *Windows ME*: A upgraded version from windows 98 but it has been historically with program errors which may be frustrating for home users.
- *Windows* 98: This was produced in two main versions. The first Windows 98 version was plagued with programming errors but the Windows 98 Second Edition which came out later was much better with many errors resolved.
- *Windows NT*: A version of Windows made specifically for businesses offering better control over workstation capabilities to help network administrators.
- *Windows* 95: The first version of Windows after the older Windows 3.x versions offering a better interface and better library functions for programs.

CENTRAL PROCESSING UNIT

SYSTEM

In the Waveform viewer, click on the Add Signals icon (or go to signals -> add signals). In the middle panel of the Component Selection window, called Chip Selection, you will see the name of the macro, MYPFA. Double click on it. In the right panel, Scan Hierarchy, all the input and output pins will be displayed. Select these pins by double clicking. When done, click the Close button.

- Open the stimulator window and define the A and B bits using the Binary counter.
- Do a functional simulation and verify the operation.

Create a macro for the Carry- Look-Ahead Logic block. Call this myclalog. Use VHDL to create this macro. You should also generate the groups generate and propagate signals, P_G and G_G, respectively. You do not need to create the carry C4. Do a simulation, as explained above. Now you can create a 4-bit CLA adder macro. In the schematic editor go to the Tools –> Symbol wizard menu and create the symbol for a Schematic macro, called MY4CLA. Once the symbol has been created, draw the schematic for the 4-bit adder using the above defined modules of PFA and MYCLALOG. The adder should have as input A[3:0], B[3:0], and CIN.

The outputs are S[3:0], P_G, and G_G. Be careful when connecting the carry signals. Since this schematic will be used as a macro, you do not need to add input/output buffers and pads. For single signals use a terminal; and for the buses (ex. A, B and S), define the bus as "input" or "output" bus (or select End Bus if the terminals have been defined already). When finished, synthesize the macro and simulate the 4-bit adder. Verify its operation and make a screen caption of the functional simulation waveforms (only one page). You are now ready to create the top level schematic of the 16-bit carry-lookahead adder. Use the block diagram of Figure. The schematic of the 16-bit adder is the top level schematic. All the input pins (A[15:0], B[15:0], CIN, sout[15:0], and COUT) need to be connected to pads and buffers. Cout is the last carry of the adder, corresponding to C16 and can be generated from the groups Propagate and Generate signals.

In order to keep the schematic and its interconnections managable, use buses as much as possible. It may be helpful to use a 16-bit wide bus for input signals A and B. This bus can be split up into segments of 4 bits that each feeds into the 4-bit inputs of each of the 4-bit CLA macros. This can be done by first drawing a 16-bit wide bus (*e.g.* AIN[15:0]). Then connect the 4-bit wide input bus (*e.g.* A[3:0]) of the first 4-bit CLA to the 16-bit wide A bus; next connect the input of the 2nd 4-bit CLA to the same A bus, etc. until all 16 inputs have been connected. Now you need to specify how the bus signals are connected. This can be done by giving the bus segment the proper name by clicking on the bus. This will open the Edit Bus window. Keep the name but change the bus width.

For instance, to specify a 4-bit wide bus segment that connects to the input of the first 4-bit adder, give it the name AIN and as width [3:0]. It is important that the name of the bus segment is the same as the name of the 16-bit bus. Do the same for the other bus segments (*e.g.* AIN[7:4], etc.). For more information about buses in the Schematic Entry window, select Help -> schematic editor help contents. In the help window select index and type "buses" or "bus connections". When done, do a functional simulation and verify that the circuit works properly. Instead of defining each input signal A0, A1... A15, B0, B1,... B15 separately, it is more convenient to use the Formulas to define the input signals of the input buses. See section on Formulas in the Logic Simulator Tutorial. When the simulation give the right result, take a screen catpure of the waveforms. When the circuit works properly, you need to implement it so that you can do a timing simulation later on. Make sure you added pads and buffers for each input and output. If you don't add pads, the mapping software will remove all the logic between input and output "connectors" and your circuit will have no logic or little logic left!

Before implementing the design, go to the Program Manager and select the implementation -> implement design menu (or ->options menu). In the Implement Design window click on the Option button. When the Options window opens, click on the Edit Options button for the Simulations (Foundation EDIF). In the Simulation Options window, click on the General Tab and De-select the option: Correlate Simulation Data to Input Design. This will prevent that the timing simulation will give undefined signals. For the implementation, see previous lab or check the tutorial on Design Implementation. Use a device speed of 4.

Check the reports and write the results in your lab notebook: Check the Map Report for the device utilization and the equivalent gate count. Check if logic has been removed during the mapping step. Check the Post Layout Timing Report. Find the maximum combinational path delay and net delay. Between which input pin and output pin does the maximum delay occur? What is the maximum frequency at which the input signals can applied without causing erroneous operation of the 16 bit adder?

Timing Simulation (Verification)

In the Project Manager click on the Verification (Timing Simulation) icon. This will open the timing simulator. Do a worst-case simulation of the CLA and determine the delay of the Sum bits and the Carry out bit cout. In case you have problems with the timing simulation and some of the signals are undefined (gray waveform), see the notes below. You do not need to go through all the possible input combinations because you have verified that the circuit works properly by doing a functional simulation above.

Apply input signals A[15:0] and B[15:0] which give a worst case scenario for the delays of the sum and carry-out signals? Measure the delays between the time the input signal is applied and the sum and carry-out signal changes (use the measurement option in the simulator). Write these numbers down in your lab notebook. Do they correspond to the ones reported in the Post Layout Timing report?

When doing the timing simulation, be careful that the period of the stimuli (*i.e.* the signals applied to the input) is larger than the longest delay of the circuit. If your input signal is changing before the output signals appear (due to the delay), you will get useless and unpredictible results. You can change the period of the binary counter output (Bc:) by going to the Options ->

preferences -> simulations; adjust the Clock Period of B0 to a value larger than the maximum delay (*e.g.* 50 ns). The input signal should not change until all the output signals have settled to the proper value.

Besides the delays of the Sum and Carry signal determine also the delay of the input and output buffers. Take a screen capture of the simulation data, including the measurement data for the delays of the Sum, Carry-out and buffer delays (max 2 screens).

Notes: In case some of the signals show as an undefined signal (gray in the waveform viewer window or blue X on the schematic) make sure that you De-select the option: Correlate Simulation Data to Input Design in the Implementation Options (Simulations) as explained above or in the timing simulation tutorial. Use the Measurement tool to determine the delay: go to Waveform -> measurment -> measurement on. This will allow you to display the delays.

STARTING OF NEXT LAB

Lab Report including:

- Course title, Lab no, Lab section, your name and date.
- Section on the lab experiments:
  - Brief description of the lab including the goals
  - Copy of the VHDL source code of the macros PFA, MYCLALOG.
  - Screen capture of the schematic of the 4 bit and 16-bit CLA adders
  - Screen catpure of the funtional simulation of the 4-bit CLA adder (label printouts)
  - Screen catpure of the timing simulation with measurements16-bit carry-look-ahead adders.
  - Summary of the Map (device utilization) and Timing Reports (delays)
  - Discussion of the measured delays using the Timing simulator.
  - Maximum frequency at which the 16 bit CLA adder can be used.

LOOKING AT CARRIES

The following is a truth table for a full adder.

Row	x	y	c_{in}	c_{out}	s
0	0	0	0	0	0
1	0	0	1	0	1
2	0	1	0	0	1
3	0	1	1	1	0
4	1	0	0	0	1
5	1	0	1	1	0
6	1	1	0	1	0
7	1	1	1	1	1

We can write the carry-out of this adder using sum of products. However, there is an alternate way of writing the carry out. Before we discuss how to write it, let's define a few terms first.

Recall that we are adding two n-bit numbers: $x_{n-1}...x_0$ to $y_{n-1}...y_0$ which results in $z_{n-1}...z_0$. In a ripple carry adder, we assign a full adder (call it adder *i*) to add x_i to y_i. We'll use the ripple carry adders which only uses full adders.

Adder *i* also has a carry in. We'll call that c_i. It generates a carry out, which we'll call c_{i+1}. When we add the least significant bits $c_0 = 0$. However, we'll simply leave it as c_0. We can write the Boolean expression for the carry-out in an alternate way:

$$c_{i+1} = x_i y_i + x_i c_i + y_i c_i$$

This Boolean expression has the same truth table as above. It even makes intuitive sense. There's a carry out when any two of the three bits (*i.e.*, x_i, y_i, or c_i) have a value of 1. Thus, $x_i y_i$ is 1 only when both x_i and y_i are 1. And since this is inclusive OR, all three bits could be 1.

We use the distributive property to rewrite the carry out as:

$$c_{i+1} = x_i y_i + c_i(x_i + y_i)$$

Let's define two terms:

$$g_i = x_i y_i$$

$$p_i = x_i + y_i$$

Then, we can rewrite c_{i+1} *using these two terms, as:*

$$c_{i+1} = g_i + p_i c_i$$

g_i is called the *generate* term. This always generates a carry out. $g_i = x_i y_i$, which is 1 only when x_i and y_i are both 1. Clearly, if two bits are 1, there's a carry. p_i is called the *propagate* term. $p_i = x_i + y_i$. This could create a carry, but it may not. We know that at least one of x_i or y_i must be 1 if $p_i = 1$. This is called *propagate* for the following reason.

If exactly one of x_i or y_i is 1, then the carry-in determines whether there is a carry-out of 1 or not. Thus, if c_i is 1, there is a carry-in of 1, which will cause a carry-out of 1. If c_i is 0, then the carry-out is 0. To propagate, in this case, means to assist.

For example, suppose you are standing in a line. Some one says to hand something forward, say, a piece of paper. Even though you did not bring the piece of paper, you can help move it along (*i.e.*, help propagate it) by passing it to the next person.

Similarly, propagating a carry means to move the carry from the previous adder to the next adder. Mostly, we only care about propagating a 1. We're not that concerned about propagating 0's. That's why we AND p_i to c_i. By itself, p_i may not cause a carry. However, it can propagate a carry-in of 1, by causing a carry-out of 1, if p_i is 1.

GENERATE AND PROPAGATE

Why generate and propagate. If you look at the Boolean expressions for p_i and g_i, you will see that they both use only x_i and y_i.

Neither depend on the carry. Sincex_i and y_i are available immediately, this gives us hope that we can avoid waiting for carries. This is how we do it. First, let's write the c_1 which is the carry out for the adding bit 0 of x and y.

$$c_1 = g_0 + p_0c_0$$

Now, we write it for c_2.

$$c_2 = g_1 + p_1c_1$$

At this point, we've used c_1, which we'd rather avoid, because it means waiting for that carry to be computed. However, we *just* defined c_1 as $g_0 + c_0p_0$.

Let's plug that in:

$$\begin{aligned} c_2 &= g_1 + p_1(g_0 + p_0c_0) \\ &= g_1 + p_1g_0 + p_1p_0c_0 \end{aligned}$$

Notice that we no longer have c_1. That means we no longer have to wait for the carry!

Let's go one more step further:

$$c_3 = g_2 + p_2c_2$$

Again, we would prefer to avoid using c_2 since this requires us to wait for the result to propagate across two adders. However, we *already* have a Boolean expression for c_2 (we just computed it a moment ago) that doesn't use any carries except c_0 which we have right away.

$$\begin{aligned} c_3 &= g_2 + p_2c_2 \\ &= g_2 + p_2(g_1 + p_1g_0 + p_1p_0c_0) \\ &= g_2 + p_2g_1 + p_2p_1g_0 + p_2p_1p_0c_0 \end{aligned}$$

Already, you should be able to detect a pattern. By following the same pattern, you'd expect:

$$c_4 = g_3 + p_3g_2 + p_3p_2g_1 + p_3p_2p_1g_0 + p_3p_2p_1p_0c_0$$

WHAT DO WE DO NOW

By now, you've noticed that we're able to compute the carries in terms of x_i's, y_i's, and c_0. These bits are available right away. We don't have to wait for any other carry to compute it. You might wonder, why? Why are we computing carries, if the idea is to avoid using carries? The idea is to construct a circuit for c_i that can be fed into the input of adder *i*. The carry-out of the adder is not used. In fact, each of the full-adders aren't directly connect to each other. We simply design the circuit for c_i and feed it in. The following is an approximate circuit.

The diagram is incomplete. It's missing the wires from x_i and y_i to the appropriate adders. As an exercise, redraw the diagram, and add those wires in. Also, draw$x_{2\text{-}0}$ as 3 separate inputs, instead of the one circle drawn in the diagram above. Do the same for $y_{2\text{-}0}$. If you want, you can even draw in the logic inside the boxes that say things like "c_3 LOGIC". What should you understand from this diagram? The key point to observe is the carry out of the full adder is *not* attached to the carry in of the next adder. Instead, there is logic (as defined by the Boolean expressions from the previous section) that has inputs from x_i's, y_i's and c_0.

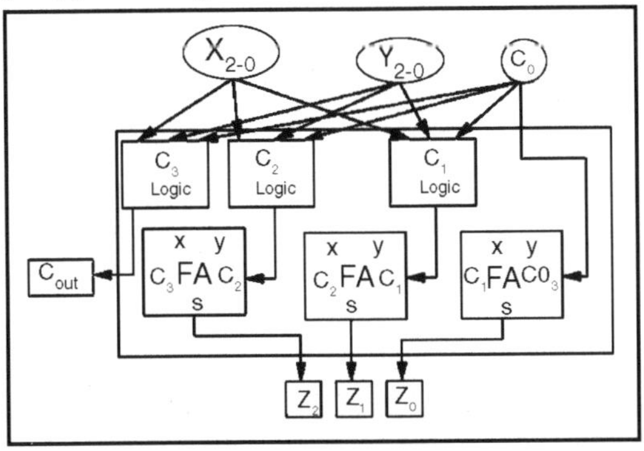

MEMORY SYSTEM

Computer memory is used to store two things: i) instructions to execute a programme and ii) data. When the computer is doing any job, the data that have to be processed are stored in the primary memory. This data may come from an input device like keyboard or from a secondary storage device like a floppy disk.

As programme or the set of instructions is kept in primary memory, the computer is able to follow instantly the set of instructions. For example, when you book ticket from railway reservation counter, the computer has to follow the same steps: take the request, check the availability of seats, calculate fare, wait for money to be paid, store the reservation and get the ticket printed out. The programme containing these steps is kept in memory of the computer and is followed for each request.

But inside the computer, the steps followed are quite different from what we see on the monitor or screen. In computer's memory both programmes and data are stored in the binary form. You have already been introduced with decimal number system, that is the numbers 1 to 9 and 0. The binary system has only two values 0 and 1. These are called *bits*. As human beings we all understand decimal system but the computer can only understand binary system. It is because a large number of integrated circuits inside the computer can be considered as switches, which can be made ON, or OFF. If a switch is ON it is considered 1 and if it is OFF it is 0. A number of switches in different states will give you a message like this: 110101....10. So the computer takes input in the form of 0 and 1 and gives output in the form 0 and 1 only. Is it not absurd if the computer gives outputs as 0's and 1's only? But you do not have to worry about. Every number in binary system can be converted to decimal system and vice versa; for example, 1010 meaning decimal 10. Therefore it is the computer that takes information or data in decimal form from you, convert it in to binary form, process it producing output in binary form and again convert the output to decimal form.

The primary memory as you know in the computer is in the form of IC's (Integrated Circuits). These circuits are called Random Access Memory (RAM). Each of RAM's locations stores one *byte* of information. (One *byte* is equal to *8 bits*). A bit is an acronym for *binary digit*, which stands for one binary piece of information. This can be either 0 or 1. You will know more about RAM later. The Primary or internal storage section is made up of several small storage locations (ICs) called cells. Each of these cells can store a fixed number of bits called *word length*.

Each cell has a unique number assigned to it called the address of the cell and it is used to identify the cells. The address starts at 0 and goes up to (N-1). You should know that the memory is like a large cabinet containing as many drawers as there are addresses on memory. Each drawer contains a word and the address is written on outside of the drawer.

CAPACITY OF PRIMARY MEMORY

The capacity is defined in terms of byte or words. Thus 64 kilobyte (KB) memory is capable of storing 64 × 1024 = 32,768 bytes. (1 kilobyte is 1024 bytes). A memory size ranges from few kilobytes in small systems to several thousand kilobytes in large mainframe and super computer. In your personal computer you will find memory capacity in the range of 64 KB, 4 MB, 8 MB and even 16 MB (MB = Million bytes).

Random Access Memory (RAM)

RAM is perhaps the most important of the input/output devices. When we talk about computer memory, we are mainly talking about RAM. In this class, when we think about the banks of light switches that can be manipulated, we are thinking of RAM memory. The term Random Access is pretty unfortunate. There is nothing random about how memory is accessed.

The programme running will determine what is in memory. (of course, the programme itself is in memory too!) RAM can be read from by the CPU. This means that the CPU can 'look' at any address in RAM and get the contents of that address. It can also be written to by the CPU, meaning that the CPU can change the value of memory cells on the fly.

One VERY important aspect of RAM memory is that it requires power. RAM can only hold values while power is going through it. If the power is interrupted, the RAM will lose ALL the values in it. This is why it is so important to save your work frequently when working on a computer. RAM memory is volatile. When the room you are working on is hit by a tsunami and the power goes out of your computer, you lose everything that was in RAM. The amount of RAM in your computer is obviously a pretty important factor. The more memory you have, the more 'room' there is in your computer for information and programmes.

Modern programmes have gotten HUGE, and the kinds of information you can work with have gotten much larger. Some early home computers had 4 or 16 K of RAM. The original IBM PC had 640 K of RAM. In its day, this was thought of as an extravagant amount of memory that would never be fully used. Modern computers with less than 16 Megabytes (16,000 K) are considered a bit lame. (pun completely intended.) Older computers can be quite happy with much less RAM, but they will not be able to run the newer programmes. If you are buying or upgrading a computer, you should seriously consider as much RAM as you can afford. There is probably no more cost-effective upgrade than RAM.

If you find that you need more memory, It is relatively cheap and easy to do a memory upgrade. Note that not all types of RAM are interchangeable. Look in the book that came with your computer for specifically which type of RAM you need when you are ready to upgrade.

Read Only Memory (ROM)

There is another memory in computer, which is called Read Only Memory (ROM). Again it is the ICs inside the PC that form the ROM. The storage of programme and data in the ROM is permanent. The ROM stores some standard processing programmes supplied by the manufacturers to operate the personal computer. The ROM can only be read by the CPU but it cannot be changed. The basic input/output programme is stored in the ROM that examines and initializes various equipment attached to the PC when the switch is made ON. The memories, which do not loose their content on failure of power supply, are known as non-volatile memories. ROM is non-volatile memory.

Memory is like the banks of switches we have been thinking about that simply contain 1/0 binary patterns. Read Only Memory (abbreviated ROM) is a special kind of memory that cannot be changed. The most basic instructions for the CPU are built in to the ROM at the factory. To the end user, there really is very little to worry about regarding ROM. The amount of ROM in your computer doesn't really matter to you. All your programmes and information will go into another kind of memory that we will learn about soon.

PROM

There is another type of primary memory in computer, which is called Programmable Read Only Memory (PROM). You know that it is not possible to modify or erase programmes stored in ROM, but it is possible for you to store your programme in PROM chip. Once the programmes are written it cannot be changed and remain intact even if power is switched off. Therefore programmes or instructions written in PROM or ROM cannot be erased or changed.

EPROM

This stands for Erasable Programmable Read Only Memory, which over come the problem of PROM and ROM. EPROM chip can be programmed time and again by erasing the information stored earlier in it. Information stored in EPROM exposing the chip for some time ultraviolet light and it erases chip is reprogrammed using a special programming facility. When the EPROM is in use information can only be read.

Cache Memory

The speed of CPU is extremely high compared to the access time of main memory. Therefore the performance of CPU decreases due to the slow speed of main memory. To decrease the mismatch in operating speed, a small memory chip is attached between CPU and Main memory whose access time is very close to the processing speed of CPU. It is called CACHE memory. CACHE memories are accessed much faster than conventional RAM. It is used to store programmes or data currently being executed or temporary data frequently used by the CPU. So each memory makes main memory to be faster and larger than it really is. It is also very expensive to have bigger size of cache memory and its size is normally kept small.

Registers

The CPU processes data and instructions with high speed, there is also movement of data between various units of computer. It is necessary to transfer the processed data with high speed. So the computer uses a number of special memory units called *registers.*

They are not part of the main memory but they store data or information temporarily and pass it on as directed by the control unit.

HIERARCHICAL MEMORY STRUCTURE

We have three levels of partition based on which we base our hierarchy.

- Registers internal to the CPU for temporary data storage-these are small in number but are really very fast and are costliest.
- External storage for data and programmes-these are relatively large in number, fast and a little cheaper.
- External permanent storage-these are much larger cheaper and really slower as compared to rest of the two.

Since we need to send data from the magnetic disks to the disk cache and then to the main memory and finally to the cache which is located near to the CPU and also to the registers inside the CPU. The memory references made by the processor, for both instructions and data, tend to cluster together as the ones for the instruction loops and subroutines cluster together and the ones for data array and tables cluster together. These clusters are kept in high speed memory to reduce the average delay in accessing data. The clusters being referenced will change as the memory management module of the OS will deal with it.

Characteristics of the Hierarchy

The basic characteristics of the memory hierarchy are:

- This consists of distinct levels of memory components as the primary, secondary or tertiary memory units.
- Each level characterizes itself by its size, access time and cost per bit which help in differentiating the elements in a hierarchical fashion.
- Each higher level in the hierarchy consists of modules of larger capacity, slower access time and lower cost per bit as depicted in the figure.

INTERNAL MEMORY/MAIN MEMORY/RAM

RAM: Random Access Memory

It is a semiconductor memory which is both readable and writable. RAM is volatile in nature and thus is mainly temporary in nature. RAM can be categorized in static and dynamic form.

- *Dynamic RAM*: Storage cell is essentially a transistor which acts as a capacitor. The charge in it dissipates over time and thus often flips to zero and thus needs to be refreshed periodically. The construction is simple and hence is less expensive. An extra refresh circuitary is essential. The main drawback is that it is slower. The address lines are active when bits are read or written.

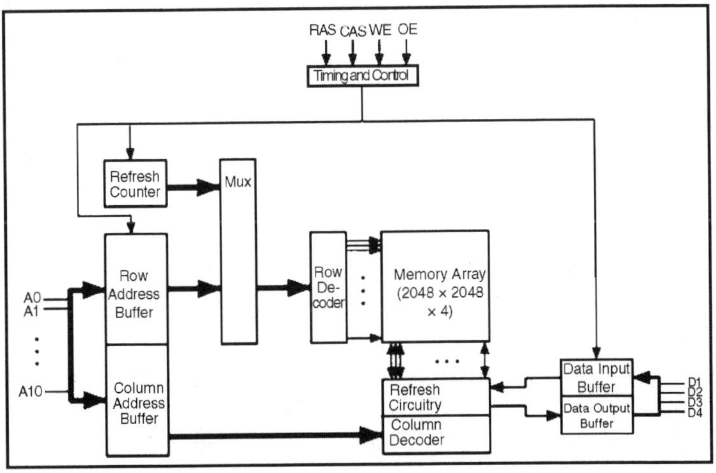

Fig. 16 Mb DRAM using (4M × 4).

- *Static RAM*: These are basically an array of flip-flop storage cells those use five to ten times more transistors than similar dynamic cell. So the packaging density is ten times lower. This RAM is although faster than a dynamic cell.

ROM: Read only Memory

It is semiconductor memory which is only readable. It is used for permanent storage and is non-volatile in nature. It is mainly used to store the library routines, system programmes(BIOS), function tables etc. The data is stored as a hard wired system during fabrication at the chip manufacturer's point. These are generally purchased in groups of 10K or more but are very expensive for small runs.

Proms

Programmable read only memory is used when the data is written once by the user employing a PROM programming device. It is useful for small production runs.

Eprom

Erasable programmable read only memory has a similar programming as that of a PROM. This is generally erased by exposing to UV light.

Eeprom

Electrically erasable programmable read only memory is generally written to many times while remaining in a system. This doesnt have to be erased first. Each individual bytes can be programmed. The writting requires several hundred microsecond per byte. This is generally used in systems for development, personalization and other tasks requiring unique information to be stored. Flash memory -This is similar to an EEPROM in using electrical erasing of data. The erasing is really fast and is done in blocks. The density is higher than EEPROM.

Cache Memory

It is the most critical component of the memory hierarchy. Cache means a safe place for hiding or storing things. The idea behind using a cache as the first level of the memory hierarchy is to keep the information expected to be used more frequently by the CPU in the cache. Thus in cache, a small portion of the main memory is actively stored. Thus when the processor sought for a memory reference, it tries to find in the cache.

Compared to the main memory, cache is relatively small. It operates near to the speed of the processor. It is although very expensive as compared to the main memory. If we assume that an access to main memory causes a block of K words to be transfered to the cache.

The block transferred from the main memory is stored in the cache as a single unit called a slot, line or a page. Once it is copied to the cache, individual words within a line can be accessed by the CPU.

Due to the high speed involved in the cache, management of the data transfer and storage in the cache is done in hardware and hence the OS has no dealings with it. Every line of data in the cache must be tagged in some way to identify what main memory block it is and thus the line of data and its tag are stored in the cache.

Factors for Designing of the Cache

- Mapping function between the main memory and the cache.
- Line replacement algorithm used.
- Various write policies (Write back, write update, write through)
- Block size.
- Number and type of caches.

Mapping Functions used in Cache

Direct Mapping

Each main memory block is assigned to a specific line in the cache. We use the function as given below-

- i=j modulo C
- i-line number assigned
- j-main memory block
- C-number of lines in cache.

This treats main memory address as 3 distinct fields namely tag identifier, Line number identifier and Word identifier(offset).

Advantages with this techniques are:

- It is easy to implement
- Relatively inexpensive to implement
- Easy to determine where a main memory reference can be found in cache.

Disadvantages are:

- Each main memory block is mapped to a specific line
- Hit ratio can be low if the blocks are swapped in and out constantly

Associative Mapping

This technique lets a block to be stored in any cache line that is not in use. Thus it must examine each line in the cache to find the right block and line numbers(ids) have no meaning in the cache. The cache is implemented in two parts namely, the lines themselves in SRAM and the tag storage in associative memory. The associative memory search is performed for overall tags to find the desired line.

Advantages are:

- Fast
- Flexible

Disadvantages are:

- Implementation is costly

Set Associative Mapping

This is an implementation which takes up the best of both the previous implementations. This implementation divides cache into a number of sets(v), each set holding a number of lines(k).

A main memory block can be stored in any one of the k lines in a set such that set number = j modulo v. If a set can hold X lines, the cache is referred to as an X-way set associative cache.

EXTERNAL MEMORY

Magnetic Disks

A hard drive is a special disk that is usually mounted permanently inside your computer's cabinet. You rarely see the hard drive, and almost never take it out. Hard drives are made of different material than floppies, and they are physically hard (although if you touched the actual hard surface, you would destroy it!) They spin much more quickly than floppies, and require much more precision. They are sealed inside a special case, and that is sealed inside the computer case.

A hard drive has a much larger capacity than a floppy, and is much faster at saving and retrieving information. Modern computers frequently have hard drives with 500 MB or more of capacity. As this capacity grows, people are beginning to measure it in terms of gigabytes. Software programmes are always becoming larger and taking more room on hard drives. It never takes long to completely fill up the capacity of a drive.

SECONDARY STORAGE

These high-speed storage devices are very expensive and hence the cost per bit of storage is also very high. Again the storage capacity of the main memory is also very limited. Often it is necessary to store hundreds of millions of bytes of data for the CPU to process. Therefore additional memory is required in all the computer systems. This memory is called *auxiliary memory* or *secondary storage.*

In this type of memory the cost per bit of storage is low. However, the operating speed is slower than that of the primary storage. Huge volume of data are stored here on permanent basis and transferred to the primary storage as and when required. Most widely used secondary storage devices are *magnetic tapes* and*magnetic disk.*

Magnetic Tape

Magnetic tapes are used for large computers like mainframe computers where large volume of data is stored for a longer time. In PC also you can use tapes in the form of cassettes.

The cost of storing data in tapes is inexpensive. Tapes consist of magnetic materials that store data permanently. It can be 12.5 mm to 25 mm wide plastic film-type and 500 meter to 1200 meter long which is coated with magnetic material. The deck is connected to the central processor and information is fed into or read from the tape through the processor. It similar to cassette tape recorder.

Advantages of magnetic tape:

- *Compact*: A 10-inch diameter reel of tape is 2400 feet long and is able to hold 800, 1600 or 6250 characters in each inch of its length. The maximum capacity of such tape is 180 million characters. Thus data are stored much more compactly on tape.
- *Economical*: The cost of storing characters is very less as compared to other storage devices.
- *Fast*: Copying of data is easier and fast.
- *Long term storage and re-usability*: Magnetic tapes can be used for long term storage and a tape can be used repeatedly with out loss of data.

Magnetic Disk

You might have seen the gramophone record, which is circular like a disk and coated with magnetic material. Magnetic disks used in computer are made on the same principle. It rotates with very high speed inside the computer drive. Data is stored on both the surface of the disk. Magnetic disks are most popular for *direct access* storage device. Each disk consists of a number of invisible *concentric circles* called *tracks*. Information is recorded on tracks of a disk surface in the form of tiny magnetic spots.

The presence of a magnetic spot represents *one bit* and its absence represents zero bit. The information stored in a disk can be read many times without affecting the stored data. So the reading operation is non-destructive. But if you want to write a new data, then the existing data is erased from the disk and new data is recorded.

Disk drives are special devices that allow us to make copies of parts of RAM and store them magnetically. If RAM memory is electronic, think of disk drives as a special kind of magnetic memory. When you save something to a disk, the electronic impulses in RAM are copied and stored to the disk as a series of magnetic impulses. All a disk drive does is translate electronic impulses and magnetic impulses back and forth. Disk drives are handy because magnetic impulses are more permanent than electronic ones. The disk drive does not require electricity to keep values in memory, so if you store something to a disk, the information will be there when the tidal wave knocks the power out to your computer. (Assuming, of course, that the disk stayed dry and clean) Disks are sometimes thought of as secondary storage for this reason.

Floppy Disk

It is similar to magnetic disk discussed above. They are 5.25 inch or 3.5 inch in diameter. They come in single or double density and recorded on one or both surface of the diskette. The capacity of a 5.25-inch floppy is 1.2 mega bytes whereas for 3.5 inch floppy it is 1.44 mega bytes. It is cheaper than any other storage devices and is portable. The floppy is a low cost device particularly suitable for personal computer system. A floppy drive is a machine that is designed to read floppy disks.

Floppy disks are the removable devices that you stick in slots in the front of the machine. Floppy disks come in hard plastic cases to make them a little more sturdy and easier to handle, but inside the plastic case, there is an actual disk. It is made of a plastic-like substance called mylar which really is floppy. Floppy disks come in two main sizes; 5 1/4 inch, and 3 1/2 inch.

The 5 1/4 disks are becoming obsolete, but you still see them from time to time. The 3 1/2 inch disks, although physically smaller, can usually hold more information! There are different flavours of floppy disks. In a modern computer, the only kind of floppy you need to purchase is High Density 1.44 MB.

Optical Disk

With every new application and software there is greater demand for memory capacity. It is the necessity to store large volume of data that has led to the development of optical disk storage medium.

Optical disks can be divided into the following categories:

- *Compact disk/Read only memory (CD-ROM)*: CD-ROM disks are made of reflective metals. CD-ROM is written during the process of manufacturing by high power *laser beam*. Here the storage density is very high, storage cost is very low and access time is relatively fast. Each disk is approximately 4 1/2 inches in diameter and can hold over 600 MB of data. As the CD-ROM can be *read only* we cannot write or make changes into the data contained in it.
- *Write once, read many (WORM)*: The inconvenience that we can not write any thing in to a CD-ROM is avoided in WORM. A WORM allows the user to write data permanently on to the disk. Once the data is written it can never be erased without physically damaging the disk. Here data can be recorded from keyboard, video scanner, OCR equipment and other devices. The advantage of WORM is that it can store vast amount of data amounting to gigabytes (10^9bytes).

Any document in a WORM can be accessed very fast, say less than 30 seconds.

- *Erasable Optical disk*: These are optical disks where data can be written, erased and re-written. This also applies a laser beam to write and re-write the data. These disks may be used as alternatives to traditional disks. Erasable optical disks are based on a technology known as *magnetic optical* (MO). To write a data bit on to the erasable optical disk the MO drive's laser beam heats a tiny, precisely defined point on the disk's surface and magnetises it.

WORLD WIDE WEB (WWW)

The World Wide Web is a system of Internet servers that supports hypertext to access several Internet protocols on a single interface. The World Wide Web is often abbreviated as the Web or www. The World Wide Web was developed in 1989 by Tim Berners-Lee of the European Particle Physics Lab (CERN) in Switzerland. The initial purpose of the Web was to use networked hypertext to facilitate communication among its members, who were located in several countries. Word was soon spread beyond CERN, and a rapid growth in the number of both developers and users ensued. In addition to hypertext, the Web began to incorporate graphics, video, and sound. The use of the Web has reached global proportions and has become a defining element of human culture in an amazingly short period of time.

MULTIMEDIA ON WEB

Today's Web presents a diversified multimedia experience. In fact, the Web has become a broadcast medium, offering live TV and radio, pre-recorded video, photos, images, and animations. Expect to encounter multimedia just about anywhere on the Web. This tutorial presents a brief overview.

Plugins, Media Players and Multimedia Types

Plugins and Media Players are software programs that allow you to experience multimedia on the Web. These terms are sometimes used interchangeably. File formats requiring this software are known as MIME types. MIME stands for Multimedia Internet Mail Extension, and was originally developed to help e-mail software handle a variety of binary (non-textual) file attachments. The use of MIME has expanded to the Web. For example, the basic MIME type handled by Web browsers is text/html associated with the file extention.html. MIME types area also used to process multimedia on the Web.

A few examples:

- *Jpeg photos*: Image/jpeg
- *Flash presentations*: Application/x-shockwave-flash

- *Quicktime movies*: Video/quicktime
- MP3s: audio/x-mpeg-3

Nowadays, many personal computers come pre-loaded with plugins and media players. This is an acknowledgement of the importance of the Web multimedia experience. If your computer doesn't have a particular piece of software, it can be easily obtained from the Web site of the company that created it. Downloading is easy and instructions are usually provided.

A common plugin used on the Web is the Adobe Reader. This software allows you to view documents created in Adobe's Portable Document Format (PDF). These documents are the MIME type "application/pdf" and are associated with the file extension.

PROTOCOLS OF WEB

The surface simplicity of the Web comes from the fact that many individual protocols can be contained within a single Web site. Internet Protocols are sets of rules that allow for intermachine communication on the Internet.

The following are a few of the protocols you can experience on the Web:

- *HTTP (HyperText Transfer Protocol)*: Transmits hyptertext over networks. This is the protocol of the Web.

- *E-mail (Simple Mail Transport Protocol or SMTP)*: distributes e-mail messages and attached files to one or more electronic mailboxes.

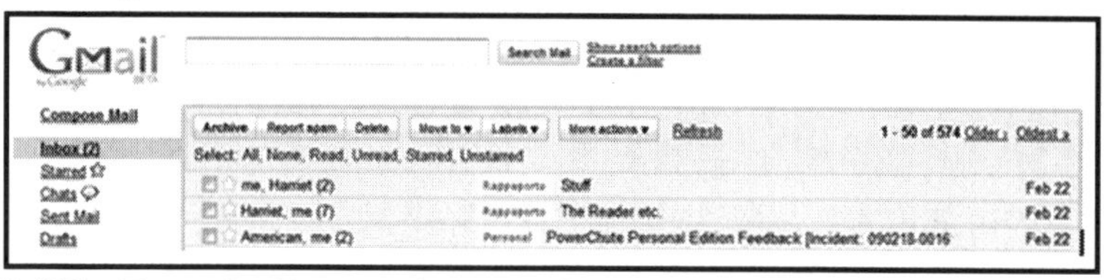

FTP (File Transfer Protocol): transfers files between an FTP server and a computer, for example, to download software.

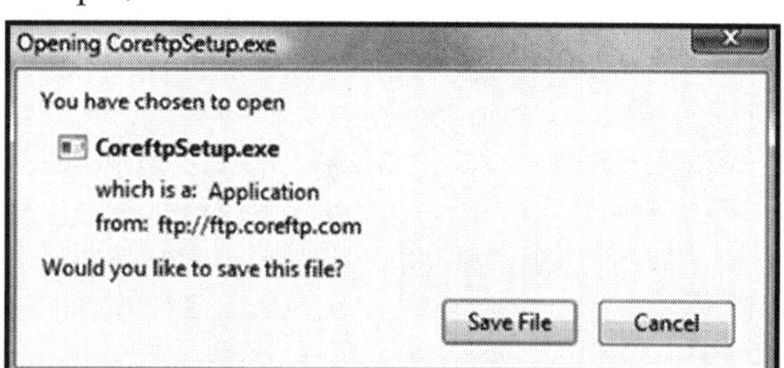

VoIP (Voice over Internet Protocol): allows delivery of voice communications over IP networks, for example, phone calls.

The Web provides a single, graphical interface for accessing these and other protocols. This creates a convenient and user-friendly environment. Once upon a time, it was necessary to know how to use protocols within separate, command-level environments. This meant you needed to know the text commands to make things happen. The Web is much easier, since it gathers these protocols together into a unified graphical system. Because of this feature, and because of the Web's ability to work with multimedia and advanced programming languages, the Web is by far the most popular component of the Internet.

COMPUTER DEVICES

A computer is a device that accepts information (in the form of digitalized data) and manipulates it for some result based on a programme or sequence of instructions on how the data is to be processed. Complex computers also include the means for storing data (including the programme, which is also a form of data) for some necessary duration. A programme may be invariable and built into the computer (and called *logic circuitry* as it is on microprocessors) or different programs may be provided to the computer (loaded into its storage and then started by an administrator or user). Today's computers have both kinds of programming.

Most histories of the modern computer begin with the Analytical Engineen visioned by Charles Babbage following the mathematical ideas of George Boole, the mathematician who first stated the principles of logic inherent in today's digital computer. Babbage's assistant and collaborator, Ada Lovelace, is said to have introduced the ideas of programme loops and subroutines and is sometimes considered the first programmer. Apart from mechanical calculators, the first really useable computers began with the vacuum tube, accelerated with the invention of the transistor, which then became embedded in large numbers in integrated circuits, ultimately making possible the relatively low-cost personal computer.

Modern computers inherently follow the ideas of the stored programme laid out byJohn von Neumann in 1945. Essentially, the programme is read by the computer one instruction at a time, an operation is performed, and the computer then reads in the next instruction, and so on. Recently, computers and programs have been devised that allow multiple programs (and computers) to work on the same problem at the same time in parallel. With the advent of the Internet and higher bandwidth data transmission, programs and data that are part of the same overall project can be distributed over a network and embody the Sun Microsystems slogan: "The network is the computer." Technically, a computer is a programmable machine. This means it can execute a programmed list of instructions and respond to new instructions that it is given.

Today, however, the term is most often used to refer to the desktop and laptop computers that most people use. When referring to a desktop model, the term "computer" technically only refers to the computer itself—not the monitor, keyboard, and mouse. Still, it is acceptable to refer to everything together as the computer. If you want to be really technical, the box that holds the computer is called the "system unit."

Some of the major parts of a personal computer (or PC) include the motherboard, CPU, memory (or RAM), hard drive, and video card. While personal computers are by far the most common type of computers today, there are several other types of computers. For example, a "minicomputer" is a powerful computer that can support many users at once. A "mainframe" is a large, high-powered computer that can perform billions of calculations from multiple sources at one time. Finally, a "supercomputer" is a machine that can process billions of instructions a second and is used to calculate extremely complex calculations. Computers are not very intelligent devices, but they handle instructions flawlessly and fast. They must follow explicit directions from both the user and computer programmer. Computers are really nothing more than a very powerful calculator with some great accessories. Applications like word processing and games are just a very complex math problem.

What a computer is in a specific, contemporary sense.Personal computers are found in most aspects of daily life, and for some it is hard to even imagine a world without them. But the term *computer* means more than simply the Macs and PCs we are familiar with. A computer is, at its most basic, a machine which can take instructions, and perform computations based on those instructions. It is the ability to take instructions — often known as programs in the parlance of computers — and execute them, that distinguishes a computer from a mechanical calculator. While both are able to make computations, a calculator responds simply to immediate input. In fact, most modern calculators are actually computers, with a number of pre-installed programs to help aid in complex tasks.

Computers range from the very small to the very large. Some are capable of doing millions of calculations in a single second, while others may take long periods of time to do even the most simple calculations. But theoretically, anything one computer is capable of doing, another computer will also be able to do. Given the right instructions, and sufficient memory, a computer found in a wristwatch should be able to accomplish anything a supercomputer can — although it might take thousands of years for the wristwatch to complete the operation.

PERSONAL COMPUTERS

Personal computers are computers that are meant to be used by individuals in homes or offices. Their retail prices, size, and capabilities make them practical for use in almost every home and office in the United States and other developed countries. The operation of personal computers relies on a small computer chip known as a microprocessor, which governs the functioning of the computer.

All personal computers have several basic components which allow the computer to function and be used. The microprocessor already mentioned oversees everything the computer does, and every process has to go through it first. Personal computers also have memory, usually in the form of random-access memory (RAM). This type of memory is used to store information that the computer is currently working with, such as open programs. The microprocessor and memory are contained as part of a large circuit board called the motherboard. The motherboard also acts as an intermediary between the microprocessor and other systems on the computer, such as drives and ports. The hard drive or hard disk is where programs and files are stored. As opposed to the RAM, the hard drive has a large capacity and is meant for long-term storage. This is where the majority of data in personal computers are located.

Another important part which is common to all personal computers is the power supply, which regulates the amount of electricity that the PC is using at a given time. Most personal computers also have sound cards and graphics cards as well. These are small circuit boards which connect to the motherboard to process audio and video data, respectively. More modern PCs also include a CD-ROM drive, where a compact disk containing programs or files can be inserted. Programs can be run directly from the CD-ROM, which acts as a form of external data storage for a PC. Personal computers were first introduced on the market in the late 1970s. Their capabilities and speed left much to be desired in comparison with modern PCs, but because of the advancement they represented, their popularity grew quickly. PCs began to be developed for everyday household use. Computer games and programs were developed which could be used on household computers, further opening up the market for these devices. By the year 2002, one billion PCs had been sold worldwide, since they were first introduced.

PCS

PCS, or a personal communications service, is the designation for a portion of theradio frequency band that is devoted to the use of wireless phone service in the United States, Canada, and Mexico. Here is some background on the development of the concept of the PCS, and how PCS continues to function today. Early in the development of cell phone technology, the need to assign particular bandwidths to the signals that would be used for cellular services was evident.

To this end, the need to carve out a radio band that would be for the exclusive use of cellular wireless networks was studied. Ultimately, the conclusions of the FCC in the United States and Industry Canada was that the designation of the 1850-1990 MHz range for use with cellular telephone service would ensure there was no interference with frequencies that were used for public broadcast or governmental functions. During 1994, both countries established the 1900 MHz band as the standard for use in any wireless network based for service in the United States or Canada. This effectively created the first unified PCS on the market. While this helped to ensure that the new technology did not interfere with other bandwidth uses, and also helped to make the process of interacting with a wired network easier, this did not address the issue of cellular phone interaction with European and Asian locations and services.

Over time, the development of dual band phones that allowed for signals to be processed that would accommodate both North American standards and other worldwide standards to be compatible. Sometimes referred to as multi-band GSMsystems, many parts of the world now use PCS as a term to describe GSM services that operate in the 1900 MHz range.

SUPERCOMPUTER

A supercomputer is a computer which performs at a rate of speed which is far above that of other computers. Given the constantly changing world of computing, it should come as no surprise to learn that most supercomputers bear their superlative titles for a few years, at best. Computer programmers are fond of saying that today's supercomputer will become tomorrow's computer; the computer you are reading this article on is probably more powerful than most historic supercomputers, for example.

The term "supercomputer" was coined in 1929 by the New York World, referring to tabulators manufactured by IBM. To modern computer users, these tabulators would probably appear awkward, slow, and cumbersome to use, but at the time, they represented the cutting edge of technology. This continues to be true of supercomputers today, which harness immense processing power so that they are incredibly fast, sophisticated, and powerful.

The primary use for supercomputers is in scientific computing, which requires high-powered computers to perform complex calculations. Scientific organizations like NASAboast supercomputers the size of rooms for the purpose of performing calculations, rendering complex formulas, and performing other tasks which require a formidable amount of computer power. Some supercomputers have also been designed for very specific functions like cracking codes and playing chess; Deep Blue is a famous chess-playing supercomputer. In many cases, a supercomputer is custom-assembled, utilizing elements from a range of computer manufacturers and tailored for its intended use.

Most supercomputers run on a Linux or Unix operating system, as these operating systems are extremely flexible, stable, and efficient. Supercomputers typically have multiple processors and a variety of other technological tricks to ensure that they run smoothly.

2

Software and Hardware

DESCRIPTION

Hardware and software work together in digital devices and systems to provide computerized functionality. Hardware includes the physical components, such as the motherboard, chips, memory, and hard drives, while software includes the programs that run on the hardware. Ergo, a computer is hardware, while anoperating system such as Microsoft XP is the software that makes the hardware functional.

Though hardware and software are most often associated with computers, software also runs on other hardware, such as cellular phones, personal digital assistants (PDAs), Global Positioning Satellite (GPS) units,medical equipment, and air traffic control systems. Modern cash registers are also computerized with software to better organize sales-related issues likeinventory, tax, and coupon discounts.

Computer technology is employed in nearly every facet of modern society. Many software programs used in industry are proprietary, which means they are designed for a specific function. This differs from computers that are generally multi-purpose, with many different kinds of software programs for various tasks.

Hardware and software are constantly improving in a kind of leapfrog fashion. Hardware is most often the bottleneck when it comes to data transfer speeds, or how fast a software programme can work. Therefore, as hardware improves, it becomes capable of running more robust software programs. Old hardware from just ten years ago may not run current software, as the software might be designed to take advantage of hardware in ways that older hardware cannot support.

INDUSTRY

The Computer Hardware and Software industry of Bangalore is regarded as the focal point of advanced technology that acts as the prime catalyst in the economic growth of the city. Housing the biggest international names of Information Technology, Bangalore is referred as the Silicon Valley of India. With the widening of the global business horizon, Bangalore has emerged as the key player in the field of Information Technology and Information Technology enabled services.

From proposed plans of Hardware Park to a thriving Business Process Outsourcing sector, Bangalore is progressing beyond leaps and bounds. The city deals with the latest models of Hardware tools Computer parts, Software programmes and accessories. The newest developments in the Software programming domain enable Bangalore to compete with the best IT brands of the world.

The major IT and ITes organizations of global repute that add credibility to the Computer Hardware and Software contours of Bangalore are:

- Microsoft Corporation
- IBM Global Services Ltd.
- Infosys Technologies Ltd.
- Intel Asia Electronics Inc.
- ITC Ltd. – Information Systems Div.
- Oracle Software (I) Ltd.
- SAP India Pvt. Ltd.
- Satyam Computer Services Ltd.
- Tata Consultancy Services
- Wipro Infotech Group
- Dell Asia Pacific SDN
- Citicorp
- CMC Ltd.
- Aptech Ltd.
- Compaq India
- Tata Infotech Ltd.
- Verifone
- TVS Electronics South Asia (P) Ltd.

The software a series of very simple computer instructions carefully organized to complete complex tasks. These instructions are written in programming languages (like BASIC, PASCAL, C.) to help simplify the development of applications. The hardware is what sits on your desk and executes the software instructions. The player piano is useless unless the roll of music has been written correctly.

ADVANCED OF COMPUTER HARDWARE

Computer hardware has advanced drastically since the early days when computers took up entire rooms and required teams of people to run. Modern computer systems fit in a small case and can draw power from a standard wall jack. It is important to learn about the components of your computer so that you can diagnose problems or replace equipment as it becomes outdated.

FUNCTION

Hardware is the corporeal and tangible portion of a computer system that you interact with to take advantage of computer programmes. It is distinct from software in that it is built of physical material and generally does not perform logical operations or change its state frequently.

Main System

The central piece of hardware for any computer is the motherboard, which is a circuit board that contains all of the sockets, slots, and chip sets that all of the other hardware devices will be connected into. The central processing unit, which handles all of the mathematical calculations that the computer needs to perform, is attached to the main socket of the motherboard. The two main companies that produce processors are AMD and Intel, each make a variety of different processor types that work with different motherboards. The random access memory attaches to slots in the motherboard and it controls the speed that computations occur. The hard drive is the component that actually stores all of the data in the computer such as files, music or games. All of these units are run by a power supply that plugs into a wall socket.

Input

In order to interact with your computer system, you will need some kind of input hardware. Most computer systems require one or more input devices to be connected or it will not boot up at all. The most popular input devices are a mouse for navigating the screen, a keyboard for typing text and a microphone for sending voice over the internet or activating voice command software.

Output

The fastest or most advanced computer in the world is useless without a means of displaying information to the user. Output hardware devices solve this problem by visually displaying graphics or text or playing sounds. A monitor is the most common type of output device. Older and bulkier cathode-ray tube monitors worked much like early televisions but most modern monitors are flat panel liquid crystal displays. Printers can also be considered output devices as they can print information from a software programme.

CONCEPT OF COMPUTER IMAGES

Computer generated images (known as CGI) have become very popular over the past two decades, and their importance and use will increase even further in the future because of their wide applicability in various fields. In the area of movies and films in general CGI has become an essential tool for filmmakers to bring their visions to the screen, be it by creating computer generated characters, props, sets, or just simplifying the process of image and sound editing. Film production has been made faster and more efficient in the postproduction phase, offering an unprecedented level of freedom and quality.

The success of 3D computer animation and CGI in general started in the early 90s, when software bundles and processing power got more affordable even for smaller companies, and since then it turned into an accepted art form by itself. Over the years the technology evolved further and further, lowering the barrier between art and technology, and even allowing these two extremes to blend seamlessly.

CREATION OF 3D GRAPHICS

The creation of CGI and computer animation requires the use of specialized software products. Several bundles have established on the market, and it is mainly a question of personal preference which one to pick. After all the biggest factor in creating convincing digital worlds is the artist himself, whereas the software is merely the tool to transfer his creativity onto the screen.

As graphics software became more user-friendly and intuitive, the process of creating CGI started to resemble its real-world counterparts, like painting, sculpting, photography and filmmaking. The area of computer animation for example requires the same steps of "real world" filmmaking, with the addition of modeling sets, props and characters first. Bringing a mass of "digital clay" into shape to form a convincing character (or any other object or location to be shown, for that matter) is the initial step. Then cameras, lights and other entities are arranged in the virtual space, and animated if necessary.

TELEVISION, FILM PRODUCTION AND COMMERCIALS

Computer animation and three-dimensional visualization is widely used in television, commercials and film production. The "small screen" has proven to be the perfect field for experimenting with newly developed technology and concepts, and many artists working in the area of television and commercials have made their way to the movie business. With software bundles getting cheaper and more accessible, independent artists and filmmakers seized the opportunity to create their own films and short films, a development, which gave the visual quality of films an enormous boost in the mid 90s. In the area of film production computer animation slowly started replacing hand-made models and puppets, and even the genre of animated films has gotten a digital counterpart.

SCIENTIFIC VISUALIZATION

Computer animation produced to present meteorological data, medical imaging,industriefilm, architecture and technology.

PRODUCT DESIGN AND ENGINEERING

Designers and engineers use special CAD (computer aided design) software for designing, developing and manufacturing consumer and industrial products. Product visualization extensively uses modern graphics technology and with the help of computers, designs can be rotated, cut and manipulated even before getting manufactured. This greatly helps engineers visualize the product that they are designing.

HARDWARE COMPONENTS

INPUT DEVICES

A keyboard and mouse are the standard way to interact with the computer. Other devices include joysticks and game pads used primarly for games. A hardware device that sends information into the CPU. Without any input devices a computer would simply be a display device and not allow users to interact with it, much like a TV. Below is a listing of different types of computer input devices.

Digital camera

A type of camera that stores the pictures or video it takes in electronic format instead of to film. There are several features that make digital cameras a popular choice when compared to film cameras. First, the feature often enjoyed the most is the LCD display on the digital camera. This display allows users to view photos or video after the picture or video has been taken, which means if you take a picture and don't like the results, you can delete it; or if you do like the picture, you can easily show it to other people. Another nice feature with digital cameras is the ability to take dozens, sometimes hundreds of different pictures.

Casio QV-R62
6.0 Mega Pixel Digital Camera

Digital cameras have quickly become the camera solution for most users today as the quality of picture they take has greatly improved and as the price has decreased. Many users however are hesitant in buying a digital camera because of the inability of getting their pictures developed. However, there are several solutions in getting your digital pictures developed. For example, there are numerous Internet companies capable of developing your pictures and send you your pictures in the mail. In addition, many of the places that develop your standard cameras film now have the ability to develop digital pictures

Joystick

A peripheral input device that looks similar to a control device you would find on an arcade game at your local arcades.

Logitech Freedom 2.4 Joystick

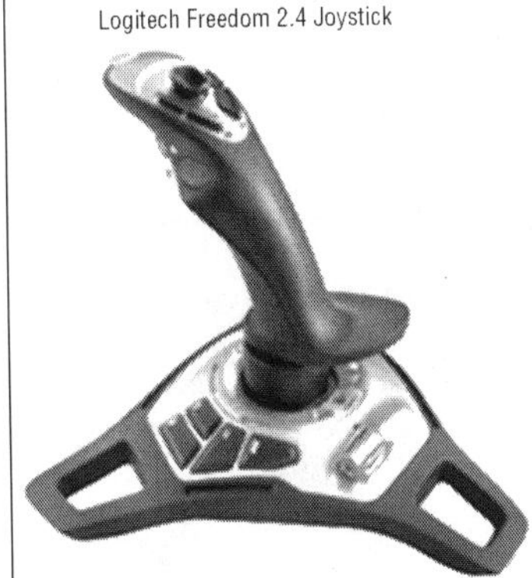

A computer joystick allows an individual to easily navigate an object in a game such as navigating a plane in a flight simulator. The image is of the Logitech Freedom 2.4 joystick and is an example of what you would expect most computer joysticks to look like.

Keyboard

One of the main input devices used on a computer, a PC's keyboard looks very similar to the keyboards of electric typewriters, with some additional keys. Below is a graphic of the Saitek Gamers' keyboard with indicators pointing to each of the major portions of the keyboard.

Saitek Gamers' Keyboard

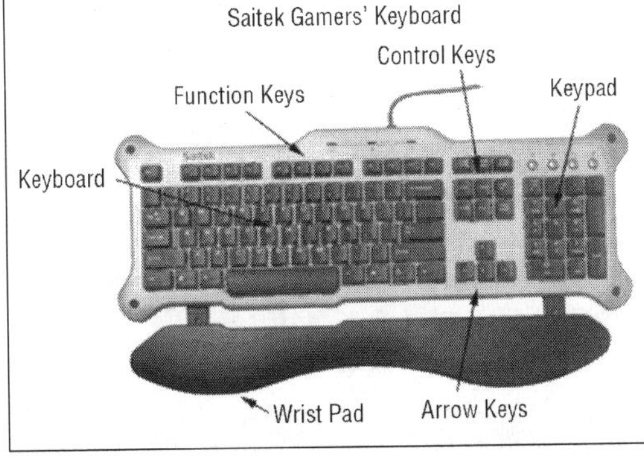

Finally, today most users use the QWERTY style keyboards. Below is a graphic illustration of where each of the keys are on a QWERTY style keyboard.

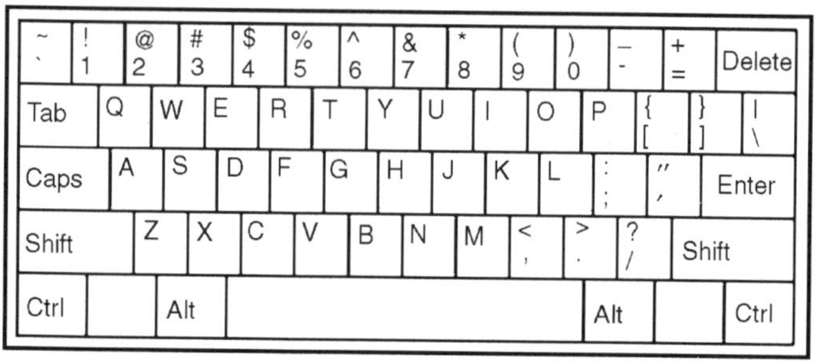

Microphone

Sometimes abbreviated as mic, a microphone is a hardware peripheral that allows computer users to input audio into their computers. To the right is a visual example of a USB headset from Logitech with a microphone. A popular solution for computer gaming.

Logitech USB headset

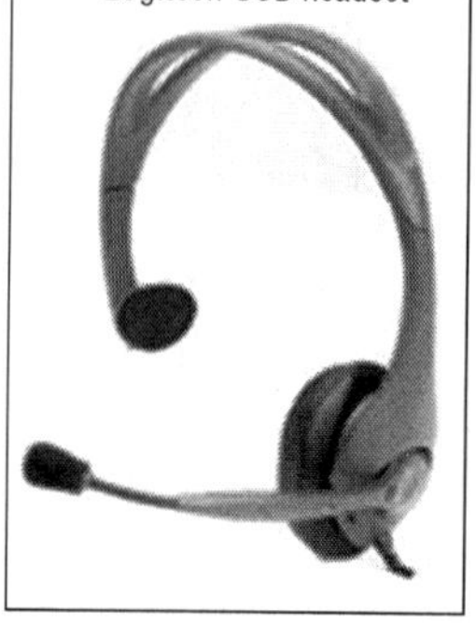

Mouse

A hardware input device that was invented by Douglas Engelbart in 1963, who at the time was working at the Stanford Research Institute, which was a think tank sponsored by University. The mouse allows an individual to control a pointer in a graphical user interface (GUI). Utilizing a mouse a user has the ability to perform various functions such as opening a programme or file and does not require the user to memorize commands, like those used in a text-based command line environment such as MS-DOS.

The Mouse was originally referred to as an X-Y Position Indicator for a Display System. Xerox later applied the mouse to its revolutionary Alto computer system in 1973. However, because of Alto's unfortunate success, it was first widely used in the Apple Lisa computer. Today, the mouse is now found on virtually every computer.

Types of computer mouse:

- Cordless
- Footmouse
- Glidepoint
- IntelliMouse
- J mouse
- Joystick
- Mechanical
- Optical
- Touchpad
- Trackball
- TrackPoint
- Wheel mouse

Scanner

Hardware input device that allows a user to take an image and/or text and convert it into a digital file, allowing the computer to read and/or display the scanned object. A scanner commonly connected to a computer USB Firewire Parallel or SCSI port.

Web Cam

A camera connected to a computer or server that allows anyone connected to the Internet to view still pictures or motion video of a user. The majority of webcam web sites are still pictures that are frequently refreshed every few seconds, minutes, hours, or days. However, there are some sites and personal pages that can supply streaming video for users with broadband.

Logitech
QuickCam Express
Model: 961183

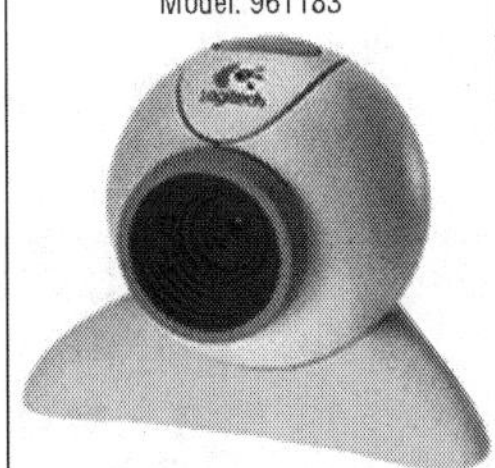

The image of the Logitech QuickCam Express and an example of what a webcam may look like. Today, most webcams are connected to the USB or Firewire port on a computer.

- There are millions of webcams around the world that allow you to view other people, places, and even events. If you're interested in looking at webcams, click here to open a search for webcams.
- If you're looking to chat with other webcam users live a great site with millions of other webcam users is Stickam.
- Parents with children should be aware of the potential dangers of children and webcams. Additional information about protecting children from harmful material on the Internet can be found on document CH000526.
- document CH000890 for additional information about users without webcams viewing users with webcams.

Output Devices

Any device that outputs information from a computer is called, not surprisingly, an output device. Since most information from a computer is output in either a visual or auditory format, the most common output devices are the monitor and speakers. These two devices provide instant feedback to the user's input, such as displaying characters as they are typed or playing a song selected from a playlist. While monitors and speakers are the most common output devices, there are many others. Some examples include headphones, printers, projectors, lighting control systems, audio recording devices, and robotic machines. A computer without an output device connected to it is pretty useless, since the output is what we interact with. Anyone who has ever had a monitor or printer stop working knows just how true this is.

Printer

Printers take information from the CPU and transfer it to paper. There are a number of different printer technologies available.

Dot Matrix

Dot Matrix printers are inexpensive and reliable, but they are loud and slow. They do not have nearly the print quality of some of the other types of printers.

Ink Jet

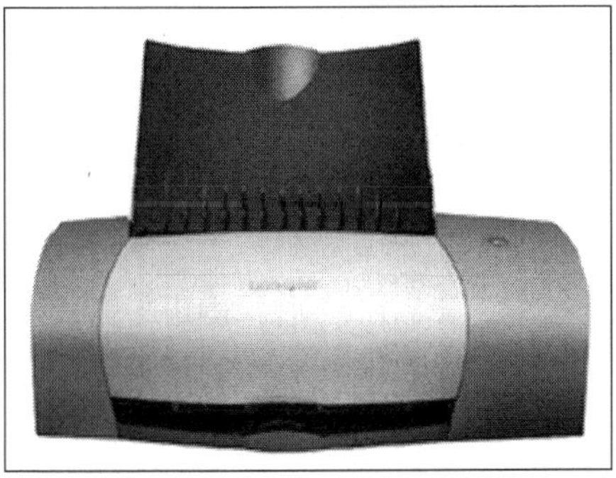

Ink Jet printers squirt small streams of ink onto the paper. They tend to be slightly more expensive than dot matrix printers, but the quiet operation and improved print quality make them very popular with buyers of home computers. Some ink jet printers can make colour prints. These can be very entertaining, but the ink becomes expensive.

Laser Printers

Laser Printers use a combination of laser and copying technology to make very clear copies. Laser printers tend to make clearer copies than the other types of printers, and operate much more quickly, but they can be quite expensive to purchase and maintain.

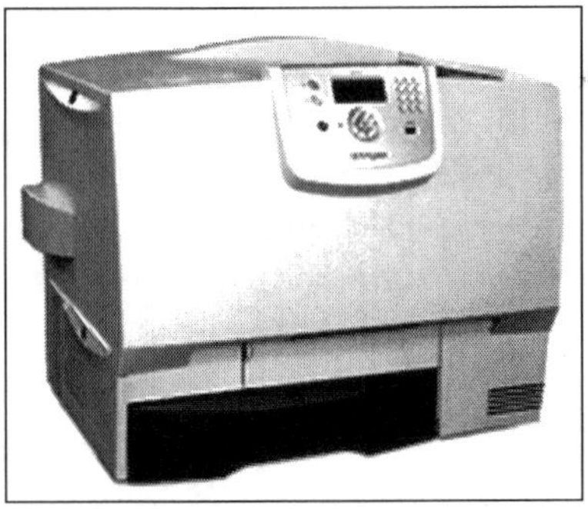

Many people try to save money on a printer purchase and are disappointed. If the main reason you will use your computer is to type letters, remember that the people you write to will not see your monitor. What they will see is only what comes out of your printer.

If printed documents are an important part of what you will use a computer for, consider a higher quality printer. Ink Jets are probably most appropriate for home use, and laser printers are more popular in an office setting. A dot matrix machine is fine for test printing or use on a kid's computer, but you will be disappointed with the results if you try to use it for business correspondence.

Monitors

Desktop Monitor

Liquid Crystal Display

The monitor is the part of the system that you look at most of the time. Monitors resemble televisions. Most computer monitors use the same technology as televisions, but with much higher resolution. Often the monitor will come packaged with a computer system, but you may wish to upgrade.

Size

The size of a monitor can make a big impact. You might get a headache squinting at a screen that is too small. The size of a monitor is measured in diagonal inches. a 15 inch monitor is 15 inches diagonally from corner to corner of the screen.

Dot Pitch and DPI

Monitors are also measured by their precision. There are two main measures, Dot Pitch, and DPI. Dot pitch is a measure of the size of each tiny dot the monitor can display. The smaller each dot is, the nicer the picture will look, but the more expensive the monitor will be. When discussing Dot Pitch, SMALLER IS BETTER!! DPI stands for Dots Per Inch. As you can guess, the smaller the dot pitch rating for a monitor is, the more of those tiny dots you could squeeze into a square inch. If you are considering DPI, LARGER IS BETTER.

Video Controller Card

Dealing with graphics takes a lot of work. Modern computers usually have a separate computer built in just to help with controlling the monitor. This little computer has its own cpu and memory! The power and speed of this little computer, as well as its memory capacity, have a huge effect on how graphics are drawn to your screen. This little computer is referred to as a graphics controller card. The most common cards now are called SVGA. Of course it gets way more complicated than this, but all you have to know is that there are fancier cards that do more and cost more, but you may not need the fanciest one out there for your first computer.

Projectors

A hardware device that enables an image, such as a computer screen, to be projected onto a flat surface. These devices are commonly used in meetings and presentations as they allow for a large image to be shown so everyone in a room can see.

A general diagram of projector as an example image of what a projector may look like is shown below. As can be seen in this image the projector is a small device often a little bigger than a toaster and typically weighs a few pounds.

Speakers

A hardware device connected to a computer's sound card that outputs sounds generated by the card. Below is a graphic image example of the general speakers with subwoofer; speakers like the ones shown below are an example of what most computer speakers resemble.

Plotters

A plotter can be used to produce very large drawings on paper sizes up to A0 (16 times as big as A4). A plotter draws onto the paper using very fine pens. There are two types of plotter. They differ in the way that the pen can be moved about on the piece of paper to draw lines:

Flatbed Plotter

The paper is fixed and the pen moves left and right and up and down across the paper to draw lines.

Drum Plotter

The pen moves up and down on the paper and the paper is moved left and right by rotating a drum on which the paper is placed. Plotters can automatically change their pens and so can produce colour output. The lines drawn by a plotter are continuous and very accurate. Plotters are very slow but produce high quality output.

They are usually used for Computer Aided Design (CAD) and Computer Aided Manufacturing (CAM) applications such as printing out plans for houses or car parts. The quality of the output produced by ink jet printers is now very good and large format (big) ink-jet printers are steadily replacing plotters for most tasks.

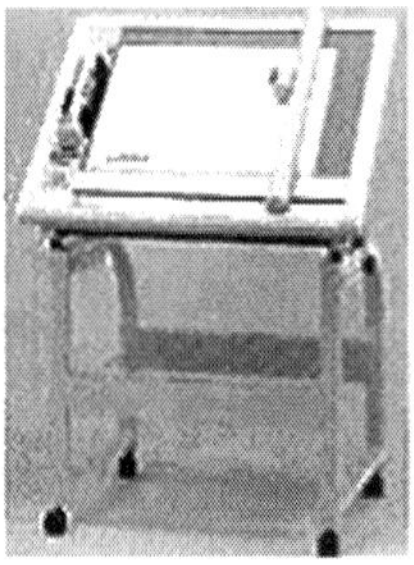
Flatbed Plotter

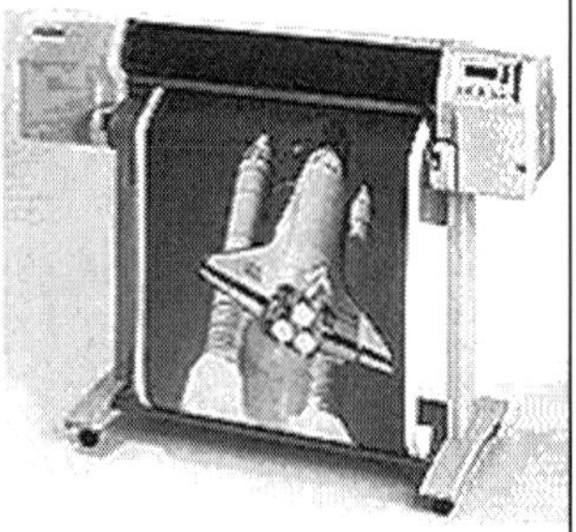
Drum Plotter

COMMON INPUT OUTPUT DEVICES

RAM

RAM is perhaps the most important of the input/output devices. When we talk about computer memory, we are mainly talking about RAM. In this class, when we think about the banks of light switches that can be manipulated, we are thinking of RAM memory. The term Random Access is pretty unfortunate. There is nothing random about how memory is accessed. The programme running will determine what is in memory. (of course, the programme itself is in memory too!) RAM can be read from by the CPU. This means that the CPU can 'look' at any address in RAM and get the contents of that address. It can also be written to by the CPU, meaning that the CPU can change the value of memory cells on the fly.

One VERY important aspect of RAM memory is that it requires power. RAM can only hold values while power is going through it. If the power is interrupted, the RAM will lose ALL the values in it. This is why it is so important to save your work frequently when working on a computer. RAM memory is volatile.

When the room you are working on is hit by a tsunami and the power goes out of your computer, you lose everything that was in RAM. This could be bad. The amount of RAM in your computer is obviously a pretty important factor. The more memory you have, the more 'room' there is in your computer for information and programs. Modern programs have gotten HUGE, and the kinds of information you can work with have gotten much larger. Some early home computers had 4 or 16 K of RAM. The original IBM PC had 640 K of RAM.

In its day, this was thought of as an extravagant amount of memory that would never be fully used. Modern computers with less than 16 Megabytes (16,000 K) are considered a bit lame. (pun completely intended.) Older computers can be quite happy with much less RAM, but they will not be able to run the newer programs.

Disk Drives

Disk drives are special devices that allow us to make copies of parts of RAM and store them magnetically. If RAM memory is electronic, think of disk drives as a special kind of magnetic memory. When you save something to a disk, the electronic impulses in RAM are copied and stored to the disk as a series of magnetic impulses.

All a disk drive does is translate electronic impulses and magnetic impulses back and forth. Disk drives are handy because magnetic impulses are more permanent than electronic ones. The disk drive does not require electricity to keep values in memory, so if you store something to a disk, the information will be there when the tidal wave knocks the power out to your computer. (Assuming, of course, that the disk stayed dry and clean) Disks are sometimes thought of as secondary storage for this reason.

Floppy Drives

A floppy drive is a machine that is designed to read floppy disks. Floppy disks are the removable devices that you stick in slots in the front of the machine. I know, they look square, not disk-shaped, and they don't look floppy at all, but they are indeed floppy disks. Floppy disks come in hard plastic cases to make them a little more sturdy and easier to handle, but inside the plastic case, there is an actual disk. It is made of a plastic-like substance called mylar which really is floppy.

Floppy disks come in two main sizes; 5 1/4 inch, and 3 1/2 inch. The 5 1/4 disks are becoming obsolete, but you still see them from time to time. The 3 1/2 inch disks, although physically smaller, can usually hold more information! There are different flavours of floppy disks.

In a modern computer, the only kind of floppy you need to purchase is High Density 1.44 MB. As you can guess, they hold 1.44 MegaBytes of information, which is a pretty good amount. (You could hold several hundred pages of text or about a dozen full colour pictures on a 1.44 MB disk) This type of disk may carry some other markings as well, such as DSHD or HD. The HD is the important part. That tells you it can handle 1.44 MB.

Hard Drives

A hard drive is a special disk that is usually mounted permanently inside your computer's cabinet. You rarely see the hard drive, and almost never take it out. Hard drives are made of different material than floppies, and they are physically hard (although if you touched the actual hard surface, you would destroy it!) They spin much more quickly than floppies, and require much more precision.

They are sealed inside a special case, and that is sealed inside the computer case. A hard drive has a much larger capacity than a floppy, and is much faster at saving and retrieving information. Modern computers frequently have hard drives with 500 MB or more of capacity. As this capacity grows, people are beginning to measure it in terms of gigabytes. Software programs are always becoming larger and taking more room on hard drives. It never takes long to completely fill up the capacity of a drive. If you can afford a large drive when you buy the computer, you won't be sorry, but you can usually add another drive or upgrade later.

Fancier kinds of Drives

There are a number of other types of drives you may encounter when buying or upgrading a computer. You may encounter such things as Bernoulli tape drives, WORM (write once, read many) drives, optical floppies, and removable hard drives. All these things are really cool, but you may want to stick with the basics until you are a little more comfortable with the technology. Any computer system ought to have at least one 3.5 inch floppy drive, as large a hard drive as possible, and a CD-ROM drive.

Drive Controller Cards

Most computers come with a small card installed that helps control all your disk drives. It is called the Drive Controller Card. There are two major kinds, IDE and SCSI. The only time you will ever care about this is when you buy a hard drive. Just know that the terms IDE and SCSI are terms that describe the drive controller card.

Network Card

In a home computer, you will generally not have a network card, but these devices are very common for computers in office settings. A network card is a special card which allows your computer to talk to other computers that are physically attached via cables. Depending on how the network is set up, you can send messages from computer to computer, run programs that are stored on different computers, and share devices like hard drives and printers. In many offices, the network also gives you access to the Internet. Network connections are generally faster than modem connections.

Modem

Modems were once thought of as somewhat extravagant, but with the advent of the Internet, they are becoming a necessity for home computers. They allow you to connect your computer to the Internet or other computer systems through a telephone connection. The term Modem stands for Modulator/Demodulator. It is a device that converts back and forth from the digital signals that computers understand to analog signals (sounds) that can be transferred over telephone lines. Modems can be internal or external. The external ones have their own little case and power supply, and are generally a little more expensive than the internal ones, which are little cards that fit inside the computer.

Modems are rated by their transmission speed, which is measured in BAUD (Bits of Audio Data/Second). If you want to do any Internet connections, you need a baud rate of 1440 BAUD (also sometimes called 14400 BPS or 14.4 KBPS) You can also purchase faster modems, but they are of course more expensive. In the near future, something will happen in this arena. It is likely that we will be switching to a completely new kind of communication technology for home computers, but nobody knows exactly what that will be just yet. Some modems also include faxing and voice mail capabilities. These features can be very convenient for people with home offices.

Sound Card

Sound cards are another peripheral device that was once thought to be extravagant, but is now pretty much standard equipment on any new machine. A sound card is a device which enables the computer to handle sounds (duh!). It can handle sounds in two major ways. It can create sound effects entirely through programming, or it can record sounds through a standard microphone. Sound cards are attached to speakers which recreate the sound. Obviously, sound cards are a big boost to computer game players, but they are frequently being used for more serious pursuits as well.

People can attach voice annotations to documents they have written, musicians can test and modify a composition with a computer, and people with visual disabilities can have screens of text read to them. The basic sound card is referred to as an 8-bit sound card, because it processes 8 bits of information at a time. You can now find 16-bit, and even 32-bit sound cards if you are willing to pay for them. As always, it depends on what you want your computer to do for you.

SOFTWARE

OVERVIEW

Various types of computer software are used to simplify the operations and applications of computer programmes. Computer software enables the computer system to perform in accordance with the given tasks. Computer software involves all types of software related applications. Electronic media content is also explained by the computer software.

EXPLANATION

Computer software, a general term used for computer programmes and data. Principally it makes up the operating system of the computer, and this computer software can either be created or purchased. Computers have vast and varied capabilities because of the many different kinds of available computer software. Computer software is held in the storage of computers for a very specific purpose and performs the function of the programme it implements, either by directly providing instructions to the computer hardware or by serving as an input to another piece of software. Computer software is described as the information processed by the systems.

Computer software can be classified into two types:

- *Systems software*: Includes basic input-output systems, device drivers etc. In most cases this software comes along in the box when the computer is purchased.
- *Applications software*: Examples of this type of software includes office suites and video games, and may be purchased separately from the computer. Computer users can also create their own computer software, including spreadsheet templates, word processor macros etc.

Once you have installed the software by following the correct instructions, the computer is then able to operate the software. The computer will pass the instructions from the application software, through the system software and on to the hardware. Each instruction carries out an operation on the computer. There is such a wide variety of computer software, I think we could successfully list pages and pages. Here is an example of a few types of different software: animated models software, communication software, desktop publishing software, ERP software, help desk software, PDF conversion software, simulation software etc. Basically there is a software on the market for nearly every human need.

Different specifications to consider when selecting your computer software:

- Firstly decipher your needs and then ensure the software fulfils all your requirements.
- Ensure the software is compatible with your computer.
- Ensure you purchase an adequate number of licenses from your supplier as prescribed.

Remember that the function of computer software is to perform a specific task you need completed! There is even dating software out there to start your own dating service, or join americansingles.com which is a dating system setup already and many members to choose from. With the innovative technology of low vision devices, it is possible for people to regain visual independence from low vision conditions. If you are having computer software problems, call an IT help line for help getting your computer working correctly.

CLASSIFICATION OF SOFTWARE

Different types of computer software are available in the global computer market. Programming software, system software and application software are the three main types of computer software used in computer networking. System software is the most commonly used variety of computer software. System software offers a protective shield to all software applications. It also provides support to the physical components of computers.

System software coordinates all external devices of computer system like printer, keyboard, displays etc. Programmers use the programming software to develop the programming languages necessary to run computer software. Compliers, interpreters, linkers and text editors are some of the basic tools used in programming software. Application software is used for commercial purpose. The application software is widely used in educational, business and medical fields. Computer games are the most popular forms of application software. Industrial automation, databases, business software and medical software prove to be of great help in the respective fields. Educational software is widely used in educational institutes across the globe.

ACCOUNTING SOFTWARE

It is critical for any business (small, medium or large) wishing to be successful in industry to have accurate accounting systems in place. Systems which diagnose and record financial transactions of an organization, such as acquisitions and sales or cost information within the organization. With this comes the installation of appropriate accounting software.

Accounting software is a class of computer programmes that perform accounting operations. The accounting software is to aid the business in developing accounting solutions that allow for accelerated and more reliable processing of their accounting information.

They may vary from simple to more complicated:

- Single-entry systems which automate check writing and record keeping.
- Double-entry systems, this includes a wider variety of functions in accounts receivable, general ledger, and accounts payable.

Some of the tasks to out look for that may be offered in various packages, is that of invoice creation, calculating sales tax, tracking of employee hours and payment. You should even be able to create tax reports to send to your accountant. Expand your accounting knowledge by taking a bookkeeping course to maximize your time and efficiency. In today's high tech society there are plenty of quality accounting software providers you can choose from. It is not always the best idea to purchase the most expensive accounting software, as programmes vary in what they offer, so maybe it is best to sit down after you have drawn up a list of what you need, and study the different packages available and purchase that best suited to your needs.

Also try and research into the support and maintenance assistance that is available on offer for accounting software packages. Track employee time and attendance with Spectrum TimeClock, web based time clock software.

Advantages of using accounting software packages:

- Back office and other functions are taken care of allowing you to focus on the primary purpose of your business-the reason you started the business.
- It improves the efficiency of your business, allowing more time.

To manage your accounts sufficiently also enables managers to determine product profitability and to investigate inefficiencies. They come to scrutinize information in a different way which is more relevant to the needs of the business.

Ecommerce Software

Ecommerce is the business of buying and selling things online. It allows a store owner to setup shop, run and maintain their online store with absolute minimum effort. There is a variety of ecommerce software available in order to make this efficient for both store owner and buyer.

Before ecommerce software the ecommerce business used to keep track of things on disks, or even hand written in books which is time consuming and not as accurate. Ecommerce software is however considered to be much more reliable. Basically you can't have ecommerce without the software, or successfully anyway. Before purchasing just any ecommerce software, research what your needs are, what is available and that your needs are met. Consider issues such as electrical failure, computer viruses, hackers on the net, and that the maintenance on the ecommerce software is kept up to date on a regular basis.

The selling for a company is only half of their battle. Current ecommerce software packages enables you the store owner to build a site where buyers can view your goods, add or delete items from their selection, and most important are able to review their final selection prior to buying.

Necessary requirements are:

- Storefront appearance
- Proper records kept of purchases made, customer details, shipping details
- Can handle currencies and tax levels

- Buyer e-mailed with purchase confirmation
- Software has a good customer base

An ecommerce store is handled via a very easy-to-use browser. There are different options to keep in mind for the buyer, *e.g.* should it include VAT and postage costs, accept all major credit cards (as people are buying online globally), search by keyword or brand, browse by a category or subcategory. The process for order facilities can include: printing off order summaries and invoices, being able to modify orders online and delivery dates, finding orders by status, date, surname or ID.

One of the most important features is the sites security, does it have a password protected admin area, firewall and daily backup, credit card orders address verification, CV credit card signature strip check as well as anti-spam and anti-virus options.

CD Burning Software

A new innovation since the development of tape recording is CD burning. A compact disc (CD) is a small disc on which audio signals, video signals, or other data can be recorded in digital form. CD burning is the production of information recorded as a succession of discrete, rather than as continuously varying parameters. There is a variety of software available for doing this including free cd burning software on the market.

The question still remains, why do people want to burn cd's and it is simple, because you would like to create mixed CD's from your current cd collection or maybe from your MP3 music collection. CD burning software purchased in the shops can be incredibly expensive and free CD burning software is often just as good.

So browse on the internet for the many sites available offering this free CD burning software, rather than wasting your money. With today's technology free CD burning software gives you an error free burn in the fastest possible time.

Some features included in free cd burning software:

- Audio recording
- Overburn feature
- Burn-proof technology to prevent CD coasters
- Creates multi-session CD's
- Creates bootable CD's
- Enables you to design your very own CD inserts and covers
- Supports all popular CD standards
- Rip audio CD's
- Burns audio CD without gaps between tracks

The above are only some of the features that can be included so when wanting to burn your CD's carefully review what is available. With free CD burning software you can burn from either CD-R, CD-RW and depending on the component set of the software the CD burner may support the creation of data CD's and audio CD's. Some may even support the burning of a CD-R/RW. To purchase this free CD burning software all you need to do is prepare this search function in your regular browser, and once you have found one that suits your needs, click on the download button. It is that simple.

Video Editing Software

We all love to capture that special moment, holiday or memory. Some of us have spent thousands on video cameras and have stacks of videos lying around, unedited and boring. However all you need is the right video editing software to change them into awe inspiring videos.

Luckily with today's computers we can kiss goodbye all those expensive and specialized equipment and say hello to the new video editing software. With this introduction editing one's videos has become easier to do, and there is a variety to choose from, basic programmes to compile the video and add simple transitions, or why not a sophisticated programme with advanced effects, sound and editing tools. There is something for everyone. The possibilities as well as the choices are endless.

Qualities to look for when seeking video editing software:

- *Ease of use*: Easy software is a key to video editing success.
- *Feature set*: They may vary in quality and quantity; but those with large feature sets are often more difficult to use than software with smaller feature sets. Purchase those with the features that closely match your needs.
- *Installation and setup*: Ensure the video editing software is easy to install, otherwise you may not even use it.
- *Help and Tech support*: this is not a bonus but in actual fact a necessity.

There is also a variety of types of video files that need editing for *e.g.* AVI, MPG. etc. So ensure you are aware what it is you will be editing. Some video editing software do include features to edit a combination. Operations that can be included in the video editing software are: deleting the frame, delete selection, crop, resize, rotate, mirror, flip, trim, text overlay, adjusting audio volume. In addition to those just mentioned some may even include powerful video enhancement and alternation. Some even include a scene content detection which automatically breaks your home movie up into scenes. Every time the camera is started and then stopped again, this is considered a scene.

Some of the more specific features of video editing software include:

- Allowing you to arrange video clips exactly as you would arrange pictures on the page of your photo album, each pic representing a separate video clip. Some allow you to display your video clips using a timeline.
- The potential to split one scene into two separate scenes.

- Video signals or animation effects that indicate that one scene has ended and another is about to begin.
- Allows you to remove the beginning or end of a sound track.

Inventory Software

Inventory is a listing of the assets of any organization, but specifically referring to it's stock. Organizations need to keep records of stocks of raw materials, semi-finished, and finished but unsold goods to help determine profitability and efficiency levels. Annual financial records need to take account of inventory costs.

In times of inflation a particular problem is how to value inventory when the value of some assets rises above the cost paid for them, but with inventory software this is done for you. If we take a look back to the past, the calculating of inventory was originally done by hand, which proved to be extremely tedious and possibly inaccurate.

Now with the introduction of inventory software it tracks the inventory of goods for sale or used in manufacturing of products for sale, saving both time and inaccurate losses. Some of the current inventory software that has been introduced is a flexible solution for inventory accounting, check depositing, sales purchase tracing and tracking. They are also implemented with high-class and quick edit functions enabling optimal formatted content to print, to export or to send out as an e-mail.

Off the shelf inventory software are easy to use bar-code based tracking solutions. They maintain a perpetual inventory so that when items are received inventory levels go up and when items are issued inventory levels go down. Uses for off the shelf inventory control includes anything that can be bar-coded such as supply rooms, food stock in shops, industrial supplies and chemicals etc.

Stand alone inventory software is available for a variety of tasks and are able to manage inventory in multiple locations, manage consignment inventory along with the company owned inventory, track and maintain the history of serial numbers, lots and batches of items and all inventory movement. Putting in place a sufficient inventory software system may be a hard task but definitely calls for success once everything is in place.

Educational Software

Educational software may be considered the relationship between formal education> and economic and social development. Research has indicated that the investment in education is necessary to effect changes in social and economic life. Educational software has thus become an essential component in today's fast moving world. Educational software has become fun, and an incredibly rich way for children to learn, no matter what their weakness, there is something to choose from:

- Phonics
- Vocabulary
- Reading Comprehension
- Spelling
- Grammar
- Writing
- Math logic
- Multiplication
- Geometry
- Mastering numeration

The above are only a very small example of what is out there, and majority of educational software can be purchased on different levels aiding children specifically in that with which they need assistance. When purchasing educational software, study the package and see by whom it is developed etc. A lot of the time it is teachers, or people in the education system designing it and thus making it all the more suitable. Today even schools are using the educational software in classrooms to aid learning. Majority of educational software builds the skills of the learner systematically due to them being designed by education experts and thereby assures success through the beneficial use of reward, reinforcement and review. They are useful teaching tools in all fields of learning due to the balance of auditory and visual activities.

The results of children using educational software is as follows:

- Children enjoy learning more
- It creates confidence in the learner
- It improves on weaknesses
- Level of understanding in the learner increases
- Children who may battle with multiplication tables, now grasp the concept, children who had difficulty in reading, now read effectively etc.

For the future in our world, labour productivity can be increased by implementing the correct education, as this is the fundamental building block. Primary education is required before effective literacy is achieved and this is what majority of the children's educational software is aimed at. Educational software is all a form of development.

Medical Billing Software

In most countries throughout the world health care is voluntary, however the billings related to one's healthcare can sometimes prove to be an absolute nightmare for both the patient and the institute. In today's society most company's etc, are moving towards a paper free society, so why not do away with patient files and invest in suitable medical billing software that takes care of everything from beginning to end. If you want your medical practice efficiently run, here are some reasons why it would be a good idea to invest in medical billing software:

- It manages medical aid authorization referrals.
- You will be able to store medical billing information for nearly all medical aid insurance.
- Mail electronic claims for error-checking that minimizes rejections thus by hurrying up payments.
- It allows you to verify the specific patients status with their healthcare plan electronically and payments are done quicker.
- Automated accounting, will keep trace of every penny going in or out.
- Printing of reports is easy-daily reports, month or year end journals and summaries can be printed.

Medical billing software leads to efficiency which in turn leads to satisfaction, smoother operation and greater profitability, reaching most people's target at the end of the day. There are phenomenal medical billing software packages available on the market place, eliminating volumes of paperwork and the chance for administrative error. Today they are not only automated but also offers customizability.

Included in the medical billing software is:

- Scheduling of patient appointments.
- Patient details, including their allergies, past medical history, diagnosis and treatments, remarks about the patient and a patient summary.

In conclusion the technology of medical billing software assists with the functions to accurately complete claim forms, thereby timeously billing insurance companies in accordance with each insurance company's policies and procedures. Obstacles are thus removed, eliminating weaknesses and increasing your revenues and at the same time giving you more time.

Mortgage Software

A mortgage is a legal contract between a mortgagor (borrower) and mortgagee (lender) secured by the assets (most commonly land or buildings) owned by the mortgagee. A mortgage is unlike a hire-purchase agreement in that the mortgaged property belongs to the borrower.

Mortgages of various kinds are typically extended by building societies, banks and insurance companies to businesses and individual house buyers. Mortgage software is available to both the mortgagor and mortgagee focusing on each sector's individual needs.

Mortgage software for the mortgagee is advisory software and usually includes some of the following features:

- Enabling calculations of mortgage payment and total costs of mortgage.
- Enabling comparison of different interest rates and mortgage amounts.

- Enables a view of a detailed breakdown of mortgage over time the with mortgage schedule.
- And very important it teaches you how to pay off your mortgage early and save yourself some money.
- With constant changes in interest rates, it enables you to view your repayment accurately with the handy mortgage grid.

This mortgage software assists you in working out complicated sums, with the inflation that is occurred over time and what you can afford. Mortgage software also has its benefits within the workplace.

Two extremely important considerations are:

- People without mortgage experience can be sufficiently trained on most mortgage billing software. With this minimization of having to employ specially skilled people in mortgage it gives flexibility and a huge advantage on cost.
- Mortgage billing software automates every step of your mortgage loan workflow.

However like most software out there, ensure you can receive 24 hour help/support, to quickly solve any problem that may occur.

The mortgage industry business is huge but it doesn't matter if you are a bank, traditional retail or wholesale lender, correspondent lender, sub-prime lender, builder subsidiary, state housing lender, there is something for everyone. Majority of mortgage software is easy to use software and parallels the entire loan process.

Real Estate Software

Real estate brokers market real property on behalf of the owner. A career in real estate may involve long, irregular hours but if the correct systems are in place it can be rewarding with huge amounts of success. With most things in life organization is of the utmost importance, and with the introduction of real estate software this can now be practiced within the industry. If you are in the industry you will now be able to sufficiently escalate the work you produce and minimize other time consuming constraints. There are some real estate software programmes that allow you to manage a number of properties all at the same time. These programmes allow the user to accomplish their appraisal in a logical set out manner, and with absolute accuracy in their figures.

If you're in the market to purchase a home or homes-Access Investment Property has a large database of investment properties to choose from. With houses and developments located all across the globe, there's no better place to turn to. If you're looking for east coast property, check out south Jersey real estate for the home of your dreams. Do you keep losing real estate deals due to incompetent real estate agents? Here at Weichert we pride ourselves in giving our clients prompt and curteous service. Our clients are our #1 priority, so if there's a home for sale that you want, we'll do everything in our power to make sure you get it! If you're looking for a southern California realtor to help you find your dream home, the Real Estate Store is waiting to work for you!

The concept behind real estate software is to make the entire process for both the seller of the house and your business as smooth as possible, from beginning to end. Some of the software goes as far as creating a virtual website for each loan transaction on which you are working. It is a safe point containing your name with access to document communication, messaging, calendars, contact details, task tracking etc... The seller of the house can log in at any given time with his log on information to view the status information of the transaction. At the end of each day you can print your management reports of all current transactions and their status.

When face to face with a client or over the phone, you have easy access to all information, no teetering through pages and pages. Within your database you can store descriptions of your properties with a matching image, all contact details, expiry dates and notifications of contracts and payment deadlines.

It even has a calculation method where any kind of calculation can be done, including mortgage calculations etc... To avoid embarrassment of forgetting something important it contains scheduling tasks that constantly remind you. There is user friendly real estate software available on the market, so research those that will best suit your individual needs.

Embroidery Software

Embroidery is a general term used to describe ornamental stitch work applied to any kind of fabric using any kind of thread. It is an extremely ancient and widespread craft, yet still popular today. And with the commencement of embroidery software has become a lot more convenient and easier to administer. The most important step is selecting the correct embroidery software for your needs, and ensuring it is user friendly.

It doesn't have to be difficult purchasing this software and some important things that need to be considered when selecting your embroidery software is as follows: ensure the software you select has a wide range of stitch types from fancy design to combining effects and first-class stitch quality, make sure the software you purchase is compatible with both your computer and sewing machine (remember applications are constantly being upgraded, it might be a good idea to purchase Microsoft certified products), select an embroidery software programme with efficient technical support with either e-mail or phone support for any problems that may occur and software that offers upgrades or expansion modules can be purchased later on as you progress. Everyone has different ideas and styles so it may be a good idea to purchase embroidery software that allows individualized techniques and editing of your designs, easily attainable methods to find and manage your designs once saved. There is such advancements in design editing and lettering power to expect, and always new innovations being lead on to the market. Embroidery software is developed by skilled digitizers and artists, bringing you a wide variety of stock designs to choose from. It is such an easy way to create masterful looking embroidery designs in no time. Embroidery has been used in the past and will continue to be used in t he future for secular purposes for designs on costumes, curtains, book covers etc.

Designing Software

Designing implies a special regard for the requirement of appearance and improvement of marketability by imparting an attractive appearance with current fashions, within the margins of variation imposed by the requirements of use and economy. The importance of consumer appeal in design is shown by the recent expansion of home design software. Home design software can assist if you are having a problem visualizing what you so desire in your home. It is a compelling tool used in the design planning and building of the ultimate home. Home design software also goes beyond what you see in planning books, by customizing your home design to match your needs!

Before purchasing your home design software research the different products available and their feature capabilities. Today a lot of these programmes come with step by step instructions, wizards, drag and drop down menus with furniture (It allows you to position interior objects such as beds, chairs and tables, appliances and more within your floor plan creating a virtual feel for the size, layout and function of each room), home fixtures, plants to add to plans, decks and patios and helpful videos.

Most of them also include both a 2-D and 3-D view. Some of the home design software successfully allows you to visualize your plan on an actual colour photo. These software programmes can help you create a brand new home or home improvement remodeling to your existing home to your wishes. After you have planned your dream house most home design software will offer you a 3-D walk through you house. You can now view how your design looks before implementing. And remember changes are easy to make however you feel necessary. If you are happy with what you see it is also possible to print off colour images. Some home design software is so advanced it goes as far as calculating beams and footings etc. As in the case with purchasing all software ensures you have a support/help centre that can assist with any glitches. I think an appealing feature of home design software is that it is fun to utilize, allowing for a gratifying designing adventure.

Bar Code Software

A bar code is an identification system that is be read by a computer. Though there are several variations they all consist of printed patterns of lines and spaces, which record information such as price and batch number as a binary code. A computer-based cash register or point of sale system are able to read bar codes optically.

There are a variety of reasons why one would require bar code software in a business:

- *Bar code production software*: Generating the actual bar codes
- *Bar code data collection software*: Collecting data from bar code readers, magnetic strip readers etc... The type of data collection software you need depends primarily on your bar code scanner output, of which there are several types.
- *Database and inventory control software*: Storing data collected from bar codes. Generally the most important part of any bar code framework is the collection of data in a database. The whole point of the introduction of bar codes is to remove slow or error given entries

Basically you can determine which product to purchase just by knowing your needs. Bar code software without much difficulty produces good quality graphic images of bar codes that can usually be imported or pasted directly into a programme *e.g.* Microsoft word or publisher, Adobe, Quark etc. It can get quite involved so its always best to research exactly what you need.

Several types of output:

- Keyboard Wedge output or USB output
- RS232 output (includes some RFID scanners)
- TCP/IP output (includes some RFID scanners)

If you are not too clued up on the technicalities of things, there are bar code software packages available that are fast, simple to install and requires not much background experience. Bar code software can be manufactured for first time databases straight from the keyboard, portable bar code scanners, current Microsoft access databases etc... The express check in or check out proficiency maintains quick and trouble-free processing of asset issues, receipts, returns or moves.

Once can assess current and past records for any items and at any time derived from location, department, employee, status or any other criteria. As in the case of all software, bar code software is licensed per computer. In other words if you will be printing from various computers in house you will have to buy multiple licenses for each computer.

Control Software

The internet is a global network that connects users together with software and protocols. The internet offers users a number of services including electronic mail, and the ability to access information even in remote areas. There are a number of high level services but unfortunately the reality of the situation is, you do find online internet predators such as pedophiles, stalkers and sex offenders.

Another problem encountered with computers is children tend to spend hours surfing or playing games, thus neglecting other areas of their life. It is said that a child's psychological growth is determined by how their parents relate to them and situations. Hopefully with parental control software the recent studies showing that children are becoming more introverted by constantly being in front of their computer, can now somewhat be curbed. Most parental control software can include any or all of the below features specifically for when a child is online:

- *Internet conversation logging*: Usually both sides of the conversation.
- Integrated scheduler enabling parents to easily but invisibly monitor their children when absent from the home.
- *Window activity logging*: Captures all information that was viewed by your child.
- Printed document logging, logs information on documents sent to the printer spool.
- Some have a VCR style playback function that detains features of what your child has been doing.
- Enables you to block websites you would prefer your child not to visit.

With parental control software you can now gain control of your child's access on the computer. You can control when they use the computer, the amount of time they spend on the computer by automatically logging your child out at a specific times, say for instance at bed time or during study times and can easily divide computer time among siblings to prevent ongoing fights. Another advantage of most parental control software is that it remains invisible to the user. Before buying research the products available on the market, and purchase the parental control software best suited to your needs. Some are easier to install and to use, others more difficult, so obviously purchase that best suited to your computer knowledge.

Retail Software

Retail trading is the sale of goods in relatively small quantities which can be fast-selling foodstuffs, toiletries, clothing or consumer durables. Most retailing is done via shops or stores and includes the vast numbers of retail chains. Current trends in retailing is the optimization of profits and fewer losses, which means it is of the utmost importance to have the correct and necessary retail software. Therefore depending on the size of the retail store, different retail software packages are designed to suit different sized stores.

Regardless of which retail software you purchase there are a number of common features to look out for:

- *Point of sale products*: Ensure they are easy to learn and use, up to date with up to date retail tools, including bar codes and credit card readers, adaptable and flexible.

- *Customer database*: Accurate in storing your customer's details such as names and a history of previous buying.
- *Inventory control and Kiosk*: This is to avoid creating disappointment in your customer by being under stocked at any stage, or overstocked which can be damaging to the company. Some retail software programmes can print sales, inventory, low-stock or over-stock reports to keep you up to date. Some retail software even comes with features that will remind you when you need to re-order certain stock.
- *Convenience features*: With keeping to your goal of increased sales, convenience features are an added bonus for *e.g.* totally touch screen suited.
- *Security features*: Needs to be incorporated at each and every level, using passwords to avoid unauthorized staff making certain transactions, including the date, time and name of sales person working at specific check out location.
- *Back office functions*: Linked to the back office making their functions easier and more accurate by transporting all necessary information.

If you are able to implement the right retail software you should constantly be able to view a thorough picture of your business and ensure you are continuously on top of things. Thus by keeping you up to date of popular products in your store, and maybe those that are not selling so great with your customers, allowing you to make profitable changes. Stay neck and tie with your competitors and up with the times, lose cash registers and join the computer revolution with retail software, it has been determined that it does save money.

Trucking Software

Trucking has become quite a necessity in the business world today. Modern trucks may be either straight or articulated; in the latter, one or more trailers are connected to the power unit by standardized couplings. Many specialized trucks have been evolved *e.g.* refrigerated vehicles for bulk distribution of food etc... With trucks becoming such a part of business and the economy, it has been necessary to introduce trucking software. If you purchase the correct trucking software it should present you with an appropriate and effortless to use multi purpose software solution. It should be able to build in all your employee records and be a complete solution in assisting you to run a profit making company.

Trucking software should also help sustain and record all the information to enable getting through each business day. The complete transportat-ion management process can be addressed by using trucking software which furnishes a business with comprehensive and integrated forms of functions and services. When selecting your trucking software ensure all your needs are met, the basic criteria to check for is dispatching, billing, accounting, payroll, settlements, maintenance, safety, brokerage and satellite tracking. Imagine being able to keep track of all these features. Of course there are different trucking software systems to meet different needs and expenses. Some come as standard packages but as in the case with most software others can be customised to suite your individual needs. Don't overlook the standard systems as some come fully featured, with a fleet management system that gives both small to medium sized carriers exceptional functionality. Another couple of options to look out for are user friendly systems, that have server compliant databases to maintain your system. Also ensure the support system of the trucking software you choose is adequate and extensive. If you purchase the right trucking software for your company it can be a powerful tool, extremely dependable, in maintaining the functions of your day to day trucking business.

Landscape Software

Landscaping involves the design and development of land by human beings for use and enjoyment. It is concerned with the beauty of natural surroundings as well as practical ways to use land and the objects on it. If you would like to turn your garden into a masterwork invest in landscape software to assist you in creating your dream garden.

If you are having trouble planning your garden, don't automatically turn to a garden architect, landscape software will help you remain in control of any construction or redesign that needs to take place to your land. You can experiment with different functions available on your software until you get the final finish you have been fantasizing about, and have fun at the same time.

Landscape software will assist you step by step as follows:

- It will aid you in exploring your options.
- You can change your mind as often as you like while in the planning phase.
- Experiment with the actual accessories before you purchase them.
- You can create a perfect and precise shopping list with landscape software by using its available tools.
- With some landscape software packages you are able to merge in an actual photo of your home and landscape in order to accurately plan.
- It will assist you in viewing your garden design from different perspectives.
- With some landscape software you can view your garden as it develops, see how the trees and plants will look in the years to come. Some packages include a landscape estimator to assist you in pricing out what your final costs will be.
- And to be on the safe side before you invest your money in those final costs some packages will give you an accurate view of final plans.
- With all these advantages of keeping you in control of your land

before commencement of construction is fully engaged, I think landscape software is worth a try. There are enough user friendly products on the market to allow you to feel comfortable with what you are doing.

All landscape software packages are different but most will contain some or all of the above mentioned features. So experiment to your hearts content with your garden with only a few mouse clicks. You can load a photo of your garden into your software package and form full-colour printable images as you go. Some will allow you a 3D walk through your entire garden, appearing as virtually real as possible. You can record how your garden looks in all the different seasons, and track the changes. Delete those you don't like in your garden, or add in things you so wish for. Some landscape software packages go as far as allowing you to plot the slope elevation of your design.

Research the different software packages available and be careful not to purchase something a landscape architect would use as it might be a little too complicated for you to work with. Even the easier packages usually have a database of hundreds of product images to choose from.

Day Care Software

Day care can be split into different sectors: namely for children and the elderly but can go as far as dog day care centres, where they are all respectively looked after. Different day care software can be purchased for the different types, however they are all run along the same lines. If you want to make a success of your institute it is of the utmost importance to keep track of what is going on, and the right day care software can help you.

It is considered as in most business sectors that the crucial area for automatation is with the managing of the accounts. Day care software should have the proficiency of tracking all money going in and out to maintain profitability. Day care centres have a huge responsibility and need to keep track of who they have in there centres, waiting lists, special needs, history etc... They also need to manage year-end records of payments and fees. With the right day care software this can be done in a hassle free way. As discussed day care software packages are all different and you need to research which one most specifically meets your needs. Different functions need to be put in place to meet the needs of different payment methods etc. Some people prefer to pay monthly and others quarterly, some prefer debit orders and others credit cards, so ensure it has accurate methods of enabling these needs.

When it comes to child day care centres, children are present for different amounts of hours in the day (depending on their parents schedule) and are obviously billed different rates, up to date day care software takes care of all this. Day care software goes as far as managing the centre's check book, produces financial statements, payroll, etc... Day care software keeps you up to date with who is present in your centre, regardless of whether its child day care or day care for the elderly. You can track meals, allergies, next of kin contact details and very important is the history of the child/adult. There are things to look out for in purchasing day care software, like most software the availability of support and help systems.

If you stumble upon a hurdle it is nice to know you can receive instantaneous help. A thorough and easy to use database is important, where necessary information can be found at the click of a button. A built in back up system is also a good idea, as it is information that needs to be stored safely and securely.

Photo Editing Software

Today an immense range of photographic materials, equipment and skills has made the photographic industry a highly articulate industry. With the introduction of digital cameras, people have hundred and thousands of un-edited or un-usable photos.

It might be a good idea to invest in good photo editing software, and get those pics out there. With photo editing software you can keep you photo looking natural, yet it includes so many functions that one can do.

See below a few examples:

- Auto trim
- Border remove
- Colour resolution
- Contour
- Contrast
- Crop
- Dilate
- Dot remove
- DPI resolution
- Edge detector
- Emboss
- Flip
- Gamma correct
- Gradient
- Hue
- Impressionist
- Invert
- Invert text
- Line remove
- Line segment
- Median
- Mirror
- Mosaic
- Multiply
- Pixelate
- Posterize
- Resample
- Resize
- Ripple
- Rotate
- Sharpen
- Shear
- Smooth
- Solarize
- Stretch intensity
- Swirl
- Unsharp mask
- Wave
- Zoom blur
- Zoom wave

And the above is just a little sample, it might be a good idea to familiarize yourself with all the photo editing terminology before you get started. Photo editing software enables suitable editing, processing or conversion to each photo image that is processed.

Some of the above functions assist you in accomplishing the following:

- Red-eye reduction
- Increasing the brightness by using an added flash
- Throw away parts of the photo that you don't want

Today when purchasing a digital camera, it mostly does come with photo editing software which is sufficient enough. However if you would like to get a little more advanced there is a variety of software available on the market to choose from. There is programmes for beginners, and seriously advanced photo editing software.

Some software programmes include a browser menu for obtaining and characterizing photos, while others are purely for intensifying and editing digital images. Photo editing software also aids one in arranging, sorting and logging all photo images. Some software has features which will allow you to execute an exercise on more than one image at a time, or to rename bunches of images. So no matter what your task is before you-e-mailing your photo, correcting poor photos or the printing of your photos, photo editing is a great tool. So why not make your own perfect prints in the comfort of your home.

Loan Software

A loan is a sum of money borrowed by one individual or organization from another. Borrowers may pay interest in addition to repaying the capital sum borrowed. Loan servicing software assists in streamlining how you keep track of all money going in and out in order to:

- Increase revenues
- Reduce expenses
- Clarify portfolio management
- Boost customer satisfaction
- Escalate management control

Loan servicing software allows lenders to do their own loan servicing and loan accounting with cost effective methods. It would not be wise to get left behind in today's fast paced and competitive environment, and loan servicing software connects you to keep up with the progression. Powerful software packages can be obtained on the market, with constant upgrades that can be conducted.

Most software companies also offer a collector's software package that can be used in conjunction with the loan software packages. Majority will have a wizard teaching you the ins and outs of the functions, otherwise they might send in an instructor to you show you the ropes or your new package. Some packages come as a standard system, but if you have more complex needs, loan servicing software packages can be custom designed. These packages will handle your most demanding financial information requirements. As in the case of you purchasing any software for your computer, ensure it is compatible with your system, meets the needs you are wanting, versatile, and offers a thorough support system either online or by phone. There are versions of loan servicing software available that will meet the needs of lenders of all types and sizes in industry including banks, private finance companies, credit unions and individual lending organizations, and includes vast capabilities that will enable you to print loan documents in-house for all your loan types and remain profitable.

If you are looking for hard money lenders and hard money loans check out the Avatar Financial Group for low rates in all 50 states. Find military loans and computer financing at the military loan company. Instant approval for our online loans and you can apply any time, day or night. Now you won't have to worry about your financial problems anymore when you're in a bind.

Music Software

Music software can assist you in the making of music. The western world has always regarded music as being the unique creation of an individual composer, and now with music software, it makes it so much easier. Music software packages allow you to work creatively, and with nearly over 5000 types of music software to choose from – audio sequences, lyric writing tools to guitar software, there is something available for everyone's interest. With music software you are able to form music from scratch, re-arrange music files oruse a composing function to develop brilliant formatting options. The most important step is to decipher what it is you would like to get out of your music software, and purchase it relatively.

Whether you are into writing and creating your own music, or no matter which instrument there is absolutely something for everybody. The entry of your notes can be made directly from your computer with most packages, and you can create them in the exact way that you would like to view them. You can print your music or view it on the screen as your notes play, you can sing or play your instrument/s as it goes along etc. Find sheet music download for new ideas to implement into your own music. Each music software package will have its own range of tools that need to be used. With most of the software packages you are also able to play back your music at any given stage. And of course as with most software ensure there is a sufficient support system. With the introduction of music software it is considered the bridging gap between technology and musical talent. If you purchase the right software you literally have your own music production studio to record your songs, and even to complete your editing.

You can compose your own songs that you will be recording, and once you have completed composing and recording you can then add in professional sounding effects. There are those music software programmes that will allow you to produce opulently layered musical compositions by recording drums, guitars, keyboards, bass guitars or what ever you so wish for. It's a safer and much more popular method of recording with music software using digital audio files on the PC as vinyl is easily scratched, and cassettes are easily ruined. The introduction of music software into the music industry is a great advantage as anybody can mix music and voice overs to create professional sounding tracks.

Stock Trading Software

The stock exchange is the market in which securities are bought and sold. Most capital cities have stock exchanges with some of the largest being in New York, Paris, Frankfurt, Tokyo and London. And with stock trading software anyone can take part in stock trading and from any where in the world. You are able to raise long-term capital if you so wish, by issuing securities to investors and can again sell them when you wish.

Stock trading software is freely available and can be purchased for day traders, short term and long term traders. You also don't need to be a computer whiz to make use of this software as most stock trading software is user friendly. With the right stock trading software you can make thousands by buying and selling stocks.

Stock trading software has been created to assist as follows:

- Spot channel breakouts
- Control your money
- Limit your inclination towards fear and greed
- Produce high prospect buy/sell signals
- Disclose trading drifts for just about any time period

Stock trading software does the research for you preventing you from making the frequent blunders of buying prematurely if the stock price tends to drop, as well as buying too late *i.e.* when prices are at the top of the cycle. Stock prices are continuously updated, giving the entry price and the stop price. When a stock is a certain distance above or below its moving average, it will eventually move back to the average. The norm is that stocks generally change back to the average.

This phenomenon is known as "reversion to the mean". With most stock market software there are filters available that down load tens of thousands of stock each day in lists. It is best to try stock trading software that offers a free trial, to see how user friendly it is. Some will offer a hundred per cent money back guarantee if you are not happy. Also look into the support system the software offers in case any problems occur.

Astrology Software

Astrology is a pseudo-science which attempts to make predictions about worldly events and people's day to day lives through interpreting the supposed influences of the position and motion of celestial bodies, principally the sun, moon and planets. Today there is astrology software to aid people interested in doing this. Astrology software is vast (although not a hard and fast rule, obviously depending on the astrology software you purchase) and comes in three types of programmes:

1. Calculations
2. Interpretation or report writing
3. Research

Astrology software packages are able to create precise and enlightening interpretations and thereafter provide a function for you to print these astrological reports. The majority of astrology software is user friendly, powerful and can calculate and integrate astrological charts with high astronomical accuracy and professional quality. There are a variety of options to choose from-house systems, zodiacal reference etc...

Before purchasing your astrology software, you will have to define your needs in order to see what you want it for and what you would like to achieve. The top priority is to ensure you purchase a well-crafted programme. Ensure you understand the product descriptions, feature lines, screen shots and read the professional reviews. Majority of astrology software will give a detailed astrological report, including interpretation help for each symbol present on the chart.

Astrological computations such as birth charts, chart comparisons and prediction methods can all be carried out through the relative calculation software programmes. After completing all your tasks it is then possible to print out all your chart wheels, tables, maps and graphs that you have created. Reports can be created for interpreting or report writing, that describes birth charts, compatibility, vocation or any other astrological topic you may think of.

We can then divide research software into an additional two categories:

1. Research features are usually automatically built into major chart calculation software programmes.
2. Dedicated research programmes which include chart databases, containing hundreds or thousands of famous people's birth data, as well as other methods of researching charts.

There are different price ranges of variations of astrology software that can be purchased for all of the above types, also ranging in advancement, so it is very dependable as to what level you are at. Majority of astrology software is designed to run under DOS or windows, so always ensure it is compatible with your PC.

Childcare Software

Child care software is a computerized schedule management system and will aid any centre in keeping track of everything-from each student enrolled (including emergency contact details, authorized guardians for pickup, permission forms, siblings etc), current and historical billing. A schedule can be entered for children and goes as far as scheduling in the holidays or temporary schedule changes.

It keeps track of day to day attendance sheets, each child care software programme having its own unique system of doing this. It is often difficult to recall each and every child present in the centre but child care software will make it easier for storing the following information: medical information, tracking and charging of extra hours, immunization tracking, door access control. It also controls enrollment of new children, adding in new applicants, placing some on a waiting list or removing children that have left the centre.

Child care software in appropriate centres also aids with the financial side of things by keeping track of billing structures, all the important information you may need about payments and billings are stored. Some can even automatically post all late fees. It can also produce financial summaries, specifically at month end. Automatic printing of client receipts on payment.

3

Computer Organization and Architecture

OVERVIEW OF COMPUTER SYSTEM

In describing computer system, a distinction is often made between computer architecture and computer organization. Computer architecture refers to those attributes of a system visible to a programmer, or put another way, those attributes that have a direct impact on the logical execution of a program. Computer organization refers to the operational units and their interconnection that realise the architecture specification.

Examples of architecture attributes include the instruction set, the number of bit to represent various data types (*e.g..*, numbers, and characters), I/O mechanisms, and technique for addressing memory. Examples of organization attributes include those hardware details transparent to the programmer, such as control signals, interfaces between the computer and peripherals, and the memory technology used. As an example, it is an architectural design issue whether a computer will have a multiply instruction. It is an organizational issue whether that instruction will be implemented by a special multiply unit or by a mechanism that makes repeated use of the add unit of the system. The organization decision may be bases on the anticipated frequency of use of the multiply instruction, the relative speed of the two approaches, and the cost and physical size of a special multiply unit. Historically, and still today, the distinction between architecture and organization has been an important one. Many computer manufacturers offer a family of computer model, all with the same architecture but with differences in organization. Consequently, the different models in the family have different price and performance characteristics. Furthermore, an architecture may survive many years, but its organization changes with changing technology.

STRUCTURE AND FUNCTION OF COMPUTERS

A computer is a complex system; contemporary computers contain million of elementary electronic components. How, then, can one clearly describe them? The key is to recognize the hierarchical nature of most complex system. A hierarchical system is a set of interrelated subsystem, each of the later, in turn, hierarchical in structure until we reach some lowest level of elementary subsystem. The hierarchical nature of complex systems is essential to both their design and their description. The designer need only deal with a particular level of the system at a time. At each level, the system consists of a set of components and their interrelationships. The behaviour at each level depends only on a simplified, abstracted characterization of the system at the next lower level.

At each level, the designer is concerned with structure and function:

- *Structure*: The way in which the components are interrelated.
- *Function*: The operation of each individual component as part of the structure.

In term of description, we have two choices: starting at the bottom and building up to a complete description, or beginning with a top view and decomposing the system, describing their structure and function, and proceed to successively lower layer of the hierarchy. The approach taken in this course follows the latter.

Function

In general terms, there are four main functions of a computer:

- Data processing
- Data storage
- Data movement
- Control

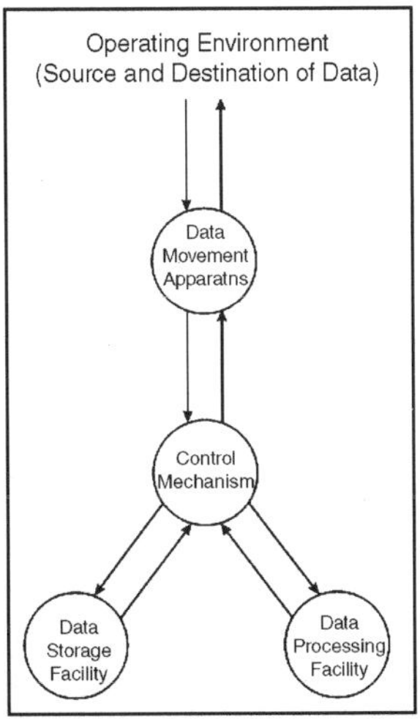

The computer, of course, must be able to process data. The data may take a wide variety of forms, and the range of processing requirements is broad. However, we shall see that there are only a few fundamental methods or types of data processing. It is also essential that a computer store data. Even if the computer is processing data on the fly (*i.e.*, data come in and get processed, and the results go out immediately), the computer must temporarily store at least those pieces of data that are being worked on at any given moment. Thus, there is at least a short-term data storage function. Files of data are stored on the computer for subsequent retrieval and update.

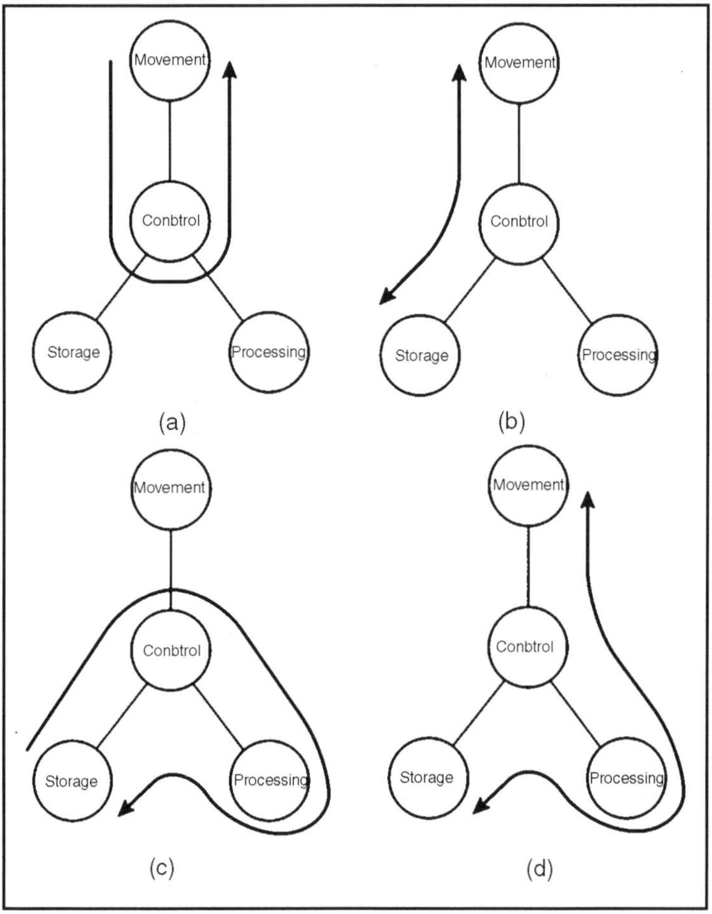

The computer must be able to move data between itself and the outside world. The computer's operating environment consists of devices that serve as either sources or destinations of data. When data are received from or delivered to a device that is directly connected to the computer, the process is known as input-output (I/O), and the device is referred to as a peripheral. When data are moved over longer distances, to or from a remote device, the process is known as data communications. Finally, there must be control of there three functions.

Ultimately, this control is exercised by the individual who provides the computer with instructions. Within the computer system, a control unit manages the computer's resources and orchestrates the performance of its functional parts in response to those instructions. At this general level of discussion, the number of possible operations that can be performed is few. The figure depicts the four possible types of operations. The computer can function as a data movement device as shown in Figure, simply transferring data from one peripheral or communications line to another.

It can also function as a data storage device as shown in Figure, with data transferred from the external environment to computer storage (read) and vice versa (write). The final two diagrams show operations involving data processing, on data either in storage or in route between storage and the external environment.

Structure

Figure above is the simplest possible depiction of a computer. The computer is an entity that interacts in some fashion with its external environment. In general, all of its linkages to the external environment can be classified as peripheral devices or communication lines.

We will have something to say about both types of linkages:

- *Central processing unit (CPU)*: Controls the operation of the computer and performs its data processing functions. Often simply referred to as processor.
- *Main memory*: Stores data.
- *I/O*: Moves data between the computer and its external environment.
- *System interconnection*: Some mechanism that provides for communication among CPU, main memory, and I/O.

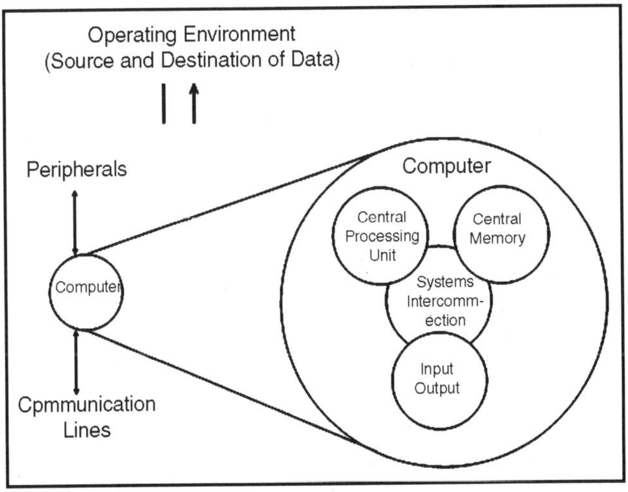

There may be one or more of each of the above components. Traditionally, there has been just a single CPU. In recent years, there has been increasing use of multiple processors, in a single system. Each of these components will be examined in some detail in later lectures. However, for our purpose, the most interesting and in some ways the most complex component is the CPU; its structure is depicted in Figure.

Its major structural components are:

- *Control unit (CU)*: Controls the operation of the CPU and hence the computer.
- *Arithmetic and logic unit (ALU)*: Performs computer's data processing functions.
- *Register*: Provides storage internal to the CPU.
- *CPU interconnection*: Some mechanism that provides for communication among the control unit, ALU, and register.

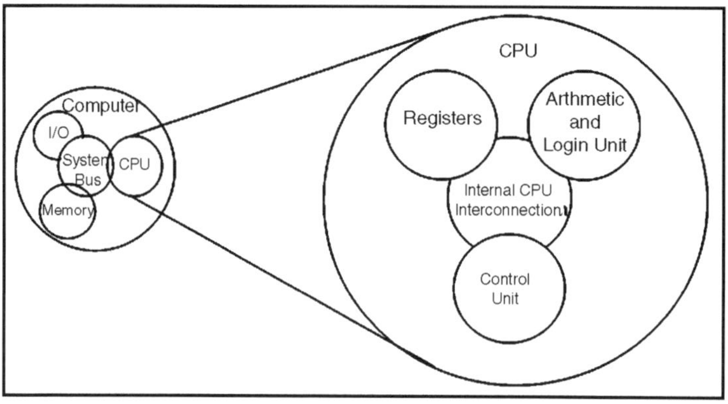

DEVELOPMENT OF COMPUTERS

FIRST GENERATION: VACUUM TUBES

ENIAC: The ENIAC (Electronic Numerical Integrator And Computer), designed by and constructed under the supervision of Jonh Mauchly and John Presper Eckert at the University of Pennsylvania, was the world's first general-purpose electronic digital computer. The project was a response to U.S. wartime needs. Mauchly, a professor of electrical engineering at the University of Pennsylvania and Eckert, one of his graduate students, proposed to build a general-purpose computer using vacuum tubes. In 1943, this proposal was accepted by the Army, and work began on the ENIAC.

The resulting machine was enormous, weighting 30 tons, occupying 15,000 square feet of floor space, and containing more than 18,000 vacuum tubes. When operating, it consumed 140 kilowatts of power. It was aloes substantially faster than any electronic-mechanical computer, being capable of 5000 additions per second. The ENIAC was decimal rather than a binary machine. That is, numbers were represented in decimal form and arithmetic was performed in the decimal system. Its memory consisted of 20 "accumulators", each capable of holding a 10-digit decimal number. Each digit was represented by a ring of 10 vacuum tubes. At any time, only one vacuum tube was in the ON state, representing one of the 10 digits. The major drawback of the ENIAC was that it had to be programmed manually by setting switches and plugging and unplugging cables. The ENIAC was completed in 1946, too late to be used in the war effort. Instead, its first task was to perform a series of complex calculations that were used to help determine the feasibility of the H-bomb. The ENIAC continued to be used until 1955.

Von Neumann Machine

The programming process could be facilitated if the program could be represented in a form suitable for storing in memory alongside the data. Then, a computer could get its instructions by reading them from memory, and a program could be set of altered by setting the values of a portion of memory. This idea, known as the Stored-program concept, is usually attributed to the ENIAC designers, most notably the mathematician John von Neumann, who was a consultant on the ENIAC project. The idea was also developed at about the same time by Turing. The first publication of the idea was in a 1945 proposal by von Neumann for a new computer, the EDVAC (Electronic Discrete Variable Computer).

In 1946, von Neumann and his colleagues began the design of a new stored-program computer, referred to as the IAS computer, at the Princeton Institute for Advanced Studies. The IAS computer, although not completed until 1952, is the prototype of all subsequent general-purpose computers. Figure shows the general structure of the IAS computer.

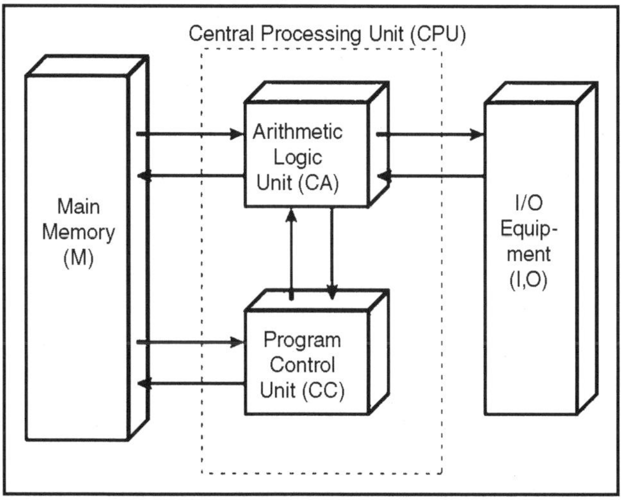

It consists of:

- A main memory, which stores both data and instructions.
- An arithmetic-logical unit (ALU) capable of operating on binary data.

- A control unit, which interprets the instructions in memory and causes them to be executed.
- Input and output (I/O) equipment operated by the control unit.

Commercial Computers

The 1950s saw the birth of the computer industry with two companies, Sperry and IBM, dominating the marketplace. In 1947, Eckert and Mauchly formed the Eckert-Maunchly computer Corporation to manufacture computers commercially. Their first successful machine was the UNIVAC I (Universal Automatic Computer), which was commissioned by the Bureau of the Census for the 1950 calculations. The Eckert-Maunchly Computer Corporation became part of the UNIVAC division of Sperry-Rand Corporation, which went on to build a series of successor machines.

The UNIVAC II, which had greater memory capacity and higher performance than the UNIVAC I, was delivered in the late 1950s and illustrates several trends that have remained characteristic of the computer industry. First, advances in technology allow companies to continue to build larger, more powerful computers. Second, each company tries to make its new machines upward compatible with the older machines. This means that the programs written for the older machines can be executed on the new machine. This strategy is adopted in the hopes of retaining the customer base; that is, when a customer decides to buy a newer machine, he is likely to get it from the same company to avoid losing the investment in programs.

The UNIVAC division also began development of the 1100 series of computers, which was to be its bread and butler. This series illustrates a distinction that existed at one time. The first model, the UNIVAC 1103, and its successors for many years were primarily intended for scientific applications, involving long and complex calculations. Other companies concentrated on business applications, which involved processing large amounts of text data. This split has largely disappeared but it was evident for a number of years.

IBM, which was then the major manufacturer of punched-card processing equipment, delivered its first electronic stored-program computer, the 701, in 1953. The 70l was intended primarily for scientific applications. In 1955, IBM introduced the companion 702 product, which had a number of hardware features that suited it to business applications. These were the first of a long series of 700/7000 computers that established IBM as the overwhelmingly dominant com puter manufacturer.

SECOND GENERATION: TRANSISTORS

The first major change in the electronic computer came with the replacement of the vacuum tube by the transistor. The transistor is smaller, cheaper, and dissipates less heal than a vacuum tube but can be used in the same way as a vacuum tube to con struct computers. Unlike the vacuum tube, which requires wires, metal plates, a glass capsule, and a vacuum, the transistor is a solid-state device, made from silicon. The transistor was invented at Bell Labs in 1947 and by the 1950s had launched an electronic revolution. It was not until the late 1950s, however, that fully transisto rized computers were commercially available. IBM again was not the first company to deliver the new technology. NCR and. more successfully. RCA were the front-run ners with some small transistor machines. IBM followed shortly with the 7000 series.

The use of the transistor defines the second generation of computers. It has become widely accepted to classify computers into generations based on the fundamental hard ware technology employed. Each new generation is characterized by greater processing performance, larger memory capacity, and smaller size than the previous one.

THIRD GENERATION: INTEGRATED CIRCUITS

A single, self-contained transistor is called a discrete component. Throughout the 1950s and early 1960s, electronic equipment was composed largely of discrete com ponents—transistors, resistors, capacitors, and so on. Discrete components were manufactured separately, packaged in their own containers, and soldered or wired together onto circuit boards, which were then installed in computers, oscilloscopes, and other electronic equipment. Whenever an electronic device called for a transistor, a little lube of metal containing a pinhead-sized piece of silicon had to be soldered to a circuit hoard. The entire manufacturing process, from transistor to circuit board, was expensive and cumbersome.

These facts of life were beginning to create problems in the computer industry. Early second-generation computers contained about 10,000 transistors. This figure grew to the hundreds of thousands, making the manufacture of newer, more power ful machines increasingly difficult. In 1958 came the achievement that revolutionized electronics and started the era of microelectronics: the invention of the integrated circuit. It is the integrated circuit that defines the third generation of computers. Perhaps the two most important members of the third generation are the IBM System/360 and the DEC PDP-8.

LATER GENERATIONS

Beyond the third generation there is less general agreement on defining generations of computers. There have been a fourth and a fifth genera tion, based on advances in integrated circuit technology. With the introduction of large-scale integration (LSI), more than 1000,000 components can be placed on a single integrated circuit chip. Very-large-scale integration (VLSI) achieved more than 1000,000,000 components per chip, and current VLSI chips can contain more than 1000.000 components.

INVENTION OF COMPUTERS

Since the invention of computers from first generation and fourth generation computers, they have been classified according to their types and how they operate that is input, process and output information. Below you will get a brief discussion on various types of Computers we have. Computer types can be divided into 3 categories according to electronic nature. Types of computers are classified according to how a particular Computer functions.

These computer types are:

- Analogue Computers
- Digital Computers
- Hybrid Computers

ANALOGUE COMPUTERS

Analogue types of Computer uses what is known as analogue signals that are represented by a continuous set of varying voltages and are used in scientific research centers?, hospitals and flight centers. The analog computer is almost an extinct type of computer these days. It is different from a digital computer in respect that it can perform numerous mathematical operations simultaneously. It is also unique in terms of operation as it utilizes continuous variables for the purpose of mathematical computation. It utilizes mechanical, hydraulic, or electrical energy or operation. With analogue types of computer no values are represented by physical measurable quantities *e.g.* voltages. Analogue computer types program arithmetic and logical operations by measuring physical changes *i.e.* temperatures or pressure.

DIGITAL COMPUTER TYPE

With these types of computers operation are on electrical input that can attain two inputs, states of ON=1 and state of OFF = 0. With digital type of computers data is represented by digital of 0 and 1 or off state and on state. Digital computer type recognizes data by counting discrete signal of (0 0r 1), they are high speed programmable; they compute values and stores results. After looking at the Digital computer type and how it functions will move to the third computer type as mentioned above.

HYBRID TYPE OF COMPUTER

Hybrid computer types are very unique, in the sense that they combined both analogue and digital features and operations. These types of computers are, as the name suggests, a combination of both Analog and Digital computers. The Digital computers which work on the principle of binary digit system of "0" and "1" can give very precise results. But the problem is that they are too slow and incapable of large scale mathematical operation. In the hybrid types of computers the Digital counterparts convert the analog signals to perform Robotics and Process control. With Hybrid computers operate by using digital to analogue convertor and analogue to digital convertor. By linking the two types of computer above you come up with this new computer type called Hybrid.

OTHER TYPES

Supercomputer and Mainframe

Supercomputer is a broad term for one of the fastest computers currently available. Supercomputers are very expensive and are employed for specialized applications that require immense amounts of mathematical calculations (number crunching). For example, weather forecasting requires a supercomputer. Other uses of supercomputers scientific simulations, (animated) graphics, fluid dynamic calculations, nuclear energy research, electronic design, and analysis of geological data (*e.g.* in petrochemical prospecting).

Perhaps the best known supercomputer manufacturer is Cray Research. Mainframe was a term originally referring to the cabinet containing the central processor unit or "main frame" of a room-filling Stone Age batch machine. After the emergence of smaller "minicomputer" designs in the early 1970s, the traditional big iron machines were described as "mainframe computers" and eventually just as mainframes. Nowadays a Mainframe is a very large and expensive computer capable of supporting hundreds, or even thousands, of users simulta-neously.

The chief difference between a supercomputer and a mainframe is that a supercomputer channels all its power into executing a few programs as fast as possible, whereas a mainframe uses its power to execute many programs concurrently. In some ways, mainframes are more powerful than supercomputers because they support more simultaneous programs. But supercomputers can execute a single program faster than a mainframe. The distinction between small mainframes and minicomputers is vague, depending really on how the manufacturer wants to market its machines.

Minicomputer

It is a midsize computer. In the past decade, the distinction between large minicomputers and small mainframes has blurred, however, as has the distinction between small minicomputers and workstations. But in general, a minicomputer is a multiprocessing system capable of supporting from up to 200 users simultaneously.

Workstation

It is a type of computer used for engineering applications (CAD/CAM), desktop publishing, software development, and other types of applications that require a moderate amount of computing power and relatively high quality graphics capabilities.

Workstations generally come with a large, high-resolution graphics screen, at large amount of RAM, built-in network support, and a graphical user interface. Most workstations also have a mass storage device such as a disk drive, but a special type of workstation, called a diskless workstation, comes without a disk drive. The most common operating systems for workstations are UNIX and Windows NT. Like personal computers, most workstations are single-user computers. However, workstations are typically linked together to form a local-area network, although they can also be used as stand-alone systems.

N.B.: In networking, workstation refers to any computer connected to a local-area network. It could be a workstation or a personal computer.

Personal Computer

It can be defined as a small, relatively inexpensive computer designed for an individual user. In price, personal computers range anywhere from a few hundred pounds to over five thousand pounds. All are based on the microprocessor technology that enables manufacturers to put an entire CPU on one chip. Businesses use personal computers for word processing, accounting, desktop publishing, and for running spreadsheet and database management applications. At home, the most popular use for personal computers is for playing games and recently for surfing the Internet. Personal computers first appeared in the late 1970s.

One of the first and most popular personal computers was the Apple II, introduced in 1977 by Apple Computer. During the late 1970s and early 1980s, new models and competing operating systems seemed to appear daily. Then, in 1981, IBM entered the fray with its first personal computer, known as the IBM PC. The IBM PC quickly became the personal computer of choice, and most other personal computer manufacturers fell by the wayside. P.C. is short for personal computer or IBM PC. One of the few companies to survive IBM's onslaught was Apple Computer, which remains a major player in the personal computer marketplace.

Other companies adjusted to IBM's dominance by building IBM clones, computers that were internally almost the same as the IBM PC, but that cost less. Because IBM clones used the same microprocessors as IBM PCs, they were capable of running the same software. Over the years, IBM has lost much of its influence in directing the evolution of PCs. Therefore after the release of the first PC by IBM the term PC increasingly came to mean IBM or IBM-compatible personal computers, to the exclusion of other types of personal computers, such as Macintoshes. In recent years, the term PC has become more and more difficult to pin down. In general, though, it applies to any personal computer based on an Intel microprocessor, or on an Intel-compatible microprocessor. For nearly every other component, including the operating system, there are several options, all of which fall under the rubric of PC Today, the world of personal computers is basically divided between Apple Macintoshes and PCs.

The principal characteristics of personal computers are that they are single-user systems and are based on microprocessors. However, although personal computers are designed as single-user systems, it is common to link them together to form a network. In terms of power, there is great variety. At the high end, the distinction between personal computers and workstations has faded. High-end models of the Macintosh and PC offer the same computing power and graphics capability as low-end workstations by Sun Microsystems, Hewlett-Packard, and DEC.

Actual personal computers can be generally classified by size and chassis/ case. The chassis or case is the metal frame that serves as the structural support for electronic components. Every computer system requires at least one chassis to house the circuit boards and wiring. The chassis also contains slots for expansion boards. If you want to insert more boards than there are slots, you will need an expansion chassis, which provides additional slots. There are two basic flavours of chassis designs–desktop models and tower models–but there are many variations on these two basic types. Then come the portable computers that are computers small enough to carry. Portable computers include notebook and sub notebook computers, hand-held computers, palmtops, and PDAs.

Tower Model

The term refers to a computer in which the power supply, motherboard, and mass storage devices are stacked on top of each other in a cabinet. This is in contrast to desktop models, in which these components are housed in a more compact box. The main advantage of tower models is that there are fewer space constraints, which makes installation of additional storage devices easier.

Desktop Model

A computer designed to fit comfortably on top of a desk, typically with the monitor sitting on top of the computer. Desktop model computers are broad and low, whereas tower model computers are narrow and tall. Because of their shape, desktop model computers are generally limited to three internal mass storage devices. Desktop models designed to be very small are sometimes referred to as slimline models.

Notebook Computer

An extremely lightweight personal computer. Notebook computers typically weigh less than 6 pounds and are small enough to fit easily in a briefcase. Aside from size, the principal difference between a notebook computer and a personal computer is the display screen. Notebook computers use a variety of techniques, known as flat-panel technologies, to produce a lightweight and non-bulky display screen. The quality of notebook display screens varies considerably. In terms of computing power, modern notebook computers are nearly equivalent to personal computers. They have the same CPUs, memory capacity, and disk drives. However, all this power in a small package is expensive. Notebook computers cost about twice as much as equivalent regular-sized computers. Notebook computers come with battery packs that enable you to run them without plugging them in. However, the batteries need to be recharged every few hours.

Laptop Computer

A small, portable computer—small enough that it can sit on your lap. Nowadays, laptop computers are more frequently called notebook computers.

Sub Notebook Computer

A portable computer that is slightly lighter and smaller than a full-sized notebook computer. Typically, subnotebook computers have a smaller keyboard and screen, but are otherwise equivalent to notebook computers.

Hand-held Computer

A portable computer that is small enough to be held in one's hand. Although extremely convenient to carry, handheld computers have not replaced notebook computers because of their small keyboards and screens. The most popular hand-held computers are those that are specifically designed to provide PIM (personal information manager) functions, such as a calendar and address book. Some manufacturers are trying to solve the small keyboard problem by replacing the keyboard with an electronic pen. However, these pen-based devices rely on handwriting recognition technologies, which are still in their infancy. Hand-held computers are also called PDAs, palmtops and pocket computers.

Palmtop

A small computer that literally fits in your palm. Compared to full-size computers, palmtops are severely limited, but they are practical for certain functions such as phone books and calendars. Palmtops that use a pen rather than a keyboard for input are often called hand-held computers or PDAs. Because of their small size, most palmtop computers do not include disk drives. However, many contain PCMCIA slots in which you can insert disk drives, modems, memory, and other devices. Palmtops are also called PDAs, hand-held computers and pocket computers.

PDA

Short for personal digital assistant, a handheld device that combines computing, telephone/fax, and networking features. A typical PDA can function as a cellular phone, fax sender, and personal organizer. Unlike portable computers, most PDAs are pen-based, using a stylus rather than a keyboard for input.

This means that they also incorporate handwriting recognition features. Some PDAs can also react to voice input by using voice recognition technologies. The field of PDA was pioneered by Apple Computer, which introduced the Newton MessagePad in 1993.

Shortly thereafter, several other manufacturers offered similar products. To date, PDAs have had only modest success in the marketplace, due to their high price tags and limited applications. However, many experts believe that PDAs will eventually become common gadgets. PDAs are also called palmtops, hand-held computers and pocket computers.

COMPUTERS CLASSIFICATION AND DATA PROCESSING

Computers are classified according to their data processing speed, amount of data that they can hold and price. Generally, a computer with high processing speed and large internal storage is called a big computer. Due to rapidly improving technology, we are always confused among the categories of computers.

Depending upon their speed and memory size, computers are classified into following four main groups.

- Supercomputer.
- Mainframe computer.
- Mini computer.
- Microcomputer.

SUPERCOMPUTER

Supercomputer is the most powerful and fastest, and also very expensive. It was developed in 1980s. It is used to process large amount of data and to solve the complicated scientific problems. It can perform more than one trillions calculations per second. It has large number of processors connected parallel.

So parallel processing is done in this computer. In a single supercomputer thousands of users can be connected at the same time and the supercomputer handles the work of each user separately.

Supercomputer are mainly used for:

- Weather forecasting.
- Nuclear energy research.
- Aircraft design.
- Automotive design.
- Online banking.
- To control industrial units.

The supercomputers are used in large organizations, research laboratories, aerospace centers, large industrial units etc. Nuclear scientists use supercomputers to create and analyse models of nuclear fission and fusions, predicting the actions and reactions of millions of atoms as they interact. The examples of supercomputers are CRAY-1, CRAY-2, Control Data CYBER 205 and ETA A-10 etc.

MAINFRAME COMPUTERS

Mainframe computers are also large-scale computers but supercomputers are larger than mainframe. These are also very expensive. The mainframe computer specially requires a very large clean room with air-conditioner. This makes it very expensive to buy and operate. It can support a large number of various equipments. It also has multiple processors. Large mainframe systems can handle the input and output requirements of several thousand of users. For example, IBM, S/390 mainframe can support 50,000 users simultaneously. The users often access then mainframe with terminals or personal computers. Tere are basically two types of terminals used with mainframe systems.

Dumb Terminal

Dumb terminal does not have its own CPU and storage devices. This type of terminal uses the CPU and storage devices of mainframe system. Typically, a dumb terminal consists of monitor and a keyboard (or mouse).

Intelligent Terminal

Intelligent terminal has its own processor and can perform some processing operations. Usually, this type of terminal does not have its own storage. Typically, personal computrers are used as intelligent terminals. A personal computer as an intelligent terminal gives facility to access data and other services from mainframe system. It also enables to store and process data locally. The mainframe computers are specially used as servers on the World Wide Web. The mainframe computers are used in large organizations such as Banks, Airlines and Universities etc. where many people (users) need frequent access to the same data, which is usually organized into one or more huge databases. IBM is the major manufacturer of mainframe computers. The examples of mainframes are IBM S/390, Control Data CYBER 176 and Amdahl 580 etc.

MINICOMPUTERS

These are smaller in size, have lower processing speed and also have lower cost than mainframe. These computers are known as minicomputers because of their small size as compared to other computers at that time. The capabilities of a minicomputer are between mainframe and personal computer. These computers are also known as midrange computers.

The minicomputers are used in business, education and many other government departments. Although some minicomputers are designed for a single user but most are designed to handle multiple terminals. Minicomputers are commonly used as servers in network environment and hundreds of personal computers can be connected to the network with a minicomputer acting as server like mainframes, minicomputers are used as web servers. Single user minicomputers are used for sophisticated design tasks.

The first minicomputer was introduced in the mid-1960s by Digital Equipment Corporation (DEC). After this IBM Corporation (AS/400 computers) Data General Corporation and Prime Computer also designed the mini computers.

MICROCOMPUTER

The microcomputers are also known as personal computers or simply PCs. Microprocessor is used in this type of computer. These are very small in size and cost. The IBM's first microcomputer was designed in 1981 and was named as IBM-PC. After this many computer hardware companies copied the design of IBM-PC. The term "PC-compatible" refers any personal computer based on the original IBM personal computer design.

The most popular types of personal computers are the PC and the Apple. PC and PC-compatible computers have processors with different architectures than processors in Apple computers. These two types of computers also use different operating systems. PC and PC-compatible computers use the Windows operating system while Apple computers use the Macintosh operating system (MacOS). The majority of microcomputers sold today are part of IBM-compatible. However the Apple computer is neither an IBM nor a compatible. It is another family of computers made by Apple computer. Personal computers are available in two models.

These are:

- Desktop PCs
- Tower PCs

A desktop personal computer is most popular model of personal computer. The system unit of the desktop personal computer can lie flat on the desk or table. In desktop personal computer, the monitor is usually placed on the system unit. Another model of the personal computer is known as tower personal computer. The system unit of the tower PC is vertically placed on the desk of table. Usually the system unit of the tower model is placed on the floor to make desk space free and user can place other devices such as printer, scanner etc. on the desktop. Today computer tables are available which are specially designed for this purpose. The tower models are mostly used at homes and offices.

Microcomputer are further divided into following categories:

- Laptop computer
- Workstation
- Network computer
- Handheld computer

Laptop computer

Laptop computer is also known as notebook computer. It is small size (85-by-11 inch notebook computer and can fit inside a briefcase. The laptop computer is operated on a special battery and it does not have to be plugged in like desktop computer. The laptop computer is portable and fully functional microcomputer.

It is mostly used during journey. It can be used on your lap in an airplane. It is because it is referred to as laptop computer. The memory and storage capacity of laptop computer is almost equivalent to the PC or desktop computer. It also has the hard dist, floppy disk drive, Zip disk drive, CD-ROM drive, CD-writer etc. it has built-in keyboard and built-in trackball as pointing device.

Laptop computer is also available with the same processing speed as the most powerful personal computer. It means that laptop computer has same features as personal computer. Laptop computers are more expensive than desktop computers. Normally these computers are frequently used in business travellers.

Workstations

Workstations are special single user computers having the same features as personal computer but have the processing speed equivalent to minicomputer or mainframe computer. A workstation computer can be fitted on a desktop. Scientists, engineers, architects and graphic designers mostly use these computers.

Workstation computers are expensive and powerful computers. These have advanced processors, more RAM and storage capacity than personal computers. These are usually used as single-user applications but these are used as servers on computer network and web servers as well.

Network Computers

Network computers are also version of personal computers having less processing power, memory and storage. These are specially designed as terminals for network environment. Some types of network computers have no storage. The network computers are designed for network, Internet or Intranet for data entry or to access data on the network. The network computers depend upon the network's server for data storage and to use software. These computers also use the network's server to perform some processing tasks.

In the mid-1990s the concept of network computers became popular among some PC manufacturers. As a result several variations of the network computers quickly became available. In business, variations of the network computer are Windows terminals, NetPCs and diskless workstations. Some network computers are designed to access only the Internet or to an Intranet. These devices are sometimes called Internet PCs, Internet boxes etc. In home some network computers do not include monitor. These are connected to home television, which serves as the output devices. A popular example of a home-based network computer is Web TV, which enables the user to connect a television to the Internet.

The Web TV has a special set-top box used to connect to the Internet and also provides a set of simple controls which enable the user to navigate the Internet, send and receive e-mails and to perform other tasks on the network while watching television. Network computers are cheaper to purchase and to maintain than personal computers.

Handheld Computer

In the mid 1990s, many new types of small personal computing devices have been introduced and these are referred to as handheld computers. These computers are also referred to as Palmtop Computers. The handheld computers sometimes called Mini-Notebook Computers. The type of computer is named as handheld computer because it can fit in one hand while you can operate it with the other hand.

Because of its reduced size, the screen of handheld computer is quite small. Similarly it also has small keyboard. The handheld computers are preferred by business traveller. Some handheld computers have a specialized keyboard. These computers are used by mobile employees, such as meter readers and parcel delivery people, whose jobs require them to move from place to place.

The examples of handheld computers are:

- Personal digital assistance
- Cellular telephones
- H/PC pro devices

Personal Digital Assistance (PDAs)

The PDA is one of the more popular lightweight mobile devices in use today. A PDA provides special functions such as taking notes, organizing telephone numbers and addresses. Most PDAs also offer a variety of other application software such as word processing, spreadsheet and games etc. Some PDAs include electronic books that enable users to read a book on the PDA's screen. Many PDAs are web-based and users can send/receive e-mails and access the Internet. Similarly, some PDAs also provide telephone capabilities.

The primary input device of a PDA is the stylus. A stylus is an electronic pen and looks like a small ballpoint pen. This input device is used to write notes and store in the PDA by touching the screen. Some PDAs also support voice input.

Cellular Phones

A cellular phone is a web-based telephone having features of analog and digital devices. It is also referred to as Smart Phone. In addition to basic phone capabilities, a cellular phone also provides the functions to receive and send e-mails & faxes and to access the Internet.

H/PC Pro Devices

H/PC Pro dive is new development in handheld technology. These systems are larger than PDAs but they are not quite as large as typical notebook PCs. These devices have features between PDAs and notebook PCs. The H/PC Pro device includes a full-size keyboard but it does not include disk. These systems also have RAM with very low storage capacity and slow speed of processor.

CONSIST OF DIGITAL COMPUTER SYSTEM

Digital computer systems consist of three distinct units.

These units are as follows:

- Input unit
- Central Processing unit
- Output unit

These units are interconnected by electrical cables to permit communication between them. This allows the computer to function as a system.

INPUT UNIT

A computer must receive both data and program statements to function properly and be able to solve problems. The method of feeding data and programs to a computer is accomplished by an input device. Computer input devices read data from a source, such as magnetic disks, and translate that data into electronic impulses for transfer into the CPU. Some typical input devices are a keyboard, a mouse, or a scanner.

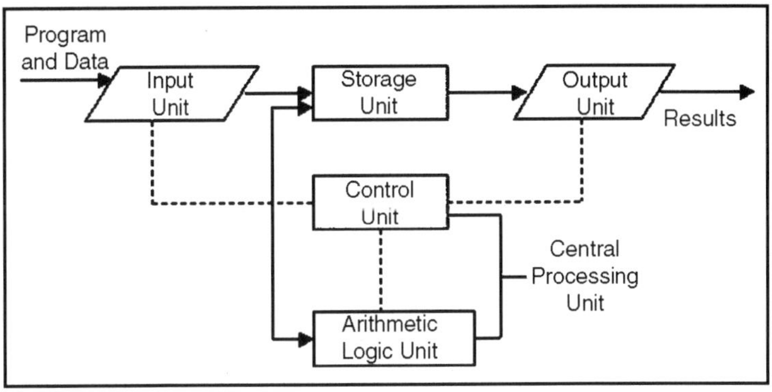

CENTRAL PROCESSING UNIT

The brain of a computer system is the central processing unit (CPU). The CPU processes data transferred to it from one of the various input devices. It then transfers either an intermediate or final result of the CPU to one or more output devices.

A central control section and work areas are required to perform calculations or manipulate data. The CPU is the computing center of the system. It consists of a control section, an arithmetic-logic section as shown in figure, and an internal storage section (main memory). Each section within the CPU serves a specific function and has a particular relationship with the other sections within the

Cpu.Control Section

The control section directs the flow of traffic (operations) and data. It also maintains order within the computer. The flow of control is indicated by dotted arrows in figure.

The control section selects one program statement at a time from the program storage area, interprets the statement, and sends the appropriate electronic impulses to the arithmetic-logic and storage sections so they can carryout the instructions.

The control section does not perform actual processing operations on the data. The control section instructs the input device on when to start and stop transferring data to the input storage area. It also tells the output device when to start and stop receiving data from the output storage area.

Arithmetic-Logic Section

The arithmetic-logic section performs arithmetic operations, such as addition, subtraction, multiplication, and division. Through internal logic capability, it tests various conditions encountered during processing and takes action based on the result.As indicated by the solid arrows in figure, data flows between the arithmetic-logic section and the internal storage section during processing. Specifically, data is transferred as needed from the storage section to the arithmetic-logic section, processed, and returned to internal storage. At no time does processing take placein the storage section.

Data maybe transferred back and forth between these two sections several times before processing is completed. The results are then transferred from internal storage to an output device, as indicated by the solid arrow in figure below.

The binary addition and multiplication tables are:

(

$0 + 0 = 0$

$0 + 1 = 1$

$1 + 1 = 10$

$1 + 0 = 1$

$0 \times 0 = 0$

$0 \times 1 = 0$

$1 \times 1 = 1$

$1 \times 0 = 0$

) (4)

Note that if carries are ignored,7 subtraction of two single-digit binary numbers yields the same bit as addition. Computers use high and low voltage values to express a bit, and an array of such voltages express numbers akin to positional notation. Logic circuits perform arithmetic operations.

Exercise: Add twenty-five and seven in base 2. Note the carries that might occur. Why is the result "nice"?

Solution: $25=11011_2$ and $7=111_2$. We find that $11001_2 + 111_2 = 100000_2=32$.

Also note that the logical operations of AND and OR are equivalent to binary addition (again if carries are ignored). The variables of logic indicate truth or falsehood. *AÂ"B*, the AND of *A* and *B*, represents a statement that both *A* and *B* must be true for the statement to be true. You use this kind of statement to tell search engines that you want to restrict hits to cases where both of the events *A* and *B* occur. *AÃ"B*, the OR of *A* and *B*, yields a value of truth if either is true.

Note that if we represent truth by a "1" and falsehood by a "0," *binary multiplication corresponds to AND and addition (ignoring carries) to OR*. The Irish mathematician George Boole discovered this equivalence in the mid-nineteenth century. It laid the foundation for what we now call Boolean algebra, which expresses as equations logical statements.

More importantly, any computer using base-2 representations and arithmetic can also easily evaluate logical statements. This fact makes an integer-based computational device much more powerful than might be apparent.

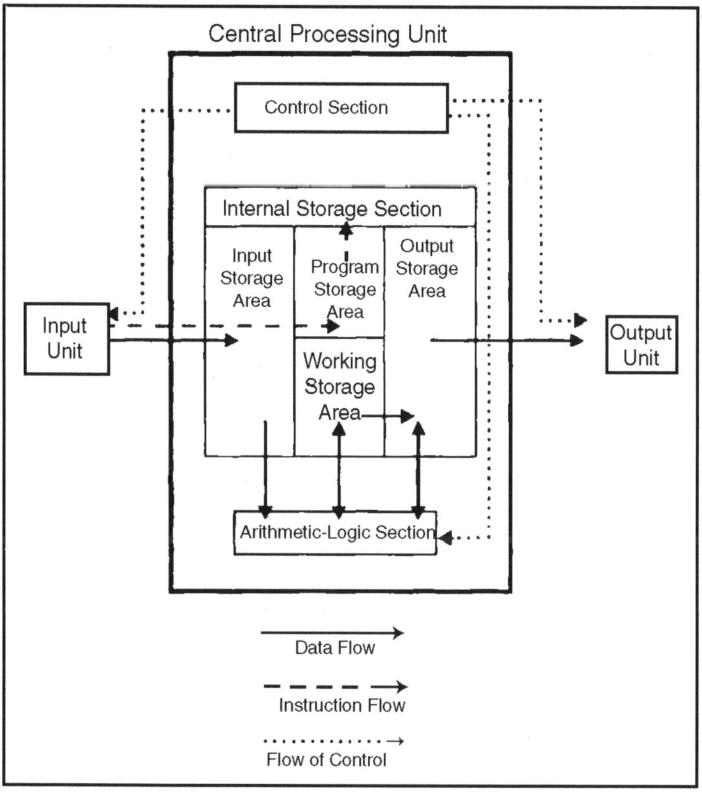

Internal Storage Section

The internal storage section is sometimes called primary storage, main storage, or main memory, because this section functions similar to our own human memory. The storage section serves four purposes; three relate to retention (holding) of data during processing.

First, as indicated by the solid arrow as shown in figure, data is transferred from an input device to the inputstorage area where it remains until the computers ready to process it. Second, a workingstorage area ("scratch pad" memory) within the storage section holds both the data being processed and the intermediate results of the arithmetic-logic operations.

Third, the storage section retains the processing results in the output storage area. From there the processing results can be transferred to an output device. The fourth storage section, the program storage area, contains the program statements transferred from an input device to process the data. Please note that the four areas (input, working storage, output, and program storage) are NOT famed in size or location but are determined by individual program requirements.

OUTPUT UNIT

As program statements and data are received by the CPU from an input device, the results of the processed data are sent from the CPU to an OUTPUT DEVICE. These results are transferred from the output storage area onto an output medium, such as a floppy disk, hard drive, video display, printer, and so on.

BUSES AND ARCHITECTURE

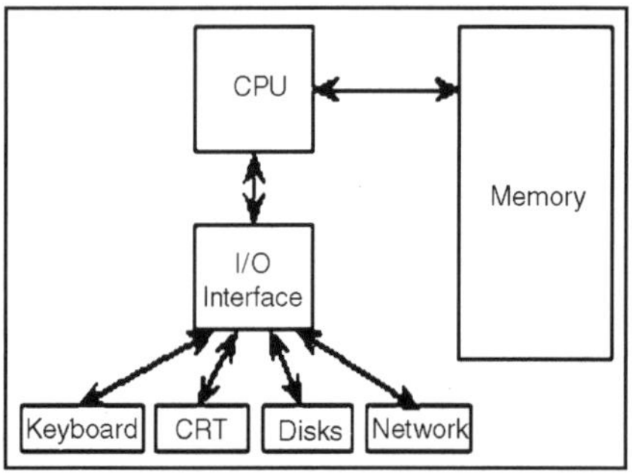

BUS

A set of parallel conductors, which allow devices attached to it to communicate with the CPU.

The bus consists of three main parts:

- Control lines
- Address lines
- Data lines

Control Lines

These allow the CPU to control which operations the devices attached should perform, *I.E.* read or write.

Address Lines

Allows the CPU to reference certain (Memory) locations within the device.

Data Lines

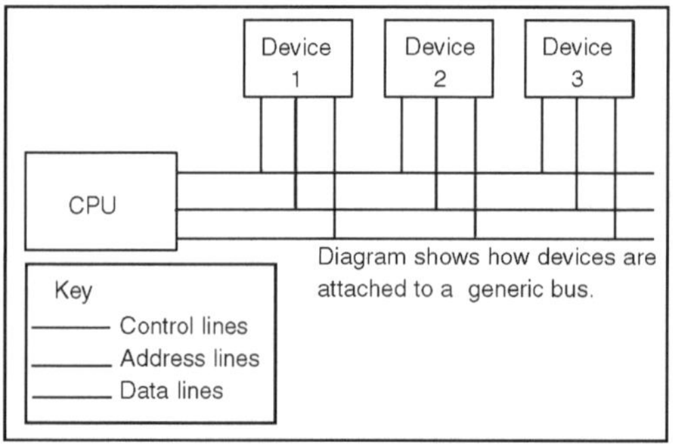

The meaningful data which is to be sent or retrieved from a device is placed on to these lines. The Bus is set to run at a specified speed which is measured in MHz.

TYPES OF BUSES

EXPANSION BUS

Expansion buses (sometimes called *peripheral buses*) are buses that have connectors that allow you to add expansion cards (peripherals) to a computer.

There are different types of standard internal buses that are characterized by:

- Their shape
- The number of connector pins
- The type of signals (frequency, data, etc.)

ISA BUS

The original version of the ISA bus (*Industry Standard Architecture*) that appeared in 1981 with PC XT was an 8-bit bus with a clock speed of 4.77 MHz. In 1984, with the appearance of PC AT (the *Intel 286* processor), the bit was expanded into a 16-bit bus and the clock speed went from 6 to 8 MHz and finally to 8.33 MHz, offering a maximum transfer rate of 16 Mb/s (in practice only 8 Mb/s because one cycle out of every two was used for addressing). The ISA bus permitted bus mastering, *i.e.* it enabled controllers connected directly to the bus to communicate directly with the other peripherals without going through the processor.

One of the consequences of *bus mastering* is direct memory access (DMA). However, the ISA bus only allows hardware to address the first 16 megabytes of RAM. Up until the end of the 1990s, almost all PC computers were equipped with the ISA bus, but it was progressively replaced by the PCI bus, which offered a better performance.

Fig. 8-bit ISA Connector

Fig.16-bit ISA Connector

MCA BUS

The MCA bus (*Micro Channel Architecture*) is an improved proprietary bus designed by IBM in 1987 to be used in their PS/2 line of computer. This 16 to 32-bit bus was incompatible with the ISA bus and could reach a throughput of 20 Mb/s.

EISA BUS

The EISA bus (*Extended Industry Standard Architecture*) was developed in 1988 by a consortium of companies (AST, Compaq, Epson, Hewlett-Packard, NEC, Olivetti, Tandy, Wyse and Zenith) in order to compete with the MCA proprietary bus that was launched by IBM the previous year. The EISA bus used connectors that were the same size as the ISA connector but with 4 rows of contacts instead of 2, for 32-bit addressing. The EISA connectors were deeper and the additional rows of contacts were placed below the rows of ISA contacts. Thus, it was possible to plug an ISA expansion board into an EISA connector. However, they did not plug as deep into the connector (because of the bezels) and thus only used the top rows (ISA) of contacts.

LOCAL BUS

Traditional I/O buses, such as ISA, MCA our EISA buses, are directly connected to the main bus and there are forced to work at the same frequency. However, some I/O peripherals need a very low bandwidth while other need higher bandwidths. Therefore there are bottlenecks on the bus. In order to solve this problem, the "local bus" architecture offers to take advantage of the system bus, or front side bus (*FSB*), by interfacing directly with it.

VLB BUS

In 1992, the VESA local bus (VLB) was developed by the *VESA* (*Video Electronics Standard Association*under the aegis of the company *NEC*) in order to offer a local bus dedicated to graphics systems. The VLB is a 16-bit ISA connector with an added 16-bit connector:

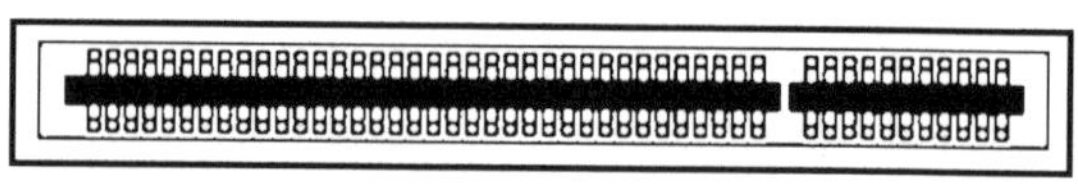

The VLB bus is a 32-bit bus initially intended to work a bandwidth of 33 MHz (the bandwidth of the first PC 486s at that time). The VESA local bus was used on the following 486 models (40 and 50 MHz, respectively) as well as on the very first Pentium processors, but it was quickly replaced by the PCI bus.

REGISTERS

Registers are fast memory, almost always connected to circuitry that allows various arithmetic, logical, control, and other manipulations, as well as possibly setting internal flags. Most early computers had only one data register that could be used for arithmetic and logic instructions. Often there would be additional special purpose registers set aside either for temporary fast internal storage or assigned to logic circuits to implement certain instructions. Some early computers had one or two address registers that pointed to a memory location for memory accesses (a pair of address registers typically would act as source and destination pointers for memory operations).

Computers soon had multiple data registers, address registers, and sometimes other special purpose registers. Some computers have general purpose registers that can be used for both data and address operations. Every digital computer using a von Neumann architecture has a register (called the program counter) that points to the next executable instruction. Many computers have additional control registers for implementing various control capabilities. Often some or all of the internal flags are combined into a flag or status register.

ACCUMULATORS

Accumulators are registers that can be used for arithmetic, logical, shift, rotate, or other similar operations. The first computers typically only had one accumulator. Many times there were related special purpose registers that contained the source data for an accumulator. Accumulators were replaced with data registers and general purpose registers. Accumulators reappeared in the first microprocessors.

- *Intel* 8086/80286: One word (16 bit) accumulator; named AX (high order byte of the AX register is named AH and low order byte of the AX register is named AL)
- *Intel* 80386: One double word (32 bit) accumulator; named EAX (low order word uses the same names as the accumulator on the Intel 8086 and 80286 [AX] and low order and high order bytes of the low order words of four of the registers use the same names as the accumulator on the Intel 8086 and 80286 [AH and AL])
- *Mix*: One accumulator; named A-register; five bytes plus sign

DATA REGISTERS

Data registers are used for temporary scratch storage of data, as well as for data manipulations (arithmetic, logic, etc.). In some processors, all data registers act in the same manner, while in other processors different operations are performed are specific registers.

- *Mix*: One extension register; named X-register; five bytes plus sign; can be concatenated on the right hand side of the A-register (accumulator)
- *Motorola* 680 × 0, 68300: 8 long word (32 bit) data registers; named D0, D1, D2, D3, D4, D5, D6, and D7

ADDRESS REGISTERS

Address registers store the addresses of specific memory locations. Often many integer and logic operations can be performed on address registers directly (to allow for computation of addresses). Sometimes the contents of address register(s) are combined with other special purpose registers to compute the actual physical address. This allows for the hardware implementation of dynamic memory pages, virtual memory, and protected memory. The number of bits of an address register (possibly combined with information from other registers) limits the maximum amount of addressable memory. A 16-bit address register can address 64K of physical memory. A 24-bit address register can address address 16 MB of physical memory. A 32-bit address register can address 4 GB of physical memory. A 64-bit address register can address 1.8446744 x 10^{19} of physical memory. Addresses are always unsigned binary numbers.

- *Mix*: One jump registers; named J-register; two bytes and sign is always positive
- *Motorola* 680 × 0, 68300: 8 long word (32 bit) address registers; named A0, A1, A2, A3, A4, A5, A6, and A7 (also called the stack pointer)

GENERAL PURPOSE REGISTERS

General purpose registers can be used as either data or address registers.

- *DEC Vax*: 16 word (32 bit) general purpose registers; named R0 through R15
- *IBM* 360/370: 16 full word (32 bit) general purpose registers; named 0, 1, 2, 3, 4, 5, 6, 7, 8, 9, A (or 10), B (or 11), C (or 12), D (or 13), E (or 14), and F (or 15)
- *Intel* 8086/80286: 8 word (16 bit) general purpose registers; named AX, BX, CX, DX, BP, SP, SI, and DI (high order bytes of the AX, BX, CX, and DX registers have the names AH, BH, CH, and DH and low order bytes of the AX, BX, CX, and DX registers have the names AL, BL, CL, and DL)
- *Intel* 80386: 8 double word (32 bit) general purpose registers; named EAX, EBX, ECX, EDX, EBP, ESP, ESI, and EDI (low order words use the same names as the general purpose registers on the Intel 8086 and 80286 and low order and high order bytes of the low order words of four of the registers use the same names as the general purpose registers on the Intel 8086 and 80286)
- *Motorola* 88100: 32 word (32 bit) general purpose registers; named r0 through r31

CONSTANT REGISTERS

Constant registers are special read-only registers that store a constant. Attempts to write to a constant register are illegal or ignored. In some RISC processors, constant registers are used to store commonly used values (such as zero, one, or negative one) — for example, a constant register containing zero can be used in register to register data moves, providing the equivalent of a clear instruction without adding one to the instruction set. Constant registers are also often used in floating point units to provide such value as pi or e with additional hidden bits for greater accuracy in computations.

- *Motorola* 88100: r0 (general purpose register 0) contains the constant 32 bit integer zero

FLOATING POINT REGISTERS

Floating point registers are special registers set aside for floating point math.

INDEX REGISTERS

Index registers are used to provide more flexibility in addressing modes, allowing the programmer to create a memory address by combining the contents of an address register with the contents of an index register (with displacements, increments, decrements, and other options). In some processors, there are specific index registers (or just one index register) that can only be used only for that purpose. In some processors, any data register, address register, or general register (or some combination of the three) can be used as an index register.

- *IBM* 360/370: Any of the 16 general purpose registers may be used as an index register
- *Intel* 80 × 86: 7 of the 8 general purpose registers may be used as an index register (the ESP is the exception)
- *Mix*: Five index registers; named I-registers I1, I2, I3, I4, and I5; five bytes plus sign
- *Motorola* 680 × 0, 68300: Any of the 8 data registers or the 8 address registers may be used as an index register

BASE REGISTERS

Base registers or segment registers are used to segment memory. Effective addresses are computed by adding the contents of the base or segment register to the rest of the effective address computation. In some processors, any register can serve as a base register. In some processors, there are specific base or segment registers (one or more) that can only be used for that purpose. In some processors with multiple base or segment registers, each base or segment register is used for different kinds of memory accesses (such as a segment register for data accesses and a different segment register for program accesses).

- *IBM* 360/370: Any of the 16 general purpose registers may be used as a base register
- *Intel* 80 × 86: 6 dedicated segment registers: CS (code segment), SS (stack segment), DS (data segment), ES (extra segment, a second data segment register), FS (third data segment register), and GS (fourth data segment register)
- *Motorola* 680 × 0, 68300: Any of the 8 address registers may be used as a base register

CONTROL REGISTERS

Control registers control some aspect of processor operation. The most universal control register is the program counter.

PROGRAM COUNTER

Almost every digital computer ever made uses a program counter. The program counter points to the memory location that stores the next executable instruction. Branching is implemented by making changes to the program counter. Some processor designs allow software to directly change the program counter, but usually software only indirectly changes the program counter (for example, a JUMP instruction will insert the operand into the program counter). An assembler has a location counter, which is an internal pointer to the address (first byte) of the next location in storage (for instructions, data areas, constants, etc.) while the source code is being converted into object code.

The VAX uses the 16th of 16 general purpose registers as the program counter (PC). Almost the entire instruction set can directly manipulate the program counter, allowing a very rich set of possible kinds of branching. The program counter in System/360 and 370 machines is contained in bits 40-63 of the program status word (PSW), which is directly accessible by some instructions.

- *IBM* 360/370: Program counter is bits 40-63 of the program status word (PSW)
- *Intel* 8086/80286: 16-bit instruction pointer (IP)
- *Intel* 80386: 32-bit instruction pointer (EIP)
- *Motorola* 680 × 0, 68300: 32-bit program counter (PC)

PROCESSOR FLAGS

Processor flags store information about specific processor functions. The processor flags are usually kept in a flag register or a general status register. This can include result flags that record the results of certain kinds of testing, information about data that is moved, certain kinds of information about the results of compations or transformations, and information about some processor states. Closely related and often stored in the same processor word or status register (although often in a privileged portion) are control flags that control processor actions or processor states or the actions of certain instructions.

- *IBM* 360/370: Program status word (PSW)
- *Intel* 8086/80286: 16-bit flag register (FLAGS); system flags, control flag, and status flags)
- *Intel* 80386: 32-bit flag register (EFLAGS); system flags, control flag, and status flags)
- *Mix*: An overflow toggle and a comparison indicator
- *Motorola* 680 × 0, 68300: 16-bit status register (SR); high byte is system byte and requires privileged access, low byte is user byte or condition code register (CCR)

A few typical result flags (with processors that include them):

- Auxilary carry Set if a carry out of the most significant bit of a BCD operand occurs (binary coded decimal addition). Also commonly set if a borrow occurs in a BCD subtract. Used in Intel 80x86 [AF].
- Carry Set if a carry out of the most significant bit of an operand occurs (addition). Also commonly set if a borrow occurs in a subtract. Used in Digital VAX [C], Intel 80x86 [CF], Motorola 680x0 [C], Motorola 68300 [C], Motorola M68HC16 [C].
- Comparison indicator contains one of three values: less, equal, or greater. Used in MIX.
- Extend Set to the value of the carry bit for arithmetic operations (used to support implementation of multi-byte arithmetic larger than that implemented directly by the hardware. Used in Motorola 680x0 [X], Motorola 68300 [X].
- Half carry Set if a carry out of bit 3 of an operand occurs during BCD addition. Used in Motorola M68HC16.
- Negative Set if the most significant bit of a result is set. Used in Digital VAX [N], Motorola 680x0 [N], Motorola 68300 [N], Motorola M68HC16 [N].
- Overflow Set if arithmetic overflow occurs. Used in Digital VAX [V], Intel 80x86 [OF], Motorola 680x0 [V], Motorola 68300 [V], Motorola M68HC16 [V].
- Overflow toggle a single bit that is either on or off. Used in MIX.
- Parity For odd parity machines, set to make an odd number of one bits; for an even parity machine, set to make an even number of one bits. Used in Intel 80x86 [PF]. The IBM 360/370 has odd parity on memory.
- Sign Set for negative sign. Used in Intel 80x86 [SF].
- Trap Set for traps. Used in Intel 80x86 [TF].
- Zero Set if a result equals zero. Used in Digital VAX [Z], Intel 80x86 [ZF], Motorola 680x0 [Z], Motorola 68300 [Z], Motorola M68HC16 [Z].

Some conditions are determined by combining multiple flags. For example, if a processor has a negative flag and a zero flag, the equivalent of a positive flag is the case of both the negative and zero flags both simultaneously being cleared.

A few typical control flags (with processors that include them):

- Decimal overflow trap enable Set if decimal overflow occurs (or conversion error on a VAX). Used in Digital VAX [DV].
- Direction flag Determines the direction of string operations (set for autoincrement, cleared for autodecrement). Used in Intel 80x86 [DF].
- Floating underflow trap enable Set if floating underflow occurs. Used in Digital VAX [FU].
- Integer overflow trap enable Set if integer overflow occurs (or conversion error on a VAX). Used in Digital VAX [IV].

- Interupt enable Set if interrupts enabled. Used in Intel 80x86 [IF].
- i/o privilege level Used to control access to I/O instructions and hardware (thereby seperating control over I/O from other supervisor/ user states). Two bits. Used in Intel 80x86 [IO PL].
- Nested task flag Used in Intel 80x86 [NF].
- Resume flag Used in Intel 80x86 [RF].
- Virtual 8086 mode Used to switch to virtual 8086 emulation. Used in Intel 80x86 [VM].

STACK POINTER

Stack pointers are used to implement a processor stack in memory. In many processors, address registers can be used as generic data stack pointers and queue pointers. A specific stack pointer or address register may be hardwired for certain instructions. The most common use is to store return addresses, processor state information, and temporary variables for subroutines.

- IBM 360/370: any of the 16 general purpose registers may be used as a stack pointer
- Intel 8086/80286: dedicated stack pointer (SP) combined with stack segment pointer (SS) to create address of stack
- Intel 80386: dedicated stack pointer (ESP) combined with stack segment pointer (SS) and the stack-frame base pointer (EBP) to create address of stack
- Motorola 680x0, 68300: dedicated user stack pointer (USP, A7) and system stack pointer (SSP, A7) for implicit stack pointer operations, as well as allowing any of the 8 address registers to be as explicit stack pointers.

CONCEPT OF MEMORY MANAGEMENT

The memory management subsystem is one of the most important parts of the operating system. Since the early days of computing, there has been a need for more memory than exists physically in a system. Strategies have been developed to overcome this limitation and the most successful of these is virtual memory. Virtual memory makes the system appear to have more memory than it actually has by sharing it between competing processes as they need it.

LARGE ADDRESS SPACES

The operating system makes the system appear as if it has a larger amount of memory than it actually has. The virtual memory can be many times larger than the physical memory in the system,

PROTECTION

Each process in the system has its own virtual address space. These virtual address spaces are completely separate from each other and so a process running one application cannot affect another. Also, the hardware virtual memory mechanisms allow areas of memory to be protected against writing. This protects code and data from being overwritten by rogue applications.

MEMORY MAPPING

Memory mapping is used to map image and data files into a processes address space. In memory mapping, the contents of a file are linked directly into the virtual address space of a process.

FAIR PHYSICAL MEMORY ALLOCATION

The memory management subsystem allows each running process in the system a fair share of the physical memory of the system,

SHARED VIRTUAL MEMORY

Although virtual memory allows processes to have separate (virtual) address spaces, there are times when you need processes to share memory. For example there could be several processes in the system running the bash command shell.

Rather than have several copies of bash, one in each processes virtual address space, it is better to have only one copy in physical memory and all of the processes running bash share it. Dynamic libraries are another common example of executing code shared between several processes.

ABSTRACT MODEL OF VIRTUAL MEMORY

Before considering the methods that Linux uses to support virtual memory it is useful to consider an abstract model that is not cluttered by too much detail. As the processor executes a programme it reads an instruction from memory and decodes it. In decoding the instruction it may need to fetch or store the contents of a location in memory. The processor then executes the instruction and moves onto the next instruction in the programme. In this way the processor is always accessing memory either to fetch instructions or to fetch and store data.

DEMAND PAGING

As there is much less physical memory than virtual memory the operating system must be careful that it does not use the physical memory inefficiently. One way to save physical memory is to only load virtual pages that are currently being used by the executing programme. For example, a database programme may be run to query a database. In this case not all of the database needs to be loaded into memory, just those data records that are being examined. If the database query is a search query then it does not make sense to load the code from the database programme that deals with adding new records. This technique of only loading virtual pages into memory as they are accessed is known as demand paging.

SWAPPING

If a process needs to bring a virtual page into physical memory and there are no free physical pages available, the operating system must make room for this page by discarding another page from physical memory. If the page to be discarded from physical memory came from an image or data file and has not been written to then the page does not need to be saved. Instead it can be discarded and if the process needs that page again it can be brought back into memory from the image or data file.

However, if the page has been modified, the operating system must preserve the contents of that page so that it can be accessed at a later time. This type of page is known as a *dirty* page and when it is removed from memory it is saved in a special sort of file called the swap file. Accesses to the swap file are very long relative to the speed of the processor and physical memory and the operating system must juggle the need to write pages to disk with the need to retain them in memory to be used again.

SHARED VIRTUAL MEMORY

Virtual memory makes it easy for several processes to share memory. All memory access are made via page tables and each process has its own separate page table. For two processes sharing a physical page of memory, its physical page frame number must appear in a page table entry in both of their page tables shows two processes that each share physical page frame number 4. For process *X* this is virtual page frame number 4 whereas for process *Y* this is virtual page frame number 6. This illustrates an interesting point about sharing pages: the shared physical page does not have to exist at the same place in virtual memory for any or all of the processes sharing it.

PROCESSORS AND MEMORY

There are two main components which have been part of nearly all computer systems ever designed and built. The first is called the processor (known also as the Central Processing Unit or CPU)and the second is called the memory. The processor is the part of a computer system which does the actual computing. That is, the part which adds, subtracts, multiplies and divides. Most processors can also compare values and perform conditional actions as a result of such comparisons. Many processors have instructions which perform various types of conversions between different representations of data. The processor itself is divided into three components that carry out the various functions that the computer is capable of performing. The first component of the processor is the controller. The controller acts as a foreman that oversees the tasks of the processor. The controller looks at the next instruction to be executed and assigns the sub-tasks that must be accomplished to carry out that instruction to the other components of the processor.

Another component of the processor is the Arithmetic-Logic Unit (ALU). This unit is the part of the processor which performs the mathematical computations and logical tasks that we expect a computer to be able to do. Addition, subtraction, comparison, etc., are all carried out by the ALU. The last component of the processor is a collection of one or more registers. Registers are special named memory cells in the processor where information is temporarily stored during various stages of a computation. The currently executing instruction, for example, resides in a register called the Instruction Register. Since modern processors can execute millions of instructions per second it is expected that information would not stay in a register for more than a few millionths of a second. A computer memory system is accessed (or read) by specifying the location (called an address) of the memory cell. The memory system then responds by producing a copy of the contents of that cell. The original value of the cell is not changed by this process. This is sometimes called a non-destructive read.

A computer memory system is changed (or written) by specifying the location of the memory cell together with the new value for that cell. The previous value stored in the cell is replaced by the new value. This is sometimes called a destructive write. The values stored in a computer memory are simply numbers. Numbers are used to represent both data and instructions. In fact, one cannot distinguish instructions from data when examining the contents of a memory system. It is up to the programmer or operating system to keep track of which memory cells hold data and which are programme instructions. Programs have been written which manipulate and produce programs. Such programs treat instructions as data. The processor and memory unit are wired together wiring connections called buses. A *bus* is a low resistance connection consisting of 1 or more wires. There are three such connections. The first, called the address bus, is used by the processor to tell the memory system the number or location of the memory cell the processor wishes to access. The second bus is used to send data out to the memory. The third bus is used to transmit data and instructions to the processor.

A typical computer might be organized as indicated in the following diagram:

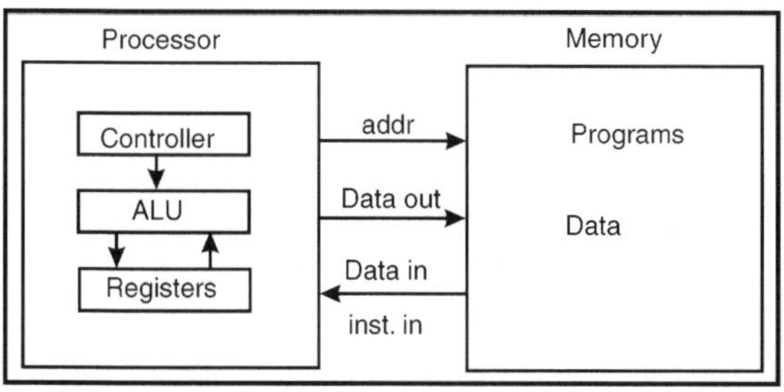

The processor contains a few memory cells, called registers, which are used for efficient temporary storage:

PROCESSOR REGISTERS

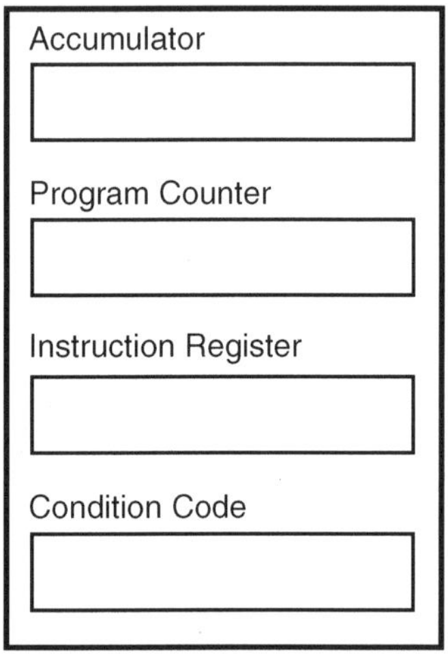

The Contents of a memory cell or a register is simply a number. For purposes of illustration, suppose that each memory cell is large enough to hold numbers up to 4 decimal digits in size.

If a memory cell holds an an instruction, use the first two decimal digits represent the operation and the remaining digits to represent the adderess or location of the instruction operand.

INSTRUCTION FORMAT

Operation	Address

Using this scheme, we could set up the following operation codes:

Operation	Code	Function
add	01	c(acc)=c(acc)+c(addr)
sub	02	c(acc)=c(acc)-c(addr)
load	03	c(acc)=c(addr)
store	04	c(addr)=c(acc)

These codes do not correspond to any known real computer, but rather, they are the operation codes for a hypothetical model computer which we will use to illustrate important aspects of computer organization.

DEFINITION OF PROCESSOR ORGANIZATION

Heretofore it has been known that the apparatus of a digital computer might be arranged in a manner such as to allow accessing to the data storage bits of the computer memory in either of two distinct modes. That is, it has been taught that a system might be developed whereby data can be written into the memory in a word-oriented mode and read from the memory in a bit-oriented mode or vice-versa. That is, data might be written into the memory such that all bits of one word are written simultaneously and one bit of all words are read simultaneously or conversely, one bit of all words are written simultaneously and all bits of one word are read simultaneously.

However, "corner-turning" problems have been inherent in prior techniques. These "corner-turning" problems are well understood by those skilled in the art. An oft-used example of such problems is the acquisition, storage, and accessing of radar data. It can be readily understood that if a radar system acquires a plurality of data at various ranges on one azimuth and stores that data in an azimuth-oriented manner and does this for several azimuths it must then devise a unique method to access this stored data if it later desires to access all data at the same range but different azimuths. In other words, if data is acquired and stored in an azimuth-oriented mode and is later to be accessed in a range-oriented mode then unique apparatus or methods must be utilized to make such accessing.

In the past, systems have required either complex logic circuitry, redundancy of circuitry or an increased number of memory access lines so as to be above to "turn the corner" from a bit-oriented access to a word-oriented access or vice-versa. Particular approaches towards circumventing the "corner-turning" problem have been numerous. A typical approach to the solution has been shown in U.S. Letter Pat. 3,277,449 for the Orthogonal Computer designed by William Shooman.

Certain articles by Mr. Showman further define andenhance the teachings of this patent. Particularly, entitled "Orthogonal Processing" of the book Parallel Processor Systems, Technologies and Applications edited by L. C. Hobbs and published by Spartan Books in 1970 basically outlines the teachings of the patent. It is readily observable from an understanding of the Shooman Patent that the invention described therein requires both vertical and horizontal accessing means, and vertical and horizontal arithmetical means. In other words, the Shooman invention, and others which have sought to circumvent the "corner-turning" problem, fundamentally teach two separate computers operating upon the same memory. Such systems are extremely expensive due to the requirements of the duplication ofaccess circuitry and arithmetic units.

Further, it has been known that computer systems known as associative processors might be designed whereby arithmetic, search, or other logical operations might be performed upon a plurality of data simultaneously. Such systems have proven themselves to be quite effective in the rapid processing of data. However, heretofore such systems have generally been quite inflexible as to mode of operation; that is, such systems have been capable of simultaneously processing all bits of one word, or one bit of all words, but no given system has been capable of performing simultaneous operations in both modes without the duplication of much of its circuitry such as to use different logic and arithmetic circuitry for each of the two modes. Therefore, it is the general object of the instant invention to present a novel solid state associative processor organization wherein a unique solid state memory array is coupled with the key apparatus of an associative processor to form an associative array wherein associative or parallel operations may be performed upon data in either a word-oriented or a bit-oriented mode and wherein each mode utilizes the same read-write lines and arithmetic unit.

A further object of the invention is to provide a solid state associative processor organization wherein a plurality of the aforementioned associative arrays may be operated upon in parallel so as to be capable of simultaneously receiving and processing data from a large number of sources. A further object of the invention is to provide a control system whereby the control programs necessary for the parallel operation of a plurality of associative arrays may themselves be processed with a speed conducive to that of the associative arrays. Still a further object of the invention is to provide a unique computer organization which is not only capable of the parallel processing of a large volume of data from various sources and capable of processing the control program with a speed conducive to the data processing speed of the system, but to do so in a manner which is accurate in operation, highly flexible, adaptable to various uses, and quite economical.

The aforesaid objects of the invention and other objects which will become apparent as the description proceeds are achieved by a digital computer wherein operations may be simultaneously performed on a plurality of data in both a bit-oriented mode and a word-oriented mode comprising a plurality of solid state memory arrays, the data storage arrangements of which are such that access may be made to the data storage bits thereof in either a bit-oriented mode or a word-oriented mode, and of suchcharacter that a single set of data input/output lines is required for writing data into the arrays or reading data from the arrays in both modes and a plurality of arithmetic units, one associated with each solid state memory array, providing the means for performing, in both word-oriented and bit-oriented modes, parallel logical and arithmetic operations on the data associated with the solid state memory arrays.

COMPUTER ARCHITECTURE

To understand digital signal processing systems, we must understand a little about how computers compute. The modern definition of a *computer* is an electronic device that performs calculations on data, presenting the results to humans or other computers in a variety of (hopefully useful) ways.

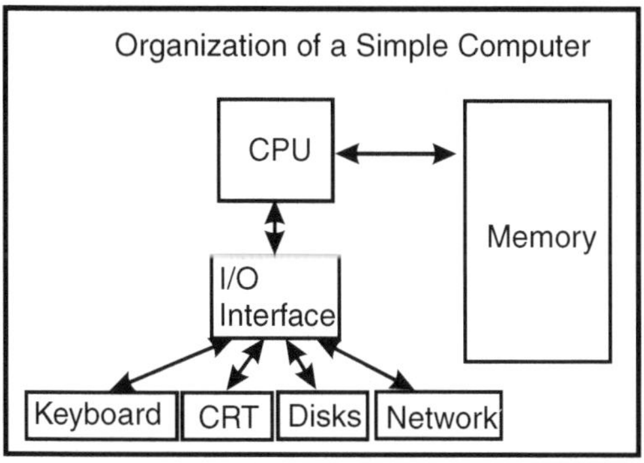

Fig. Generic Computer Hardware Organization.

The generic computer contains *input* devices (keyboard, mouse, A/D (analog-to-digital) converter, etc.), a *computational unit,* and output devices (monitors, printers, D/A converters). The computational unit is the computer's heart, and usually consists of a *central processing unit* (CPU), a *memory,* and an input/output (I/O) interface. What I/O devices might be present on a given computer vary greatly.

A simple computer operates fundamentally in discrete time: Computers are *clocked* devices, in which computational steps occur periodically according to ticks of a clock. This description belies clock speed: When you say "I have a 1 GHz computer," you mean that your computer takes 1 nanosecond to perform each step. That is incredibly fast! A "step" does not, unfortunately, necessarily mean a computation like an addition; computers break such computations down into several stages, which means that the clock speed need not express the computational speed. Computational speed is expressed in units of millions of instructions/second (Mips). Your 1 GHz computer (clock speed) may have a computational speed of 200 Mips.

Computers perform integer (discrete-valued) computations: Computer calculations can be numeric (obeying the laws of arithmetic), logical (obeying the laws of an algebra), or symbolic (obeying any law you like). Each computer instruction that performs an elementary numeric calculation — an addition, a multiplication, or a division — does so only for integers. The sum or product of two integers is also an integer, but the quotient of two integers is likely to not be an integer. How does a computer deal with numbers that have digits to the right of the decimal point? This problem is addressed by using the so-called *floating-point* representation of real numbers. At its heart, however, this representation relies on integer-valued computations.

REPRESENTING NUMBERS

Focusing on numbers, all numbers can represented by the *positional notation system.* 2 The *b*-ary positional representation system uses the position of digits ranging from 0 to *b*-1 to denote a number. The quantity *b* is known as the *base* of the number system. Mathematically, positional systems represent the positive integer *n* as

$$\forall d_k, d_k \in <apply> \{0,\ldots,b-1\}.</apply>:$$

$$\left(n = \sum_{k=0}^{\infty} \left(d_k b^k\right) \right)$$

and we succinctly express *n* in base-*b* as $n_b = d_N d_{N''1} \ldots d_0$. The number 25 in base 10 equals $2 \times 10^1 + 5 \times 10^0$, so that the*digits* representing this number are $d_0=5$, $d_1=2$, and all other d_k equal zero. This same number in *binary* (base 2) equals 11001 ($1 \times 2^4 + 1 \times 2^3 + 0 \times 2^2 + 0 \times 2^1 + 1 \times 2^0$) and 19 in hexadecimal (base 16). Fractions between zero and one are represented the same way.

$$\forall d_k, d_k \in <apply> \{0,\ldots,b-1\}.</apply>:$$

$$\left(f = \sum_{k=-\infty}^{-1} \left(d_k b^k\right) \right)$$

All numbers can be represented by their sign, integer and fractional parts. Complex numbers can be thought of as two real numbers that obey special rules to manipulate them. Humans use base 10, commonly assumed to be due to us having ten fingers. Digital computers use the base 2 or *binary* number representation, each digit of which is known as a *bit* (*b*inary dig*it*).

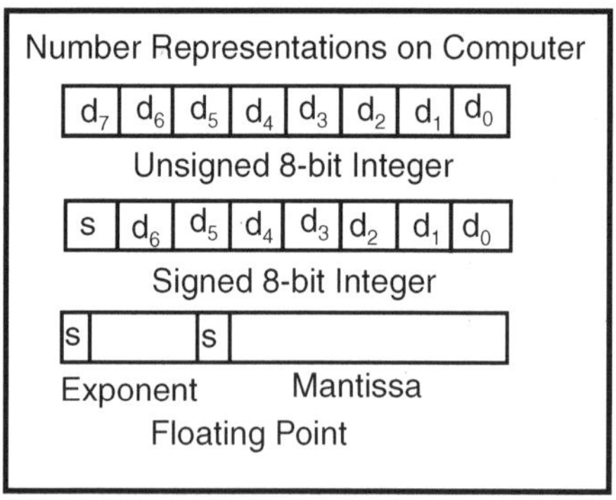

Fig. The Various ways Numbers are Represented in binary are Illustrated. The Number of Bytes for the Exponent and Mantissa Components of floating Point Numbers Varies.

Here, each bit is represented as a voltage that is either "high" or "low," thereby representing "1" or "0," respectively. To represent signed values, we tack on a special bit—the *sign bit*—to express the sign. The computer's memory consists of an ordered sequence of *bytes,* a collection of eight bits. A byte can therefore represent an unsigned number ranging from 0 to255. If we take one of the bits and make it the sign bit, we can make the same byte to represent numbers ranging from "128to 127. But a computer cannot represent *all* possible real numbers.

The fault is not with the binary number system; rather having only a finite number of bytes is the problem. While a gigabyte of memory may seem to be a lot, it takes an infinite number of bits to represent ð. Since we want to store many numbers in a computer's memory, we are restricted to those that have a *finite*binary representation. Large integers can be represented by an ordered sequence of bytes. Common lengths, usually expressed in terms of the number of bits, are 16, 32, and 64. Thus, an unsigned 32-bit number can represent integers ranging between 0 and2^{32}"1 (4,294,967,295), a number almost big enough to enumerate every human in the world.

COMPUTER ARITHMETIC AND LOGIC

The binary addition and multiplication tables are:

(

0 + 0 = 0

0 + 1= 1

1 + 1 = 10

1 + 0 = 1

0 × 0 = 0

0 × 1 = 0

1 × 1 = 1

1 × 0 = 0

)

Note that if carries are ignored, subtraction of two single-digit binary numbers yields the same bit as addition. Computers use high and low voltage values to express a bit, and an array of such voltages express numbers akin to positional notation. Logic circuits perform arithmetic operations.

4

Network Communication and Sharing Technology

DEFINITION OF NETWORK

A group of computers & associated peripheral devices connected by a communicational channel, capable of sharing files & other resources between several users is known as networking. Networking provides us the facility to share distant resources such as database, processor or software. It provides high reliability by having alternate resources for providing distribution of processing so that load sharing can be achieved. Networks are used to save money by using a network of computer, which is cheaper, that using a single mainframe. A Mainframe is 100 times faster than a PC but thousand times costlier than a PC.

DESCRIPTION

If you have two or more computers, including laptops, Why not network them together and share music, pictures, files and folders, printers,scanners etc? The big advantage of your own network will be that all of your computers on the network can share one internet connection and view different pages at the same time. You can also link in your game console and play online. There are two main networks.

LOCAL AREA NETWORK (LAN)

LAN is a group of computers & associated peripheral devices connected by a communication channel, capable of sharing files & other resources between several users. Using LAN we can get the high speed the connections among computers but sacrificing the ability to cover long distance. LAN can operate between 10 Mbps (mega bit per second) to 2 Gbps.

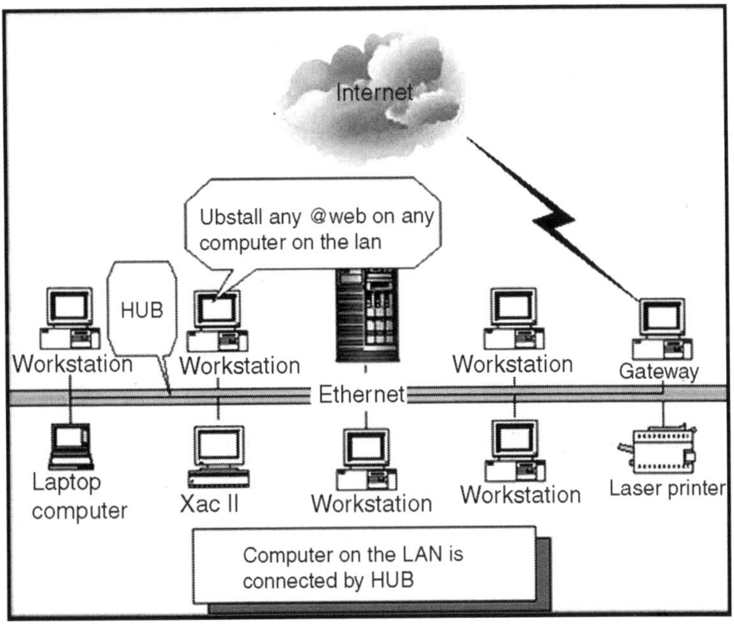

WIDE AREA NETWORK/GLOBAL AREA NETWORK (WAN/GAN)

A network that connects users across larger distances, often crossing geographical boundaries of cities, states, or countries is known as WAN. WANs normally use public telephone network & satellite links for data transmission. Data transmission rates are bellow 1 Mbps for WAN. It is normally owned by multiple organizations. The transmission time is more for WAN because of longer distances & different transmission medium used.

VIRTUAL PRIVATE NETWORK

Many organizations use virtual private networks (VPN) to establish to secure intranet & extranets. A VPN is a secure network that uses the internet as its main backbone network, but relies on network firewalls, encryption and other security features of its internet and intranet connection and those of participating organizations.

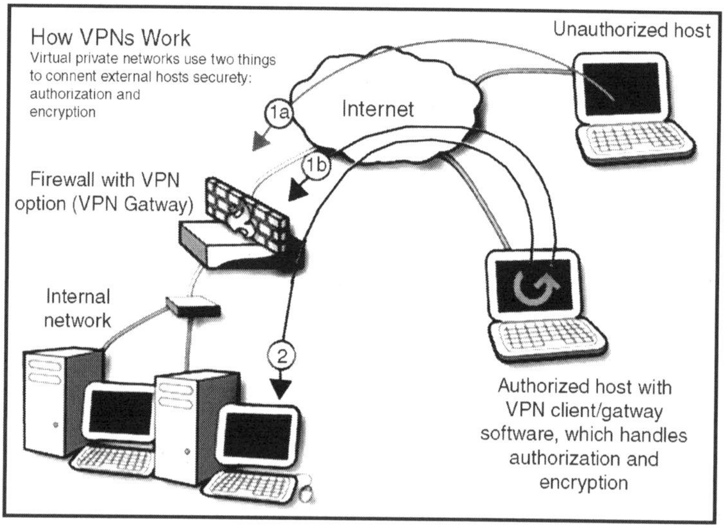

CLIENT SERVER NETWORKS

Client Sever have become the predominant information architecture of enterprise computing. In a client/server network, end user PC or NC work stations are the clients. They are interconnected by local area network & share application processing with network server, which also manage the network.

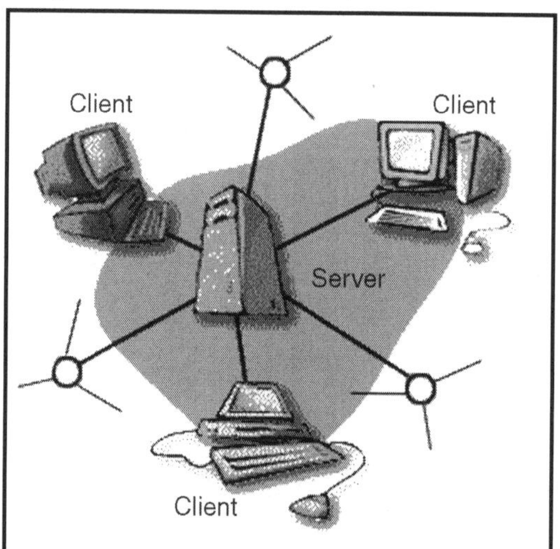

INTRANET

An intranet is a network inside an organization that uses internet technologies (such as Web browsers & servers, TCP/IP network protocols, HTML hypermedia document publishing and databases & so on) to provide an internet like environment within the enterprise for information sharing, communications, collaboration, and the support of business process. An intranet is protected by security measures such as passwords, encryption, and firewalls & thus can be accessed by authorized users through the internet. A companies intranet can also be accessed through the internets of customers, suppliers, and other business partners via *extranet links*.

WIRED NETWORK

A wired network is the most reliable type but the only disadvantage is hiding the cables that network your computers together. However, with a little forward planning, this can be easily overcome.

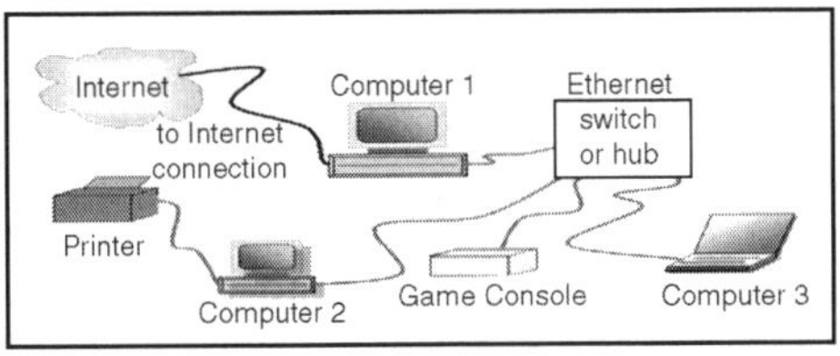

WIRELESS NETWORK

A wireless network operates on radio waves, so a lot depends on the environment the system is installed in. Other radio objects, such as cordless phones, can interfere with your network signal. But wireless is still a reliable system of networking.

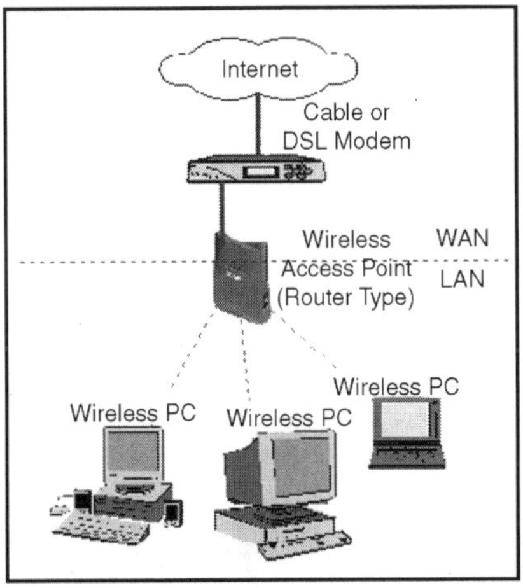

NETWORKING

Because a computer can never be complete, it can complement itself by using resources that other, also incomplete, computers have. In order for two computers to share what they have, they must establish some type of communication. This is easily done using a cable and an appropriate object (a network card, also called NIC) inserted in each computer. This means that a cable would go from this object of one computer to the same type of object on the other computer (In the illustration below, we are using an object between the computers, this object is called a hub. It is perfectly possible to connect two computers using one cable that goes from one computer to the other but this works only if you have two computers. If you have more than one computer, then you use a type of intermediary object whose job is to "direct traffic". For example, when one computer A requests to use or open a piece of text that is located in a computer B but to print it in a printer that is connected to a computer C, this intermediary object is able to know what computer has the text, what computer has the printer, and what computer needs these two services. For these reasons, most connections use this intermediary object: the hub):

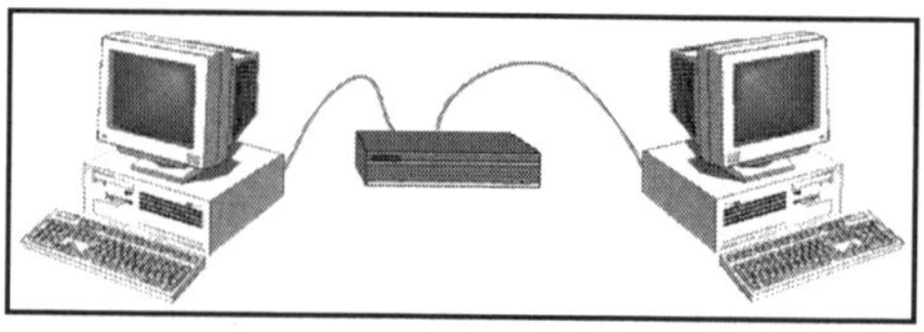

Only computers that are connected can share what they have. A computer A that is connected to a computer B can access what computer B has. When two or more computers are connected, the idea is to let them share and exchange what they contain. If the computers are small, like regular desktop computers, they may become overwhelmed and they may not have enough to share. The next step is to have a "bigger" central computer that holds even more things that other small computers would need (the word big here doesn't necessarily mean that this computer is physically big; it implies that this computer can do more things, for example it can perform more and faster calculations, than the other small computers). Such a central computer is called a server, because its job is to serve other computers (these other small computers are then called workstations):

Once again, only a computer that is a member of this network can take advantage of what the network has to offer. If a computer is not connected to this network, it cannot access the information (and/or resources) of this network. As information and resources (things to share) became more and more useful and in demand, servers of different companies started establishing types of connections among themselves, of course following some rules. In fact, in some situations, some big computers (servers) were made simply to provide information to other computers, without needing to know who owned these small computers, why these small computers needed this information, or what to do with them. The internet was born.

INTERNETWORKING

The Internet is a group of big computers connected to share the information they hold. Some of these computers belong to the government. Some of these computers belong to schools (mostly universities). Some of these computers belong to big companies (corporations). Some of these computers belong to small companies. And some of these computers belong to individuals (located in the basement of their mother). There are two things that may already come to your mind: This is wonderful, and this can be messy; right on both accounts. The computers that are connected may not have anything at all in common. To make sure that this communication is possible, a few rules (called protocols) were established so that anybody who wants to make his or her information available to other people through the Internet must follow these rules, no matter what he or she does with the server or computer.

NETWORKING TOPOLOGIES

DEFINITION

Network topology refers to the way that your computer network is arranged. The network can have a physical or a logical topology. The physical topology describes the layout of computers and where the workstations are positioned. The logical network topology describes how the information flows through the network.

Choosing your physical topology is important because if it is not chosen correctly, this could cause your network to not operate properly. There are several terms that describe the type of physical topology that a network can have. The most common topologies are bus, ring, star, and mesh. In a bus topology, all of the computers are attached to a single cable using terminators.

The terminators work to absorb the energy from the signals in the network. The bus topology is easy to install, but it is not reliable because a single default can bring down your network. In a ring topology, each computer is connected directly to two other computers on the network. As with a bus topology, a single fault can disrupt a ring network. This type of network does have advantages, however, and does not require a network server. In a star topology, each computer is connected using its own separate cable. This set up is more reliable than a bus topology because its design makes it fault tolerant and susceptible to errors. The information on the network is transmitted from one system to another and the data flows in one single direction. The topology is expensive to maintain and is not reliable because removing one computer can disrupt your entire network.

In a mesh topology, a path is present from one computer to another computer in the network. The mesh topology is usually used in internet structure. The mesh topology can be complicated to construct because it has multiple connection between locations. For every computer that you have you will need at least one and a half connections for each one. This contributes to the expensive structure.

In choosing a network topology, understand that each one has its advantages and disadvantages. Research each one and see which one fits within your budget and which one fits your network layout. Also consider the amount of maintenance required in each topology. When setting up a network at home, consider a network topology that is simple and easy to maintain. You will also want a topology that is inexpensive to set up. If you are choosing a topology for a business, you will want to consider a topology that is reliable and resistant to errors. Your customers will need a network that is free of downtime; therefore, be sure that your topology is one that withstands disruption.

TYPES OF NETWORKING TOPOLOGIES

Bus Topology

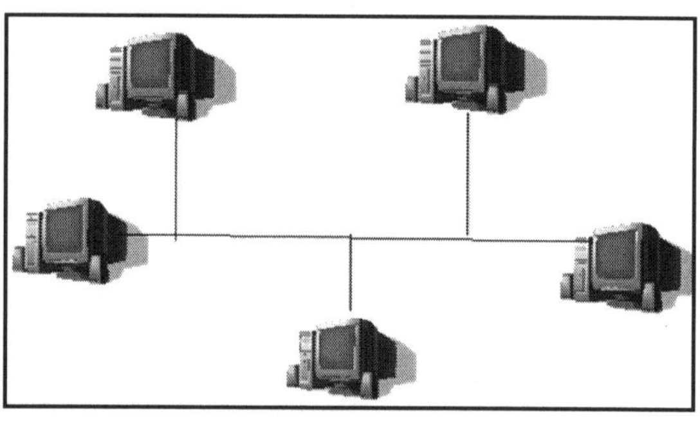

A bus topology is a method of transmission on networks that uses a common vehicle for transmissions and thus it is categorized as shared communication. Imagine a bus picking up various people from one stop and dropping of people as it travels and then picking a few more. That is what happens in a bus network exactly. A bus network uses a multi-drop transmission medium, all node on the network share a common bus and thus share communication. This allows only one device to transmit at a time. A distributed access protocol determines which station is to transmit. Data frames contain source and destination addresses, where each station monitors the bus and copies frames addressed to itself. A bus topology connects each computer (nodes) to a single segment trunk (a communication line, typically coax cable, that is referred to as the 'bus'. The signal travels from one end of the bus to the other. A terminator is required at each to absorb the signal so as it does not reflect back across the bus. A media access method called CSMA/MA is used to handle the collision that occur when two signals placed on the wire at the same time. The bus topology is passive. In other words, the computers on the bus simply 'listen' for a signal; they are not responsible for moving the signal along. However in a Bus topology only one device is allowed to transmit at a given point of time. The DAP or the Distribute Access Protocol has the information about which station has to transmit the data. The data that is being transmitted have frames that will have the source name and the network address.

Function of Bus Topology

The bus topology connects each computer on the network into something called the segment trunk. A bus is usually referred to a cable that connects end to end and this is used to transmit the signals from one end to the other end. At every end a terminator is placed so that it understands in which direction the data is traveling and also the terminator is used to absorb the signals. If the terminator does not absorb the signal then the same signal is reflected back to the bus confusing the whole data flow. The bus is considered to be a passive network because the computers are largely dependant on the signal that is being transmitted.

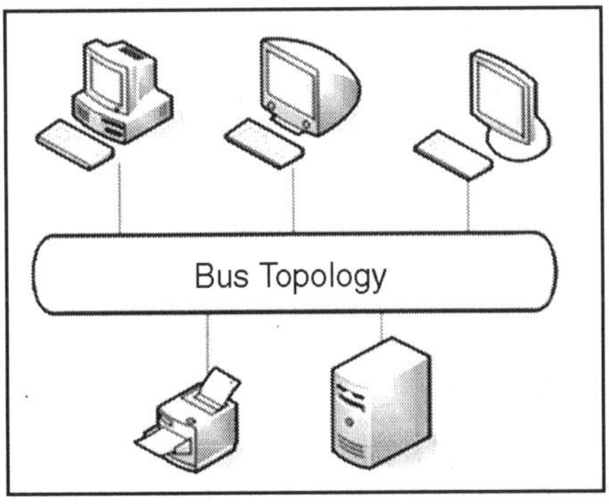

Advantages

The advantage of the Bus network is that if one computer fails in the network the others are still not affected and they continue to work. Bus network is very simple and easy to set up. If there is an urgent need to set up a network and perhaps be used on a short term basis then the Bus network is the best possibility. Bus networks use the least amount of cable to set up making it cost effective.

Limitations

In the bus network you will need a network connection in order to determine if the data is being transferred between two nodes. If the data transfer rate is high then the Bus network does not perform very well because the data travels in a stream and cannot be overloaded. The bus network is a bit challenging when you have to troubleshoot the problems. Bus networks are not suitable as large networks as there are limitations to the number of nodes you can set up for one single cable. As the number of computers increase in the network the data transfer rate goes down accordingly and noticeably.

Conclusion

The bus networks in spite of its limitations is considered to be the easiest and the fastest network that can be set up compared to the other kinds of network. In bus networks there is a collision handling system which ensures that data travels without errors and data is delivered correctly. There is a bus master on the network which ensures that data is flowing in the right direction and order. All the computers on the bus network however listen for the signals and they do not hold the responsibility to move the signal forward. The signal carries forward on its own. So if one computer is not receiving any signals the signal still carries forward without stopping at the computer that has failed. These days bus networks are less common due to the advancement of networks and there are much lesser complicated networks that are easy to operate and efficient. However even these newer technologies derive their basics from older technologies like the Bus Topology.

Ring Topology

Definition

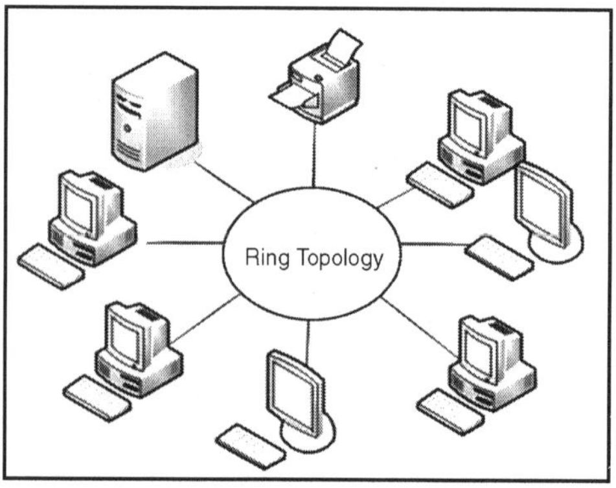

A ring topology is a network topology or circuit arrangement in which each network device is attached along the same signal path to two other devices, forming a path in the shape of a ring. Each device in the network that is also referred to as node handles every message that flows through the ring. Each node in the ring has a unique address. Since in a ring topology there is only one pathway between any two nodes, ring networks are generally disrupted by the failure of a single link.

The redundant topologies are used to eliminate network downtime caused by a single point of failure. All networks need redundancy for enhanced reliability. Network reliability is achieved through reliable equipment and network designs that are tolerant to failures and faults. The FDDI networks overcome the disruption in the network by sending data on a clockwise and a counterclockwise ring. In case there is a break in data flow,the data is wrapped back onto the complementary ring before it reaches the end of the cable thereby maintaining a path to every node within the complementary ring.

Ring network connects computers in a circle of point-to-point connections, with no central server, such as a series of desktop computers in an office. Each node handles its own applications and also shares resources over the entire network. If one node becomes inoperative, the other nodes are still able to maintain contact with one another. Such a network is best for decentralized systems in which no priorities are required

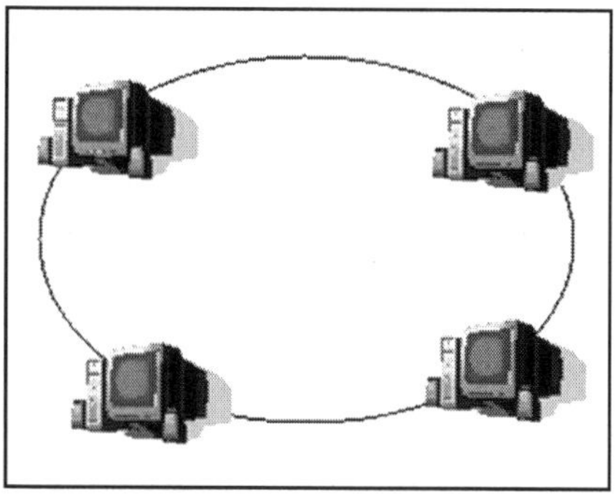

Under the network, a signal is transferred sequentially via a "token" fro one station to the next. When a station wants to transmit, it "grabs" the token, attaches data and an address to it, and then sends it around the ring. The token travels along the ring until it reaches the destination address. The receiving computer acknowledges receipt with a return message to the sender. The sender then releases the token for the token for use by another computer. Each station on the ring has equal access but only one station can talk at a time. To allow an orderly access to the ring, a single electronic token passes from one computer to the next around the ring as seen in (token ring). A computer can only transmit dat

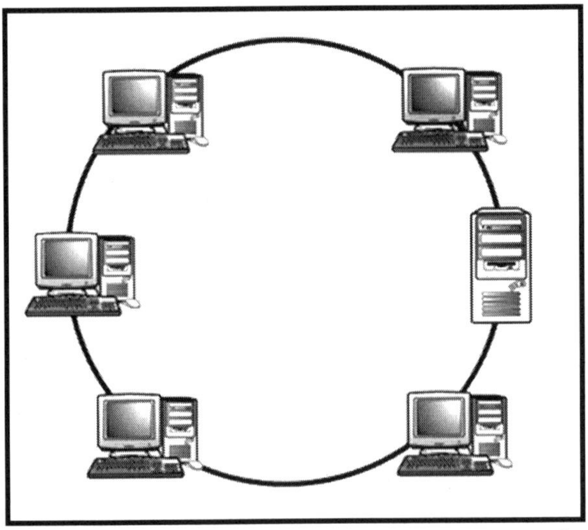

In a true ring topology, if a single computer or section of cable fails, there is an interruption in the signal. The entire network becomes inaccessible. Network disruption can also occur when computers are added or removed from the network, making it an impractical network design in environments where there is constant change to the network.

Ring networks are most commonly wired in a star configuration. In a Token Ring network, a multistation access unit (MSAU) is equivalent to a hub or switch on an Ethernet network. The MSAU performs the token circulation internally. To create the complete ring, the ring in (RI) port on each MSAU is connected to the ring out (RO) port on another MSAU. The last MSAU in the ring is then connected to the first, to complete the ring.

Token Ring Topology

Unlike Ethernet, Token Ring uses a ring topology whereby the data is sent from one machine to the next and so on around the ring until it ends up back where it started. It also uses a token passing protocol which means that a machine can only use the network when it has control of the Token, this ensures that there are no collisions because only one machine can use the network at any given time.

Figure below shows the basic of a Token Ring Topology. Although 16Mbps is the standard ring speed these days (and Fast Token Ring is being developed) we will consider a 4Mbps Token Ring in this tutorial to explain the basic concepts. At the start, a free Token is circulating on the ring, this is a data frame which to all intents and purposes is an empty vessel for transporting data. To use the network, a machine first has to capture the free Token and replace the data with its own message. In the example above, machine 1 wants to send some data to machine 4, so it first has to capture the free Token. It then writes its data and the recipient's address onto the Token.

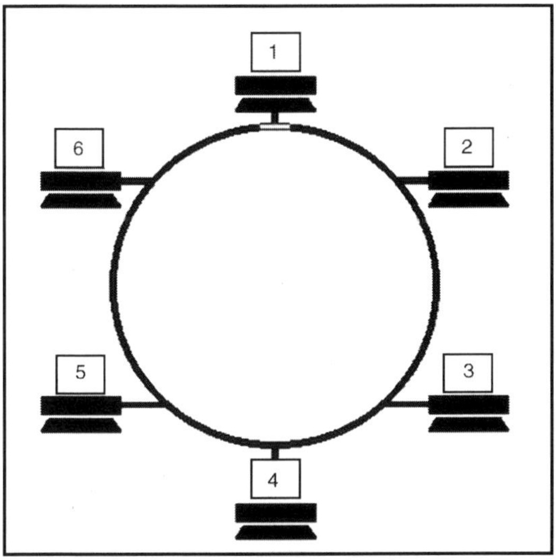

The packet of data is then sent to machine 2 who reads the address, realises it is not its own, so passes it on to machine 3. Machine 3 does the same and passes the Token on to machine 4. This time it is the correct address and so number 4 reads the message. It cannot, however, release a free Token on to the ring, it must first send the message back to number 1 with an acknowledgement to say that it has received the data (represented by the purple flashing screen).

The receipt is then sent to machine 5 who checks the address, realises that it is not its own and so forwards it on to the next machine in the ring, number 6. Machine 6 does the same and forwards the data to number 1, who sent the original message. Machine 1 recognizes the address, reads the acknowledgement from number 4 (represented by the purple flashing screen) and then releases the free Token back on to the ring ready for the next machine to use.

Token Ring Self Maintenance

When a Token Ring network starts up, the machines all take part in a negotiation to decide who will control the ring, or become the 'Active Monitor' to give it its proper title. This is won by the machine with the highest MAC address who is participating in the contention procedure, and all other machines become 'Standby Monitors'.

The job of the Active Monitor is to make sure that none of the machines are causing problems on the network, and to re-establish the ring after a break or an error has occurred. The Active Monitor performs Ring Polling every seven seconds and ring purges when there appears to be a problem. The ring polling allows all machines on the network to find out who is participating in the ring and to learn the address of their Nearest Active Upstream Neighbour

(NAUN). Ring purges reset the ring after an interruption or loss of data is reported. Each machine knows the address of its Nearest Active Upstream Neighbour. This is an important function in a Token Ring as it updates the information required to re-establish itself when machines enter or leave the ring. When a machine enters the ring it performs a lobe test to verify that its own connection is working properly, if it passes, it sends a voltage to the hub which operates a relay to insert it into the ring.

If a problem occurs anywhere on the ring, the machine that is immediately after the fault will cease to receive signals. If this situation continues for a short period of time it initiates a recovery procedure which assumes that its NAUN is at fault, the outcome of this procedure either removes its neighbour from the ring or it removes itself.

Token Ring Operation Using a Hub

A Token Ring hub simply changes the topology from a physical ring to a star wired ring. The Token still circulates around the network and is still controlled in the same manner, however, using a hub or a switch greatly improves reliability because the hub can automatically bypass any ports that are disconnected or have a cabling fault.

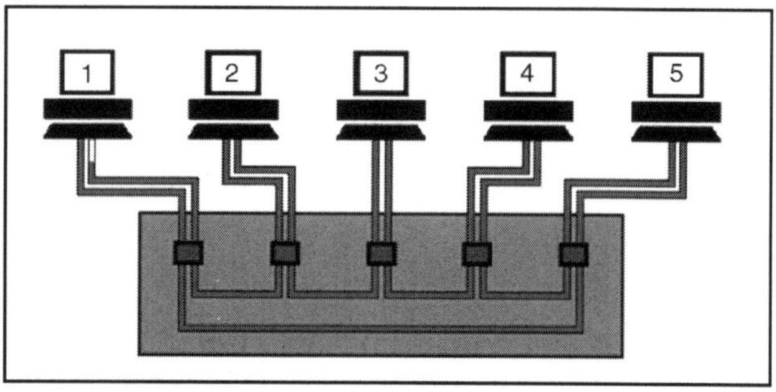

Further advancements have been made in recent years with regard to Token Ring technology, such as early Token release and Token Ring switching but as this site is primarily concerned with cabling issues we will not go into any more detail here.

Star Topology

Star topology is the most commonly used physical technology in Ethernets LANS, when installed, the star topology resembles spokes I n a bicycle wheel. The star topology is made up of a central connection point that is a device such as a hub, switch, or router, where all the cabling segments meet. Each host in the network is connected to the central devices with its own cables although a physical star topology costs more to implement than the physical bus topology , the advantage of star topology make it worth the additional cost.

Because each host it connected to the central device with its own cable, when that cable has a problem, only that host is affected, the rest of the network remains operational this benefit is extremely important and is why virtually every newly designed Ethernet a central connection point might be desirable for security or restricted access, but this is also a main disadvantage of a star topology.if the central device fails, the whole network become disconnected.when a star network is expanded to include an additional networking device that is connected for the main networking device, it is called an extended star topology.

Description

A star topology is designed with each node (file server, workstations, and peripherals) connected directly to a central network hub or concentrator. Data on a star network passes through the hub or concentrator before continuing to its destination. The hub or concentrator manages and controls all functions of the network.

It also acts as a repeater for the data flow. This configuration is common with twisted pair cable; however, it can also be used with coaxial cable or fibre optic cable. Many businesses and home networks use the star topology. A star network features a central connection point called a "hub" that may be an actual hub or a switch as shown below:

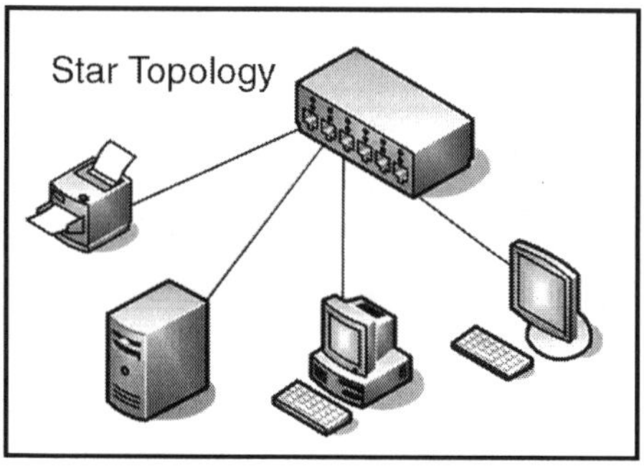

Devices typically connect to the hub with Unshielded Twisted Pair (UTP) Ethernet cables also known as RJ45 cables. Compared to the bus topology, a star network generally requires more cable, but a failure in any star network cable will only take down one computer's network access and not the entire LAN.

Star topology has the following advantages:

- Easy to manage
- Easy to locate problems (cable/workstations)
- Easier to expand than a bus or ring topology
- Easy to Install and Wire
- No disruptions to the network then connecting or removing devices.
- Easy to detect faults and to remove parts.

Star topology has following disadvantages:

- It is susceptible to a single point of failure be it the server or hub/ switch
- With Increased devices and traffic can make the network slow
- Requires more Cable Length.
- If the hub or concentrator fails, nodes attached are disabled.
- More expensive than linear bus topologies because of the cost of the concentrators.

Tree Topology

Among all the Network Topologies we can derive that the Tree Topology is a combination of the bus and the Star Topology. The tree like structure allows you to have many servers on the network and you can branch out the network in many ways.

This is particularly helpful for colleges, universities and schools so that each of the branches can identify the relevant systems in their own network and yet connect to the big network in some way.

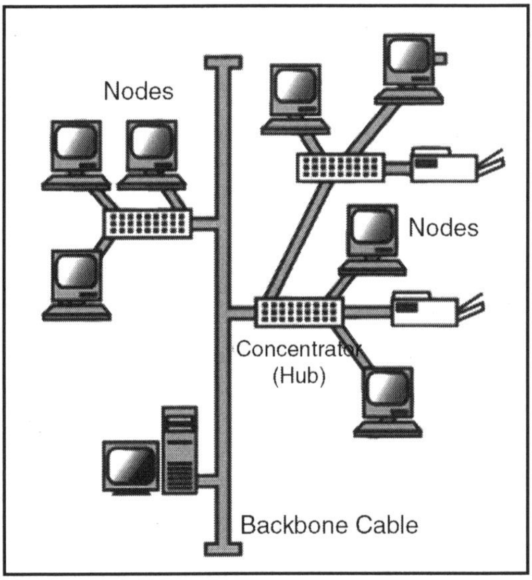

A Tree Structure suits best when the network is widely spread and vastly divided into many branches. Like any other topologies, the Tree Topology has its advantages and disadvantages. A Tree Network may not suit small networks and it may be a waste of cable to use it for small networks. Tree Topology has some limitations and the configuration should suit those limitations.

Benefits

A Tree Topology is supported by many network vendors ad even hardware vendors. A point to point connection is possible with Tree Networks. All the computers have access to the larger and their immediate networks. Best topology for branched out networks.

Limitations

In a Network Topology the length of the network depends on the type of cable that is being used. The Tree Topology network is entirely dependant on the trunk which is the main backbone of the network. If that has to fail then the entire network would fail. Since the Tree Topology network is big it is difficult to configure and can get complicated after a certain point.

The Tree Topology follows a hierarchical pattern where each level is connected to the next higher level in a symmetrical pattern. Each level in the hierarchy follows a certain pattern in connecting the nodes. Like the top most level might have only one node or two nodes and the following level in the hierarchy might have few more nodes which work on the point to point connectivity and the third level also has asymmetrical node to node pattern and each of these levels are connected to the root level in the hierarchy. A Tree Structured network is very similar to this and that is why it is called the Tree Topology.

Features

There will be at least three levels of hierarchy in the Tree Network Topology and they all work based on the root node. The Tree Topology has two kinds of topology integral in it, the star and the linear way of connecting to nodes. The Tree Topology functions by taking into account the total number of nodes present in the network. It does not matter how many nodes are there on each level. Nodes can be added to any level of the hierarchy and there are no limitations a far as the total number of nodes do not exceed. The higher levels in the hierarchy are expected to perform more functions than the lower levels in the network.

Advantages of a Tree Topology

- Point-to-point wiring for individual segments.
- Supported by several hardware and software venders.

Disadvantages of a Tree Topology

- Overall length of each segment is limited by the type of cabling used.
- If the backbone line breaks, the entire segment goes down.
- More difficult to configure and wire than other topologies.

Mesh Topology

A type of network setup where each of the computers and network devices are interconnected with one another, allowing for most transmissions to be distributed, even if one of the connections go down. This type of topology is not commonly used for most computer networks as it is difficult and expensive to have redundant connection to every computer. However, this type of topology is commonly used for wireless networks. The *mesh* topology incorporates a unique network design in which each computer on the network connects to every other, creating a point-to-point connection between every device on the network. The purpose of the mesh design is to provide a high level of redundancy. If one network cable fails, the data always has an alternative path to get to its destination.

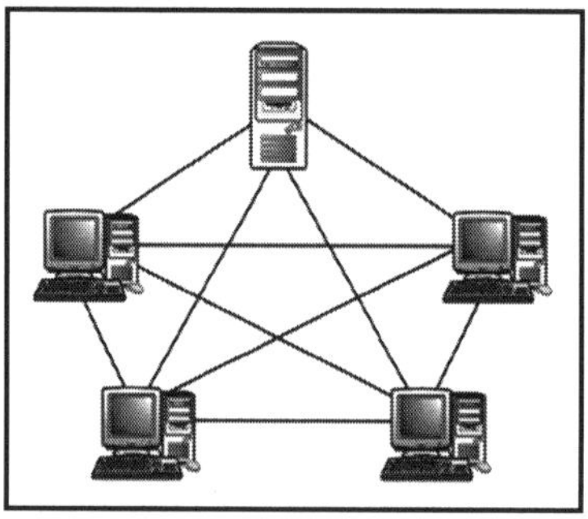

As seen in the above figure, the wiring for a mesh network can be very complicated. Further, the cabling costs associated with the mesh topology can be high, and troubleshooting a failed cable can be tricky. Because of this, the mesh topology is rarely used. A variation on a true mesh topology is the hybrid mesh. It creates a redundant point-to-point network connection between only specific network devices.

Wireless Mesh Networks

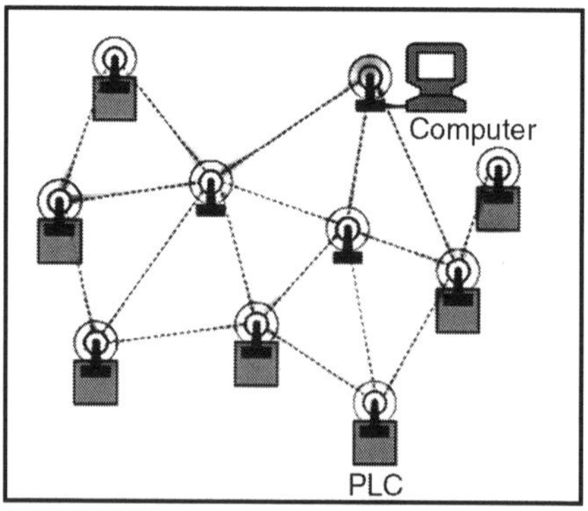

Wireless Mesh Networks work based on the radio frequencies and was originally developed by the army to be able to communicate. The reliability factor is high in any kind of Mesh Network. There are three types of wireless Mesh Topologies.

- Fixed Wireless Connections
- Peer to Peer or Adhoc Networks
- Node to Node

Fixed Mesh Networks

The fixed Mesh Networks will work only in the specified location and they are not mobile networks. They are meant to be used in a limited surrounding with boundaries. The location of nodes in affixed Mesh Network is all pre determined and they are not interchangeable. The fixed Mesh Network does not work on line of sight like the other types of Mesh Networks. The total number of hops in a fixed Mesh Network is usually fixed and also short. There may not be many nodes as this kind of Mesh Networks exist within an office or building. More often than not the data travels ion a specific direction.

Peer to Peer Mobile Networks

In a peer to peer mobile network the individual devices connect to each other using the Mesh Network. The peer does not require connecting to the main node and they can still communicate from one device to another device by taking the shortest possible data transfer route. However many experts believe that in the peer to peer Mesh Networks the problems with scalability in terms of time taken for data transfer is questionable. The device has to know to transmit the data in the most optimal path and the entire data transfer or depends on this single factor. If the device is incapable then the whole purpose of using it in a peer to peer connection is lost.

TELEPHONE NETWORK IN COMPUTING

PSTN

The PSTN or Public Switched Telephone Network refers to the originally telephone network. From a communications perspective it was slow and unreliable. Some of the exchanges on a PSTN may still make use of mechanical switches to route telephone calls. These add additional noise to the line. When lines are noisy, signals have to be resent repeatedly between the source and the destination. The PSTN makes use of analogue technology. Analogue technology uses continuously variable signals. An example of an analogue signal is ordinary speech. Newer digital technologies make use of pulses of fixed magnitude and duration.

In order to improve connections, it is possible to have an analogue leased line. This is a dedicated permanent telephone connection between two computers using the PSTN. In order to connect a computer to a telephone network, you need a modem. This is an abbreviation for modulator-demodulator. The function of the modem is to convert the digital signals from the computer into an analogue form suitable for transmission on the PSTN.

ISDN

ISDN or Integrated Services Digital Network is a technological development that is able to make use of the existing PSTN cabling to transmit digital signals. Technically ISDN is an international standard for the transmission of data, voice and video or normal voice or digital telephone lines. ISDN supports rates of up to 64Kbps. An ISDN connection consists of two lines which can be used independently or together to give a combined rate of 128Kbps. If you wish to connect a computer to an ISDN line you need a special ISDN modem. This is a different type of modem to the one used with an analogue line. Its purpose, however, is the same, to convert the digital signals of the computer into a form suitable for transmission on an ISDN line. It is possible to get a dedicated connection between two computers using ISDN. This is called a diginet connection. The older telephone systems make use of electrical currents transmitted through copper cabling. As electric signals are subject to interference, they are not the ideal method of transmitting data.

ADSL

ADSL or Asymmetric Digital Subscriber Lines allow the transmission of high speed digital data over ordinary telephone lines using a modulation technology called DMT or Discrete MultiTone. Ideally, fibre-optic is the ideal medium for high speed digital transmission. As the installation of fibre-optic is expensive, ADSL provides solution until copper cable is replaced by fibre-optic.

COMMUNICATIONS TERMINOLOGY

Analogue Signals

Analogue signals are used on the PSTN as well as for normal AM and FM radio transmissions. An analogue signal is one which varies continuously as, for example, in ordinary speech.

Digital Signals

Digital signals are used in ISDN and ADSL connections. Newer television and radio transmission techniques are also making using of digital technology. Digital signals are two state signals corresponding to a switch which is on or off. The same two state signal can also represent TRUE and FALSE or 1 and 0. Graphically a digital signal is represented as in the diagram above.

Modems

A modem or modulator-demodulator is a device connected between a computer and a telephone line. Its function is to convert the digital signals of the computer into a form suitable for transmission over a telephone line. It must also do the reverse and convert the telephone line signals into a form suitable for the computer. Note that the modem used to connect to an ISDN line is different to that used to connect to an analogue line.

Fig. External Modem

Data Transfer Rates

Each 1 or 0 that is transferred is referred to as a bit. The speed of a data transfer is measured by the number of bits that can be transferred each second or bps (bits per second). This is also sometimes called the baud rate or bandwidth.

High speed lines have their speed measured in kbps or Mbps:

- 1 kbps = 1 024 bps (roughly 1 000 bps)
- 1 Mbps = 1 024 kbps = 1 048 576 bps (roughly 1 000 000 bps)

To put these figures in perspective, the maximum theoretically attainable speed with an analogue line is 56kbps. This figure is very seldom attained and the reality is usually substantially lower. ISDN lines operate at 64 kbps.

NETWORK SERVER

The word "server" often appears in discussions concerning the Internet (Web server, mail server and chat server for example) and company networks (print server and document server for example). But how does a server differ from the computer sitting beneath your desk? What are servers used for and how might you benefit from using one?

A server is a computer, often a mid-to-high end system, which offers some kind of service or resource to a number of users, most often over a network. A server differs from a desktop system in that a server usually provides a small number of specific services to its users. Desktop systems are designed for everyday use, allowing users to perform a large number of tasks, from checking e-mail or writing documents, to watching streaming video or archiving data.

Servers are used to support a number of users who may need to share a single service or resource. This resource is placed in a single location, on the server, allowing for easy configuration and management, while also allowing for access by a large number of users. Take, for example, a Web server. A Web server can hold a multitude of information regarding an organization, such as product information, contact information, investor information, and support documents, just to name a few. Because all of this information resides in a single place, you can easily change, update, and manage it, while allowing any number of users to access that information by simply visiting the Web site. However, there are many other uses for servers outside of Web hosting. Servers can be used for data storage or archival, for running centralized applications, for sending and receiving mail, or even as simply an efficient way to organize and manage a network infrastructure.

HP and Compaq offer a wide range of server solutions to meet your organization's needs, from small Web hosting solutions to mid-sized data storage to scalable cutting-edge critical systems and beyond.

- *Compaq Proliant Servers*: comprehensive computing systems that include all the necessary components — processor, memory, and network connections — on a single plane called a blade. These systems are designed to reduce space requirements in high-density computing centers while offering a rack-mountable system that utilizes shared components, such as cabling, power-supplies and cooling fans.
- *HP Tower Servers*: offered in standalone and rack-mountable versions and with 1 to 6 CPUs per server, these systems are designed to accommodate a large amount of internal storage and I/O expansion. These systems are an excellent server solution for small-to-medium organizations.
- *Compaq AlphaServers*: high performance systems for Tru64 Unix, OpenVMS and Linux, offering entry-level, mid-range, and high-performance Alpha architecture solutions, with 1 to 32 processors. These systems are available in both rack-mount and desktop configurations.
- *HP rack-optimized servers*: high availability servers with a unique space-saving design, offering 1 to 16 CPUs per server and available in a number of different architectures. These systems offer robust service and management features in a scalable package.
- *HP super-scalable servers*: ideal for large-scale applications and databases, these servers are extremely powerful and flexible, offering high-available solutions with 1 to 64 CPUs per server. These servers are designed to meet high-end demands.
- *Compaq NonStop Integrity Servers*: providing the highest levels of availability and scalability for critical applications, these servers include fault tolerance reliability, data integrity, and continuous availability.

VIRTUAL PRIVATE NETWORK (VPN)

A VPN or a Virtual Private Network is a dedicated communications channel which is streamlined using another network. A VPN is useful for companies which need their own space on the internet. For example a business community that needs to secure its own network on the internet and wants to carry out various business activities within this environment can use a VPN. The VPN operates on a different and more complicated topology than a point to point network. Also VPN dos not stress on security features and rather the network on which it is based may tend to have extreme security features. Virtual Private Networks have gained a lot of popularity in the recent past because it not only reduce costs but also increases and expands the network capabilities. Because of the functionalities of VPN, employees can connect from anywhere in the world to the company's network and carry out important and sensitive task on time. It keeps the employees connected to the company's intranet.

What is a Virtual Private Network

A Virtual Private Network is a system that keeps the computers connected even if there are long distances or physical barriers. The VPN is categorized as a form of a wide area network. The VPN supports functions like remote access for clients; it can network one LAN to another LAN, and also keeps the functions limited to the intranet. Companies find it easier to use VPN because it needs to give special access or create special access for their employees who have to be mobile. It is globally active intra network so employees from anywhere can connect to the company's intranet

VPN Functionality

VPN supports many protocols like PPTP, L2TP, IPSec and SOCKS. These protocols help the authentication process in the VPN. The VPN clients can establish a connection and identify the authorized people on the network. The VPN networks are also encrypted which means that they are usually invisible on the bigger networks. Being encrypted enhances the security feature for the VPN. The Virtual Private Networks also have paved the way for Wi-Fi and private wireless connections networks. More and more technologies are basing their developments in the VPN because of the mobility it provides.

Virtual Private Network Features

Virtual Private Networks are cost effective solutions for large business organizations instead of dedicated network facilities It increases the mobility for organizations by instantly connecting home networks or mobile workers to the organization. Security features can be customised.

VPN Disadvantages

By providing access to employees globally the security is at risk. This also puts the sensitive information of the company accessible globally. For a VPN extra care has to be taken and the security should be clearly defined.

VN for remote access can be set up for employees who are constantly travelling and have to stay connected to the company's intranet. Even when the remote access is established the employee or the person have to connect top the local internet service provider first in order to be able to connect to the virtual private network of the organization. That is why the VPN is known to work on an underlying network and cannot work independently.

VPN Solutions

There are many solutions that a VPN can provide like long distance connectivity, file sharing, video conferencing and other services related to networks. The features that are already being offered on the internet through various services can be offered through VPN in perhaps a cost effective way. The VPN is so flexible that it can work on private networks and public networks.

LAN/WAN/MAN

VeriCenter's network services span the gamut, from providing just the physical link to offering full network management. Depending on your requirements and the level of responsibility you want to offload, we can customise a solution for your specific needs.

NETWORK MONITORING

To keep your network at peak availability and performance-and to proactively manage potential issues-you need real-time knowledge, visibility, and control of your IT environment. VeriCenter offers a flexible suite of services that allows you to monitor your IT infrastructure, including routers, switches, and servers. Our network monitoring services range from simple up/down status to customised threshold monitoring (such as server CPU and disk utilization) to I/O queue length. VeriCenter provides monitoring and real-time detection of both exception and normal operating conditions for monitored elements. We notify you if pre-defined thresholds are exceeded, allowing you to proactively address potential problems before your customers call you.

Network monitoring is provided through a secure connection to your environment, and reporting information is accessed via our Web-based Customer Portal. This portal not only offers a snapshot of your current system state, but also provides trending analysis to help you manage your environment. VeriCenter's network management services provide comprehensive turnkey support for your local and wide area networks (LANs and WANs). This service is backed by a highly trained team of technicians and engineers with proven expertise in network management and maintenance.

VeriCenter remotely manages your network infrastructure, including routers, hubs, and switches, for the highest reliability and optimized performance. When a problem is detected and isolated, VeriCenter takes the steps necessary to coordinate with hardware vendors and carrier partner(s) for problem resolution. At all times, you're able to access critical information about your network through our secure Web-based Customer Portal.

Our services are designed to provide you with complete management of critical network devices within your environment, using the tools and expertise of our Network Operations Center (NOC). Every productive data network is made up of two intergral parts-infrastructure (communications environment) and active elements, which utilise the communications environment. The infrastructure can be made up of a structured cabling system based on melicke or optical lines, wireless transfer system etc. The quality and performance of the infrastructure directly affects the resulting attributes and output of the data network.

With the rapid development of Internet applications and technology, more and more emphasis is being put on securing access to data networks and on protection of the actual data with systems against misuse or attack. There is an evident trend of integrating various security functions into basic network elements, such as switches, routers etc. The convergence trend for data and telephony into one communications infrastructure has brought the need to secure the necessary quality of service (QoS) for operations sensitive to the quality of the data network (IP telephony, video-conferencing). A modern data network is capable of working with several classes of operations and each of these classes is capable of securing the necessary quality of service.

Since it was established, GiTy has been oriented to the most up-to-date technologies, which guarantee the maximum possible output for data networks and their long technological lifetime. Key components of data networks developed by us are products from the foremost technological manufacturers, such as Siemon, Cisco Systems, Enterasys Network, 3COM, Allied Telesyn and Crossbeam. Data networks developed by us provide users with high performance, the maximum level of security and the tools needed for management of the quality of services for individual applications.

THE HISTORY OF LANS

The advent of personal computers changed the type of information sent over office computer networks. Terminals were no longer "dumb," but contained the power to perform their own instructions and maintain their own memories. This took considerable pressure off mainframe devices, whose energies could now be devoted to more complex tasks.

LANs allowed for the transmission of data between workers. In turn, they enabled this shared data to be directed to a common printer, serving a larger group of users. This eliminated the need for each worker to have a printer and ensured that the one printer provided was not underutilized. In addition, LANs allowed data to be called up directly on other workers' computers, providing immediate communication and eliminating the need for paper. The most common application was in interoffice communications, or electronic mail (e-mail). Messages could be directed to one or several people and copied to several more over the LAN. As a result, an e-mail system became something of an official record of communications between workers. Addressees became obligated to respond to e-mail messages in a timely manner because their failure to answer could be easily documented for supervisors.

Personal computers transformed LANs from mere shared processors to fully integrated communication devices. With processing power distributed among several computers, the mainframe's main role was eclipsed and complex processing, administrative functions, and data file storage became the job of a new device, the file server. Today, there are many different types of LANs. For example, many Macintosh computers use Appletalk, while IBM computers commonly use Ethernets.

Physical Components

The physical properties of a LAN include network access units (or interfaces) that connect the personal computer to the network. These units are actually interface cards installed on computer motherboards. Their job is to provide a connection, monitor availability of access to the LAN, set or buffer the data transmission speed, ensure against transmission errors and collisions, and assemble data from the LAN into usable form for the computer.

The next part of a LAN is the wiring, which provides the physical connection from one computer to another, and to printers and file servers. The properties of the wiring determine transmission speeds. The first LANs were connected with coaxial cable, the same type used to deliver cable television. These facilities are relatively inexpensive and simple to attach. More importantly, they provided great bandwidth (the system's rate of data transfer), enabling transmission speeds initially up to 20 megabits per second.

Another type of wiring, developed in the 1980s, used ordinary twisted wire pair (commonly used for telephones). The primary advantages of twisted wire pair are that it is very cheap, simpler to splice than coaxial, and is already installed in many buildings. The downside of this simplicity is that its bandwidth is more limited.

A more recent development in LAN wiring is optical fibre cable. This type of wiring uses thin strands of glass to transmit pulses of light between terminals. It provides tremendous bandwidth, allowing very high transmission speeds and because it is optical rather than electronic, it is impervious to electromagnetic interference. Still, splicing it can be difficult and requires a high degree of skill. The primary application of fibre is not between terminals, but between LAN buses (terminals) located on different floors. As a result, fibre distributed data interface is used mainly in building risers. Within individual floors, LAN facilities remain coaxial or twisted wire pair. When a physical connection cannot be made between two LANs, such as across a street or between buildings, microwave radio may be used. However, it is often difficult to secure frequencies for this medium. Another alternative in this application is light transceivers, which project a beam of light similar to fibre optic cable, but through the air rather than over cable. These systems do not have the frequency allocation or radiation problems associated with microwave, but they are susceptible to interference from fog and other natural obstructions.

LAN Topologies

LANs are designed in several different topologies, or physical patterns, connecting terminals. These shapes can range from straight lines to a ring. Each terminal on the LAN contends with other terminals for access to the system. When it has secured access to the system, it broadcasts its message to all the terminals at once. The message is picked up by the one or group of terminal stations for which it is intended. The branching tree topology is an extension of the bus, providing a link between two or more buses.

A third topology, the star network, also works like a bus in terms of contention and broadcast. But in the star, stations are connected to a single, central node (individual computer) that administers access. Several of these nodes may be connected to one another. For example, a bus serving six stations may be connected to another bus serving 10 stations and a third bus connecting 12 stations. The star topology is most often used where the connecting facilities are coaxial or twisted wire pair.

The ring topology connects each station to its own node, and these nodes are connected in a circular fashion. Node 1 is connected to node 2, which is connected to node 3, and so on, and the final node is connected back to node 1. Messages sent over the LAN are regenerated by each node, but retained only by the addressees. Eventually, the message circulates back to the sending node, which removes it from the stream.

Transmission Methods Used By LANs

LANs function because their transmission capacity is greater than any single terminal on the system. As a result, each station terminal can be offered a certain amount of time on the LAN, like a timesharing arrangement. To economize on this small window of opportunity, stations organize their messages into compact packets that can be quickly distributed. When two messages are sent simultaneously, they could collide on the LAN causing the system to be temporarily disrupted. Busier LANs usually utilize special software that virtually eliminates the problem of collisions by providing orderly, non-contention access.

The transmission methods used on LANs are either baseband or broadband. The baseband medium uses a high-speed digital signal consisting of square wave DC voltage. While it is fast, it can accommodate only one message at a time. As a result, it is suitable for smaller networks where contention is low. It also is very simple to use, requiring no tuning or frequency discretion circuits. This transmission medium may be connected directly to the network access unit and is suitable for use over twisted wire pair facilities.

By contrast, the broadband medium tunes signals to special frequencies, much like cable television. Stations are instructed by signaling information to tune to a specific channel to receive information. The information within each channel on a broadband medium may also be digital, but they are separated from other messages by frequency. As a result, the medium generally requires higher capacity facilities, such as coaxial cable. Suited for busier LANs, broadband systems require the use of tuning devices in the network access unit that can filter out all but the single channel it needs.

The File Server

The administrative software of the LAN resides either in a dedicated file server; in a smaller, less busy LAN; or in a personal computer that acts as a file server. In addition to performing as a kind of traffic controller, the file server holds files for shared use in its hard drives, administers applications such as the operating system, and allocates functions.

When a single computer is used as both a workstation and a file server, response times may lag because its processors are forced to perform several duties at once. This system will store certain files on different computers on the LAN. As a result, if one machine is down, the entire system may be crippled. If the system were to crash due to undercapacity, some data may be lost or corrupted.

The addition of a dedicated file server may be costly, but it provides several advantages over a distributed system. In addition to ensuring access even when some machines are down, its only duties are to hold files and provide access.

Other Lan Equipment

LANs are generally limited in size because of the physical properties of the network including distance, impedance, and load. Some equipment, such as repeaters, can extend the range of a LAN. Repeaters have no processing ability, but simply regenerate signals that are weakened by impedance. Other types of LAN equipment with processing ability include gateways, which enable LANs operating dissimilar protocols to pass information by translating it into a simpler code, such as ASCII. A bridge works like a gateway, but instead of using an intermediate code, it translates one protocol directly into another. A router performs essentially the same function as a bridge, except that it administers communications over alternate paths. Gateways, bridges, and routers can act as repeaters, boosting signals over greater distances. They also enable separate LANs located in different buildings to communicate with each other.

The connection of two or more LANs over any distance is referred to as a wide area network (WAN). WANs require the use of special software programs in the operating system to enable dial-up connections that may be performed by a telephone lines or radio waves. In some cases, separate LANs located in different cities—and even separate countries—may be linked over the public network.

LAN Difficulties

LANs are susceptible to many kinds of transmission errors. Electromagnetic interference from motors, power lines, and sources of static, as well as shorts from corrosion, can corrupt data. Software bugs and hardware failures can also introduce errors, as can irregularities in wiring and connections. LANs generally compensate for these errors by working off an uninterruptable power source, such as batteries, and using backup software to recall most recent activity and hold unsaved material. Some systems may be designed for redundancy, such as keeping two file servers and alternate wiring to route around failures. Security problems can also be an issue with LANs. They can be difficult to manage and access because the data they use is often distributed between many different networked sources. In addition, many times this data is stored on several different workstations and servers. Most companies have specific LAN administrators who deal with these issues and are responsible for the use of LAN software. They also work to backup files and recover lost files.

WAN/MAN CONNECTIVITY

Once you move your hosted environment to VeriCenter's Tier 1 data center, how do you access it? Through one of our network solutions. Whether you want secure access for administrative purposes only or gigabit metro area network (MAN) connections to extend the LAN from your site to VeriCenter's, we can accommodate your needs. We can also custom-design a solution to meet specific security or redundancy concerns. VeriCenter's standard offerings include private network access, with speeds from DS1 to DS3. In addition, through our partners, we can offer private Ethernet connections ranging from 10 Mbps to 1,000 Mbps.

LAN

Definition: A local area network (LAN) supplies networking capability to a group of computers in close proximity to each other such as in an office building, a school, or a home. A LAN is useful for sharing resources like files, printers, games or other applications. A LAN in turn often connects to other LANs, and to the Internet or other WAN. Most local area networks are built with relatively inexpensive hardware such as Ethernetcables, network adapters, and hubs. Wireless LAN and other more advanced LAN hardware options also exist.

Specialized operating system software may be used to configure a local area network. For example, most flavours of Microsoft Windows provide a software package called Internet Connection Sharing (ICS) that supports controlled access to LAN resources. The term LAN party refers to a multiplayer gaming event where participants bring their own computers and build a temporary LAN.

WAN

Definition: A WAN spans a large geographic area, such as a state, province or country. WANs often connect multiple smaller networks, such as local area networks (LANs) or metro area networks (MANs). The world's most popular WAN is the Internet. Some segments of the Internet, like VPN-based extranets, are also WANs in themselves. Finally, many WANs are corporate or research networks that utilize leased lines. WANs generally utilize different and much more expensive networking equipment than do LANs. Key technologies often found in WANs include SONET, Frame Relay, and ATM.

BRIDGE

DEFINITION

The bridges used in computer networking are not like your typical bridge. This type of bridge is a internetworking device used to help conserve the bandwidth on the network. When LANs are really starting to grow, network data traffic begins to become a little overwhelming to the available bandwidth on the network media. One way of conserving this network traffic is to slice the network up into smaller segments. These segments are connected to a bridge. Bridges are smarter than hubs and repeaters. They also use software to help get the job done.

Bridges are able to read MAC addresses, which are also known as hardware addresses that are burned onto the NIC inside every computer on the network, of each data packet the is circulated on the network segments connected on the bridge. It is by learning which MAC addresses are live on the network that the bridge is able to control traffic that is local to a particular segment and keep it from spreading to other network segments that are being serviced by another bridge. A bridge device filters data traffic at a network boundary. Bridges reduce the amount of traffic on a LAN by dividing it into two segments. Bridges operate at the data link layer (Layer 2) of the OSI model. Bridges inspect incoming traffic and decide whether to forward or discard it. An Ethernet bridge, for example, inspects each incoming Ethernet frame-including the source and destination MAC addresses, and sometimes the frame size-in making individual forwarding decisions.

Bridges serve a similar function as switches, that also operate at Layer 2. Traditional bridges, though, support one network boundary, whereas switches usually offer four or more hardware ports. Switches are sometimes called "multi-port bridges" for this reason. Computer networks serve the purpose of connecting many different computers or terminals to each other, host computers, printers, file servers etc. so that expensive computing assets, programs, files and other data may be shared among many users. A large network may typically contain one or more gateways, routers and bridges operating in conjunction with one or more network segments.

A segment is section of a network connected to a group of machines which may communicate with each other via repeater operations without having to traverse a bridge or router. Bridges and routers are useful in that they allow connections of multiple segments such that more computers may communicate with each other than would otherwise be possible given the limited bandwidth of the media. A network bridge is a transmission device for carrying out bidirectional data transmission across a plurality of networks connected via ports. The function of the bridge is to monitor frames transferred over the LAN and to transfer them from one network to another on the basis of the physical address of the data packets.

Only frames having a destination address indicating transmission to the side of the other network are able to cross the bridge. The bridge thus acts as an insulator which reduces the load in other network portions. A LAN bridge interconnects a LAN with one or more other LANs, through an interconnecting link or links, to form a larger network in which messages can be sent from a device on one LAN to one or more devices on another LAN. Each network bridge and router requires certain other peripheral circuitry to support it such as LAN controllers, a CPU, a power supply, a network management process, memory to store bridge source and destination address tables and various other things like status registers etc. Typically, a network bridge is connected to a hub by a separate local area network segment which itself requires two port interface circuits such as LAN controllers and AUI's (generic network interfaces) with appropriate port drivers adapted for the specific media used for the bridge-hub LAN segment.

HUB

DEFINITION

One of the most commonly used networking hardware devices are hubs.

However, the inexpensive switch is rapidly replacing the hub. Anyway, hubs serve as central connection points for local area networks (LANs) that typically embrace the star topology. The basic hub contains no active electronics and cannot be used to extend a LAN past its cabling distance specifications. Yet, hubs organize your cables and relay data signals to all computers that exist on your LAN.

Hubs are used on networks where twisted-pair cabling is used. The ports, which are available on the hub, provide connection points for the devices on the network. Computers and devices are connected to the hub via network cables to individual ports. In cases where a LAN outgrows the size of its hub, a new hub can be attached by daisy-chaining them together using a short connection cable, which is often referred to as a rattail. The FS100 series Fast Ethernet switches brings the 100 Mbps switching technology and simplifies it for the small office marketplace. These products provide a cost effective way to instantaneously boost network performance while preserving your network infrastructure, including installed cabling and desktop software and hardware. Since each port is auto-speed- sensing, installation is plug and play and each connection can easily be upgraded from 10 to 100 Mbps. Manufacturer Part No. FS108NA. SKU# 070423.

Features: 5 or 8 switched 10/100 Mbps ports Each port provides dedicated 10 or 100 Mbps bandwidth for connecting one or multiple PCs, servers, and hubs. In full-duplex mode, each port supports up to 200 Mbps of throughput. Automatic speed and full/half-duplex sensing The switch supports n-way auto negotiation, and each port automatically senses and operates at the proper speed and duplex mode, taking the burden of configuration off the user.

vistajacks with built-in LEDs clearly indicate port status, simplifying installation and troubleshooting. The switch is plug and play with no software to configure. Versatile and compatible The switch is protocol independent and is compatible with all popular networks such as the Internet or TCP/IP, NetWare, Microsoft Windows, or LANTASTIC

ROUTER

DEFINITION

Routers are physical devices that join multiple wired or wireless networks together. Technically, a wired or wireless router is a Layer 3 gateway, meaning that the wired/wireless router connects networks (as gateways do), and that the router operates at the network layer of the OSI model.

Home networkers often use an Internet Protocol (IP) wired or wireless router, IP being the most common OSI network layer protocol. An IP router such as a DSL or cable modembroadband router joins the home's local area network (LAN) to the wide-area network (WAN) of the Internet.

By maintaining configuration information in a piece of storage called the routing table, wired or wireless routers also have the ability to filter traffic, either incoming or outgoing, based on the IP addresses of senders and receivers. Some routers allow the home networker to update the routing table from a Web browser interface. Broadband routers combine the functions of a router with those of a network switch and a firewall in a single unit. A hardware device designed to take incoming packets, analyzing the packets and then directing them to the appropriate locations, moving the packets to another network, converting the packets to be moved across a different type of network interface, dropping the packets, or performing any other number of other types of actions. To the right is a picture of the Linksys BEFSR11 router and is similar to what most home users would use for their home network.

A router has a lot more capabilities than other network devices such as a hub or a switch that are only able to perform basic network functions. For example, a hub is often used to transfer data between computers or network devices, but does not analyse or do anything with the data it is transferring. Routers however can analyse the data being sent over a network, change how it is packaged and send it to another network or over a different type of network. For example, routers are commonly used in home networks to share a single Internet connection with multiple computers.

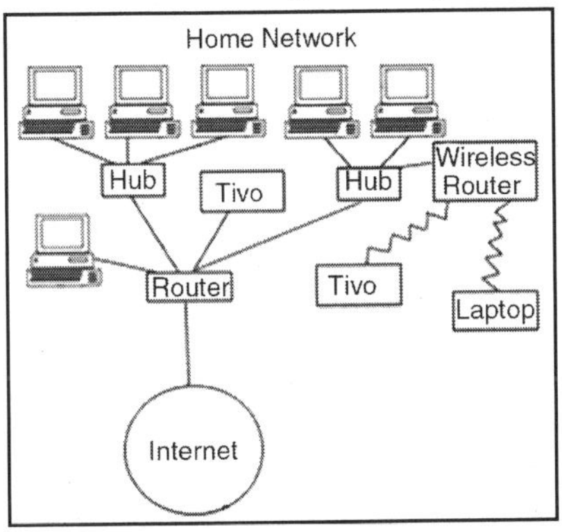

In the above example of a home network there are two different examples of a router, the router and the wireless router. As can be seen in the example the router is what allows all the computers and other network devices access the Internet. Below are some additional examples of different types of routers used in a large network.

Brouter

Short for Bridge Router, a "brouter" is a networking device that serves as both abridge and a router.

Core router

A core router is a router in a computer network that routes data within a network but not between networks.

Edge router

An edge Router is a router in a computer network that routes data between one or more networks.

Virtual router

A Virtual Router is a backup router used in a VRRP setup:

- Document CH001200 for additional information about adjusting the settings on your home router.

DYNAMIC ROUTING

Dynamic routing protocols not only perform these path determination and route table update functions but also determine the next-best path if the best path to a destination becomes unusable. The capability to compensate for topology changes is the most important advantage dynamic routing offers over static routing.

Obviously, for communications to occur the communicators must speak the same language. There are eight major IP routing protocols from which to choose; if one router speaks RIP and another speaks OSPF, they cannot share routing information because they are not speaking the same language. Subsequent chapters examine all the IP routing protocols in current use, and even consider how to make a router "bilingual," but first it is necessary to explore some characteristics and issues common to all routing protocols—IP or otherwise.

All dynamic routing protocols are built around an algorithm. Generally, an *algorithm* is a step-by-step procedure for solving a problem. A routing algorithm must, at a minimum, specify the following:

- A procedure for passing reachability information about networks to other routers
- A procedure for receiving reachability information from other routers
- A procedure for determining optimal routes based on the reachability information it has and for recording this information in a route table

- A procedure for reacting to, compensating for, and advertising topology changes in an internetwork

A few issues common to any routing protocol are path determination, metrics, convergence, and load balancing.

PATH DETERMINATION

All networks within an internetwork must be connected to a router, and wherever a router has an interface on a network that interface must have an address on the network. This address is the originating point for reachability information. Each router knows about its directly connected networks from its assigned addresses and masks.

Metrics

When there are multiple routes to the same destination, a router must have a mechanism for calculating the best path. A *metric* is a variable assigned to routes as a means of ranking them from best to worst or from most preferred to least preferred. Consider the following example of why metrics are needed. Different routing protocols use different, and sometimes multiple, metrics. For example, RIP defines the "best" route as the one with

Hop Count

A hop count metric simply counts router hops. For instance, from router A it is 1 hop to network 192.168.5.0 if packets are sent out interface 192.168.3.1 (through router B) and 2 hops if packets are sent out 192.168.1.1 (through routers C and B). Assuming hop count is the only metric being applied, the best route is the one with the fewest hops, in this case, A-B. But is the A-B link really the best path? If the A-B link is a DS-0 link and the A-C and C-B links are T-1 links, the 2-hop route may actually be best because bandwidth plays a role in how efficiently traffic travels through the network.

Bandwidth

A bandwidth metric would choose a higher-bandwidth path over a lower-bandwidth link. However, bandwidth by itself still may not be a good metric. What if one or both of the T1 links are heavily loaded with other traffic and the 56K link is lightly loaded? Or what if the higher-bandwidth link also has a higher delay?

Load

This metric reflects the amount of traffic utilizing the links along the path. The best path is the one with the lowest load. Unlike hop count and bandwidth, the load on a route changes, and therefore the metric will change. Care must be taken here. If the metric changes too frequently, *route flapping*—the frequent

Delay

Delay is a measure of the time a packet takes to traverse a route. A routing protocol using delay as a metric would choose the path with the least delay as the best path. There may be many ways to measure delay. Delay may take into account not only the delay of the links along the route but also such factors as router latency and queuing delay.

On the other hand, the delay of a route may be not measured at all; it may be a sum of static quantities defined for each interface along the path. Each individual delay quantity would be an estimate based on the type of link to which the interface is connected.

Reliability

Reliability measures the likelihood that the link will fail in some way and can be either variable or fixed. Examples of variable-reliability metrics are the number of times a link has failed or the number of errors it has received within a certain time period. Fixed-reliability metrics are based on known qualities of a link as determined by the network administrator. The path with highest reliability would be selected as best.

Cost

This metric is configured by a network administrator to reflect more- or less-preferred routes. Cost may be defined by any policy or link characteristic or may reflect the arbitrary judgment of the network administrator. The term *cost* is often used as a generic term when speaking of route choices. For example, "RIP chooses the lowest-cost path based on hop count." Another generic term is *shortest,* as in "RIP chooses the shortest path based on hop count." When used in this context, either *lowest-cost* (or *highest-cost*) and *shortest* (or *longest*) merely refer to a routing protocol's view of paths based on its specific metrics.

SWITCH

DEFINITION

A network switch is a small hardware device that joins multiple computers together within one local area network (LAN). Technically, network switches operate at layer two (Data Link Layer) of the OSI model. Network switches appear nearly identical to network hubs, but a switch generally contains more intelligence (and a slightly higher price tag) than a hub. Unlike hubs, network switches are capable of inspecting data packets as they are received, determining the source and destination device of each packet, and forwarding them appropriately. By delivering messages only to the connected device intended, a network switch conservesnetwork bandwidth and offers generally better performance than a hub. As with hubs, Ethernet implementations of network switches are the most common. Mainstream Ethernet network switches support either 10/100 Mbps Fast Ethernet or Gigabit Ethernet (10/100/1000) standards.

Different models of network switches support differing numbers of connected devices. Most consumer-grade network switches provide either four or eight connections for Ethernet devices. Switches can be connected to each other, a so-called daisy chaining method to add progressively larger number of devices to a LAN.

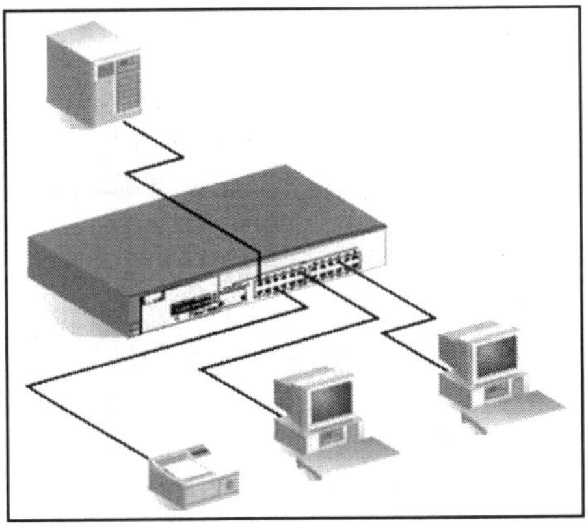

A switch is another internetworking device used to manage bandwidth on a large network. Switches are rapidly becoming one of the most used internetworking devices from connecting even smaller networks because they allow you to have some control over the use of the bandwidth on the network. A switch, which is referred to as a "bridge on steroids" controls how data flows by using the MAC addresses that are placed on each data packet. Remember that this MAC address on the data packet is the same MAC address on the network card of that particular computer.

Switches divide networks into what is known as a Virtual LAN or VLAN. The best thing about a VLAN, which is also a logical grouping of computers on a network into what is described as some sort of communication group, is that the computers really do not have to be in close proximity or even on the same floor. This is because it allows the computers to be grouped by the similarities in the types of users in the VLAN. Switches use a combination of software and hardware to switch packets between computers and other devices on the network.

This software is the switches operating system. And, because switches offer a higher density of connection ports, they can easily replace hubs on the network. This means that each computer on the network can be connected to its own port on the switch. When the computers are directly connected to the switch, the switch can supply each of the computers with a dedicated amount of bandwidth. For example, say users are on a 100Mbps Ethernet network via a switch. Each user can realise a bandwidth of 100Mbps and don't have to compete for the bandwidth the way computers do on a network via a hub because each port on the switch has a dedicated 100Mbps. This is why switches are rapidly replacing hubs. Inexpensive switches are even available to accomodate small networks and home network markets.

Some of the switch hardware can also take advantage of full-duplex access to the network media, which allows for the sending and receiving of data simultaneously. Essentially, this provides access to an Ethernet network that is collision free, when an Ethernet network is pretty much known to have data collisions. A computer existing on a Fast Ethernet network, typically running at 100Mbps, would see a 200Mbps throughput because sending and receiving would occur simultaneously on a full-duplex media.

Since switches are becoming very popular on both the small and large networks, they have all but replaced bridges as the internetworking devices for conserving network bandwidth and expanding LANs into larger corporate internetworks. But, they are also making hubs a device of the past for smaller networks. A network switch is a device that provides a switching function in a data communications network. Data communication in a computer network involves the exchange of data between two or more entities interconnected by communication links and subnetworks. A network switch is an intermediate station which interconnects the communication links and subnetworks to enable transmission of data between the end stations. Switching involves transferring information, such as digital data packets or frames, among entities of the network. A switch functions as an interchange and provides path switching for data being transported over a network. Typically, a switch supports one network protocol (*e.g.* Ethernet), meaning that the switch manages data in a particular format. Switched local area networks use a network switch for supplying data frames between network stations or other network nodes (such as routers or gateways), where each network node is connected to the network switch by a media.

A network switch for routing packets between network buses includes a set of input switch ports for receiving packets arriving on the network buses, a set of output switch ports for forwarding packets outward on the network buses, and a switch fabric for routing packets between the input and output switch ports. Each input switch port includes a memory for storing packets arriving on a network until the switch fabric can forward them to an output switch port. The input port may convert each packet arriving on a network bus to a sequence of cells of uniform size which can be efficiently stored in uniformly-sized buffer memory storage locations until the input port can forward them in proper sequential order through the switch fabric to one of the switch's output ports. Each output switch port may also include a memory for storing packets it receives via the switch fabric until the port can forward them outward on a network bus. Each output switch port stores each cell sequence arriving from an input port in its own buffer memory. The output port later reassembles them into the packet from which they were derived, then forwards the packet outward on an another network bus.

GETAWAYS CELL RELAY

CELL RELAY

A concept in which data is sent over a network in relatively small, fixed-size packets, or cells (ATM is based on cell relay). This contrasts with networks based on frames, which may be chunks of data of variable lengths. The frame relay specifications, for instance, set a maximum frame length of about 4,000 octets. This can cause problems with transmissions where delay might cause distortion or even dropped information at the receiving end, for example, in voice calls. In a cell relay network, if the cells are sufficiently small, then so are the odds that one cell will occupy the transmission facilities long enough to cause an unacceptable delay. With cell relay it's important to note that the cells may be of any size as long as all of the cells within that closed system are the same size. And the slower the transmission speed, the smaller the optimal cell size. Using relatively short cells makes it easier to mix data, which is not sensitive to minor delays, with highly delay-sensitive voice. A statistically multiplexed interface protocol for packet switched data communications that uses fixed-length packets, *i.e.*, cells, to transport data. Note 1: Cell relay transmission rates usually are between 56 kb/s and 1.544 Mb/s, *i.e.*,the data rate of a DS1 signal. Note 2: Cell relay protocols:

- Have neither flow control nor error correction capability,
- Are information-content independent, and
- Correspond only to layers one and two of the ISO Open Systems Interconnection--Reference Model.

Note: Cell relay systems enclose variable-length user packets in fixed-length packets, *i.e.*, cells, that add addressing and verification information. Frame length is fixed in hardware, based on time delay and user packet-length considerations. One user data message may be segmented over many cells.

FRAME RELAY

OVERVIEW

Frame relay is a synchronous HDLC protocol based network. Data is sent in HDLC packets, referred to as "frames". The diagram below of an HDLC frame may be familiar, since without adding specific definitions of how the Address, Control and CRC is used, the diagram is applicable to IBM's SDLC, to X.25, to HDLC, to Frame Relay, as well as other protocols. The protocol is similar to that of an X.25 network, except all circuits are permanently assigned. What is a circuit? A circuit is a link between user end points. In frame relay and X.25 networks, circuits are known as "permanent virtual circuits", or PVC's. The circuits are known as virtual because they are not electrical ciruits where there is a direct electrical connection from end to end. Rather, there is a "logical" connection, or virtual connection, where the user data moves from end to end, but without a direct electrical circuit. X.25 circuits can be initiated and ended from the users terminals. Frame relay circuits are set up at the time of installation and are maintained 24 hours per day, 7 days per week.

Frame relay circuits are not created and ended by user at their terminals or PC's. However, the user may have an application running over a frame relay circuit where computer to terminal sessions are initiated and ended by the user. These sessions are related to the application, not to the underlying frame relay network. Frame relay relies on the customer equipment to perform end to end error correction. Each switch inside a frame relay network just relays the data (frame) to the next switch. X.25, in contrast, performs error correction from switch to switch. The networks of today are sufficiently error free to move the burden of error correction to the end points. Most modern protocols do error correction anyway, protocols such as SDLC, HDLC, TCP/IP, stat mux protocols, etc. Because frame relay passes blocks of data from switch to switch without error correction, propagation from customer end to customer end through the network is very fast. Propagation time in a DCB mux test at Wiltel (LDDS Worldcom) indicated a 70 millisecond round trip delay from Tulsa, Oklahoma to New York City and back.

Network Characteristic	**Frame Relay**	**X.25**
Propagation Delay	Low	High
Error Correction	None, done by the terminal equipment at each end of the link	Node to Node
Protocol family	HDLC	HDLC
Good for interactive use?	Yes	Barely acceptable. Rather slow with one second or more round trip delay.
Good for polling protocols?	OK, sometimes, requires "spoofing"	Slow, even with spoofing
Good for LAN file transfer	Yes	Slow
Good for voice?	Good, standards developing	No
Ease of implementation	Easy	Difficult

This is equal to or less than the propagation time through 9600 bps modems over the same distance. Similar propagation times have been measured by DCB over Sprint, AT&T and MCI frame relay networks. An X.25 network would experience a delay of a least one half second, and probably a second or more for the same distance.

Topology

Topology is the map, or visual layout of the frame relay network. Frame relay network topology must be viewed from several perspectives to fully understand the network and the equipment used to construct the network. Topological views include an overview map, a logical connection map, perhaps a functional map, a map showing the detail equipment and channel links, an address map. The map below is an overview where the frame relay switching is in the cloud in the center. The lines going out from the cloud represent the connections from the frame relay provider (phone company) to the customer premises. These are typically lines ranging in speed from 56000 bps to T-1 (1.544 Mbps) and faster. One or more DLCI numbers is assigned to each line end point. DLCI is discussed in more detail below. Over 900 DLCI's can be assigned, but frame relay networks rarely have that many, because a user does not need that many in most cases. There may also be limits due to constraints in the frame relay switching equipment. Also, a single network that is too large will be difficult to maintain.

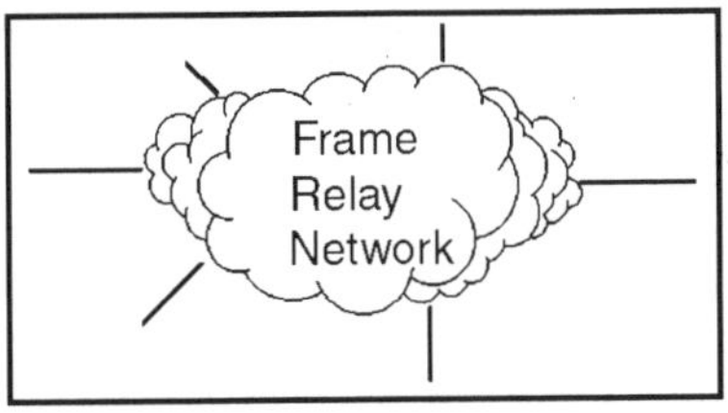

The frame relay network shown above as a cloud can also be shown as a connection of end points tied to a central site, or a number of end points that are all meshed together. End points tied to a central site is the traditional host to terminal model.

The map below has 6 end points, just as in the previous map. Below, the end points are given meaning by defining one end as the host, the other 5 as the remotes. *DLCI addressing could be assigned as follows:*

Location	DLCI #
Host end	16,17,18,19,20
Remote 1	16
Remote 2	16
Remote 3	16
Remote 4	16
Remote 5	16

At the frame relay switch, all remotes are mapped back to the host. At the host, Host 16 is mapped to Remote 1, Host 17 to Remote 2, Host 18 to Remote 3, Host 19 to Remote 4, and Host 20 to Remote 6. In practice, data from the host for Remote 5 arrives at the frame relay switch, from the customer equipment, with the destination address of 20.

The frame relay switch, using its internal lookup table, finds that the data is for Remote 5, a physical port on the frame relay switch, that has a local address of 16. In the frame relay switch, address 20 is replaced with address 16 and the data is then delivered to Remote.

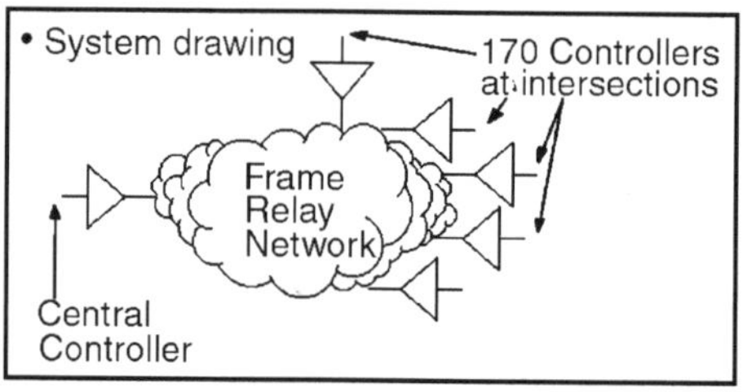

The frame relay network above is a typical installation. This drawing represents a system of traffic industry controllers known as "the model 170" (we know them as "intersection red lights" and a central control computer. It can also be shown as a traditional multidrop host to remotes, with lines bridged in the middle, as shown below:

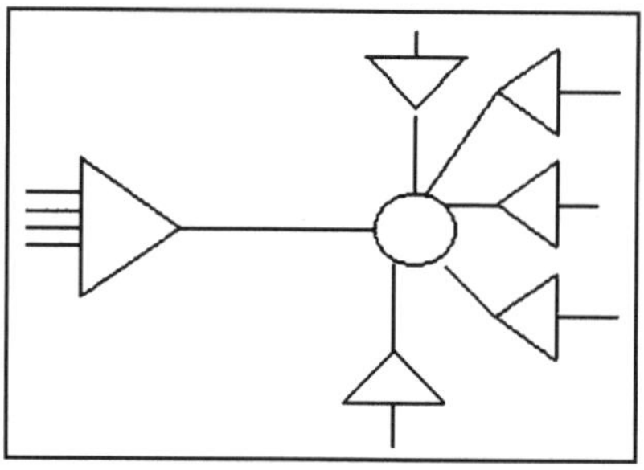

Frame relay also allows meshed networks. Since each endpoint can have one or more DLCI addresses, each user location can be connected to one other location, several locations, or all locations. If every location were connected to every other location, the network would be said to be "fully meshed". An illustration with all locations interconnected is below, next page.

Meshed Network

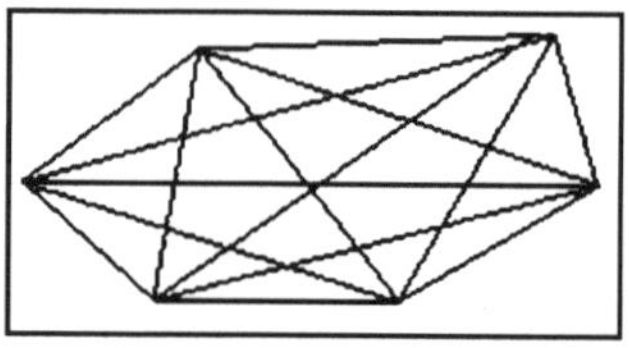

The fully meshed network mapping of DLCI's looks like this:

Location	DLCI #
Location 1	16,17,18,19,20
Location 2	16,17,18,19,20
Location 3	16,17,18,19,20
Location 4	16,17,18,19,20
Location 5	16,17,18,19,20
Location 6	16,17,18,19,20

This addressing can also be shown as a mapping table showing the addresses from the perspective of each one of the 6 locations. A frame relay switch requires this type of cross reference map. The switch uses the map to route the frame relay packets from one internal port of the switch to another port. The following table shows the local port number and the DLCI destination mapping that would be typical for a meshed network.

FRAD

Frame Relay Assembler/Disassembler. A FRAD is a piece of networking equipment that assembles and disassembles data frames. For example, the DCB SR and SRX series of multiplexers assemble asynchronous data into frame relay frames. Hence, the SR is a FRAD for async data. Async data packaged by DCB multiplexers onto frame relay networks includes "dumb" terminal data. It includes PC data for remote control software of programs like PC Anywhere, Reachout, Carbon Copy and CoSession. DCB multiplexers are used to encapsulate in frame relay PPP protocol between host systems and PC's, between routers that use async PPP. There are many examples of devices that encapsulate other protocols into frame relay protocol, and hence are know as FRADs. Frads are used to encapsulate ethernet MAC layer protocol, TCP/IP protocol, IPX protocol, IBM SDLC protocol, bisync protocol, Poll/Select polling protocols. Voice is being encoded for transmission over frame relay, especially voice that has been compressed via CELP, VSELP and similar methods.

PVC

Permanent Virtual Circuits. PVC's contrast with Switched Virtual Circuits (SVC). A connection to a network that allows connection and disconnection to various points is a switched virtual circuit. Circuits that are routed through software switching devices like X.25 pads and frame relay networks are virtual. A hard wired connected in a plain old circuit, not a virtual circuit.

DLC

Data Link Connections

DLCI

Data Link Connection Identifier. This number identifies a virtual circuit.

For a stat mux applications, a head end DCB SRX multiplexer might have 4 DLCI,s associated with it, while each of 4 remotes would have just a single DLCI. The example illustrates that DCLI numbers have significance at the user's end point only.

Chicago has 4 addresses, 16, 17, 18 and 19. At each remote, each location has the same number 16. The telephone company providing the frame relay service has a frame relay switch that translates the addresses. When these permanent virtual circuits are established, the relationship of the physical ports is mapped and then assigned DLCI numbers.

DCB Frame Relay Multiplexers

Vendors of frame relay services focus almost exclusively on LANs when explaining and selling frame relay. They also expect that a typical application with a single host site has a single line coming into the site, often at a high speed that is many times that of the remote locations. For example, the host may have a 256 Kbps router, and remotes (5, 10, 15 or more) at 56 Kbps each. DCB frame relay multiplexers, such as the SRX-32, have a limited number of ports. Therefore, DCB may have the customer put in several 56 or 64 Kbps lines at the host, each serving a limited number of remote sites, typically between 2 and 8 (4 to 16 ports per remote site).

Special DLCI numbers

- DLCI 0 (zero) and 1023 are reserved for management
- DLCI 1 to 15 and 1008 to 1022 have been reserved for future use.
- DLCI 992 to 1007 are reserved for layer 2 management of frame relay bearer service.
- DLCI numbers 16 to 991 are available for subscribers for each user frame relay network

Management Protocols

Protocols for exchanging information between a user FRAD and the frame relay network equipment. *The protocols are*: LMI-The original interim management protocol, uses DLCI 1023. LMI was specified by the Frame Relay Forum. Annex D-An ANSI T1.617 management protocol standard, uses DLCI 1. Annex D was specified by the ANSI T1.617 specification. Annex A-Nearly identical to Annex D, used in Europe.

Status Inquiry

The is an inquiry from the frame relay user to the network every x seconds. The time value can be 5 to 30 seconds. The default value is 10 seconds for LMI and for Annex D. If the user does not make this inquiry every 10 seconds, the carrier network equipment will generate an alarm. The network equipment default value is 15 seconds. That is, the user should make an inquiry every 10 seconds, and the network expects the request every 15 seconds. The 5 second difference is a buffer time that allows for a small delay. The status inquiry returns status about the network. Sending the inquiry tells the network that the user FRAD is in service. When a status inquiry is not sent, the network will generate an alarm. An alarm may result in a "pro active" call to the customer from the service vendor. Status information is often collected by a FRAD and formatted into a MIB (management information base) for reporting via SNMP (simple network management protocol). Agents interface to the devices to collect the MIB's to deliver them to a manager.

Full Status Inquiry

This inquiry gets more information returned by network than is obtained in the Status Inquiry. Full status responses to the user from the network also returns all of the active DLCI numbers. The value can range from 1 to 255. The default value is 6, which means the user equipment sends 5 regular status inquiries, then the full status inquiry.

Link Integrity Verification Timer

Indicates how frequently the FRAD should initiate a Status Inquiry Message. This is the 10 second timer referred to under the term "Status Inquiry".

MIB

Management Information Base, a piece of information collected for an SNMP manager.

Agent

A device that collects MIB's to report them to SNMP managers. HP's Open View is an example of a manager. The DCB product PA2000 is an agent, specifically a proxy agent that collects data from non-SNMP devices and reports the data to an SNMP manager like HP Open View, reporting the data in SNMP fomat.

VIRTUAL CIRCUITS

The Frame Relay frame is transmitted to its destination by way of virtual circuits (logical paths from an originating point in the network) to a destination point. Virtual circuits may be permanent (PVCs) or switched (SVCs). PVCs are set up administratively by the network manager for a dedicated point-to-point connection; SVCs are set up on a call-by-call basis.

ADVANTAGES OF FRAME RELAY

Frame Relay offers an attractive alternative to both dedicated lines and X.25 networks for connecting LANs to bridges and routers.

The success of the Frame Relay protocol is based on the following two underlying factors:

- Because virtual circuits consume bandwidth only when they transport data, many virtual circuits can exist simultaneously across a given transmission line. In addition, each device can use more of the bandwidth as necessary, and thus operate at higher speeds.
- The improved reliability of communication lines and increased error-handling sophistication at end stations allows the Frame Relay protocol to discard erroneous frames and thus eliminate time-consuming error-handling processing.

These two factors make Frame Relay a desirable choice for data transmission; however, they also necessitate testing to determine that the system works properly and that data is not lost.

FRAME RELAY STRUCTURE

Standards for the Frame Relay protocol have been developed by ANSI and CCITT simultaneously. The separate LMI specification has basically been incorporated into the ANSI specification. The following discussion of the protocol structure includes the major points from these specifications. The Frame Relay frame structure is based on the LAPD protocol. In the Frame Relay structure, the frame header is altered slightly to contain the Data Link Connection Identifier (DLCI) and congestion bits, in place of the normal address and control fields. This new Frame Relay header is 2 bytes in length and has the following format:

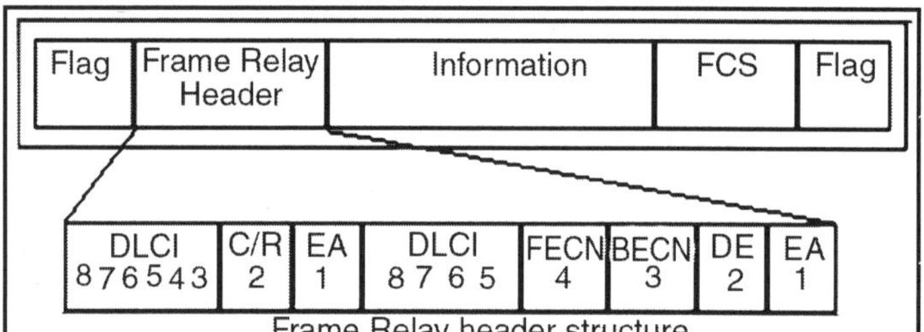

Frame Relay header structure

DLCI

10-bit DLCI field represents the address of the frame and corresponds to a PVC.

C/R

Designates whether the frame is a command or response.

EA

Extended Address field signifies up to two additional bytes in the Frame Relay header, thus greatly expanding the number of possible addresses.

FECN

Forward Explicit Congestion Notification.

BECN

Backward Explicit Congestion Notification.

DE

Discard Eligibility.

Information

The Information field may include other protocols within it, such as an X.25, IP or SDLC (SNA) packet.

EXPLICIT CONGESTION NOTIFICATION (ECN) BITS

When the network becomes congested to the point that it cannot process new data transmissions, it begins to discard frames. These discarded frames are retransmitted, thus causing more congestion. In an effort to prevent this situation, several mechanisms have been developed to notify user devices at the onset of congestion, so that the offered load may be reduced. Two bits in the Frame Relay header are used to signal the user device that congestion is occurring on the line: They are the Forward Explicit Congestion Notification (FECN) bit and the Backward Explicit Congestion Notification (BECN) bit. The FECN is changed to 1 as a frame is sent downstream towards the destination location when congestion occurs during data transmission. In this way, all downstream nodes and the attached user device learn about congestion on the line.

The BECN is changed to 1 in a frame traveling back towards the source of data transmission on a path where congestion is occurring. Thus the source node is notified to slow down transmission until congestion subsides.

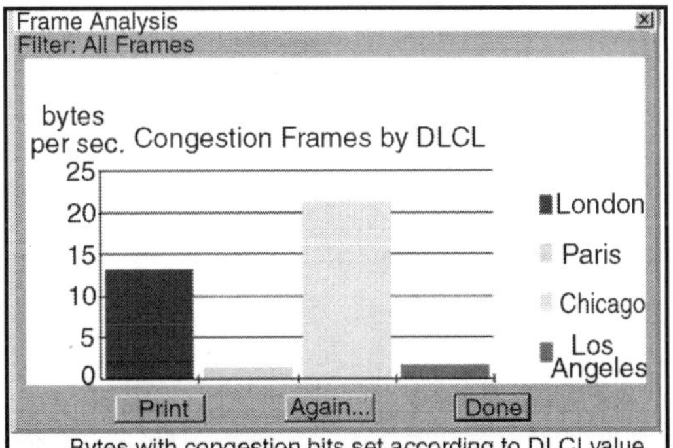

Bytes with congestion bits set according to DLCI value

CONSOLIDATED LINK LAYER MANAGEMENT

It may occur that there are no frames traveling back to the source node which is causing the congestion. In this case, the network will want to send its own message to the problematic source node. The standard, however, does not allow the network to send its own frames with the DLCI of the desired virtual circuit. To address this problem, ANSI defined the Consolidated Link Layer Management (CLLM). With CLLM, a separate DLCI (number 1023) is reserved for sending link layer control messages from the network to the user device. The ANSI standard (T1.618) defines the format of the CLLM message. It contains a code for the cause of the congestion and a listing of all DLCIs that should act to reduce their data transmission to lower congestion.

STATUS OF CONNECTIONS (LMI)

Each DLCI corresponds to a PVC (Permanent Virtual Circuit). It is sometimes necessary to transmit information about this connection (*e.g.*, whether the interface is still active) the valid DLCIs for the interface and the status of each PVC. This information is transmitted using the reserved DLCI 1023 or DLCI 0, depending on the standard used. A multicast status may also be sent with the LMI. Multicasting is where a router sends a frame on a reserved DLCI known as a multicast group. The network then replicates the frame and delivers it to a predefined list of DLCIs, thus broadcasting a single frame to a collection of destinations.

DISCARD ELIGIBILITY (DE)

When there is congestion on the line, the network must decide which frames to discard in order to free the line. Discard Eligibility provides the network with a signal to determine which frames to discard. The network will discard frames with a DE value of 1 before discarding other frames. The DE bit may be set by the user on some of its lower-priority frames. Alternatively, the network may set the DE bit to indicate to other nodes that a frame should be preferentially selected for discard, if necessary.

FRAME RELAY STANDARDS

ANSI T1.618

T1.618 describes the protocol supporting the data transfer phase of the Frame Relay bearer service, as defined in ANSI T1.606. T1.618 is based on a subset of ANSI T1.602 (LAPD) called the "Core Aspects" and is used by both switched and permanent virtual calls. T1.618 also includes the Consolidated Link Layer Mechanism (CLLM). The generation and transport of CLLM is optional. With CLLM, DLCI 1023 is reserved for sending link layer control messages. T1.618 issues implicit congestion notification from the network to the user device. The congestion notification contains a code indicating the cause of the congestion and lists all DLCIs that have to reduce their traffic in order to lower congestion.

ANSI T1.617

To establish a Switched Virtual Circuit (SVC) connection, Frame Relay users must establish a dialog with the network using the signalling specification in T1.617. The procedure results in the assignment of a DLCI. Once the dialog is established, the T1.618 procedures apply. To establish a Permanent Virtual Circuit (PVC), a setup protocol is used which is identical to the ISDN D-channel protocol and defined in T1.617. With ISDN, users can use the D-channel for setup. For non-ISDN callers, there is no D-channel, so the dialog between the user and the network must be separated from the ordinary data transfer procedures. In T1.617, DLCI 0 is reserved. T1.617 also contains specifications on how Frame Relay service parameters are negotiated.

ANSI LMI

ANSI LMI is a Permanent Virtual Circuit (PVC) management system defined in Annex D of T1.617. ANSI LMI is virtually identical to the Manufacturers' LMI, without the optional extensions. ANSI LMI uses DLCI 0.

Manufacturers' LMI

Manufacturers' LMI is a Frame Relay specification with extension-document number 001-208966, September 18, 1990. Manufacturers' LMI defines a generic Frame Relay service based on PVCs for interconnecting DTE devices with Frame Relay network equipment. In addition to the ANSI standard, Manufacturers' LMI includes extensions and LMI functions and procedures. Manufacturers' LMI uses DLCI 1023.

B-ISDN

DEFINITION

There may be many popular meanings for BISDN with the most popular definition being that of Broadband Integrated Services Digital Network. We searched our database and could not find a definition other than Broadband Integrated Services Digital Network for BISDN

If you have more information or know of another definition for BISDN, please let us know so that we can review it and add that information to our database. Every attempt has been made to provide you with the correct acronym for BISDN. If we missed the mark, we would greatly appreciate your help by entering the correct or alternate meaning in the box below. Definitions have been compiled from popular search engines and multiple results provided for your review.

A standard for transmitting voice, video and data at the same time over fibre telephone lines. Broadband ISDN can support data rates of 1.5 million bits per second (bps), but it has not been widely implemented.

ISDN (Integrated Services Digital Network) development began in the 1980s as part of a plan by the carriers to develop a single integrated network transmitting voice, video, and data communications. B-ISDN development began in 1988 as developers saw a need for bandwidth above 155 Mbits/sec in anticipation of future video and multimedia services. ATM was developed from this work as the underlying transport, with B-ISDN being the overlying technology for controlling the network. Figure B-10 illustrates the B-ISDN architecture. ATM cells are delivered across a physical SONET network.

In general, ISDN is based on 64-Kbit/sec channels. These channels are just wide enough to handle a digitized voice call. All other ISDN implementations are some multiple of this basic service. A typical user signs up for basic rate ISDN, which consists of two 64-Kbit/sec channels (called the B channels) and one 16-Kbit/sec D channel used for signaling. The B channels can be used individually for separate voice calls or combined to create a 128-Kbit/sec data channel. Primary rate ISDN consists of 23 B channels and one 64-Kbit/sec signaling channel. ISDN is useful for networking because the customer can add bandwidth in increments of 64 Kbits/sec as needed. ISDN is a switched service and is designed around intelligent switching components in the carrier network. It allows users to dial any other ISDN point on the network and create a high-speed digital link that can mimic point-to-point T1 lines. However, T1 lines are usually permanently established between two points, while ISDN allows the switching of the line between many different points by the customer. This is due to the intelligent network components. The intelligent network also supports a variety of other services, including call forwarding, caller ID, and channel bonding.

B-ISDN provides the intelligent telecommunications services above ATM. It manages the establishment of point-to-point and point-to-multipoint connections through the switched network. It supports on-demand, reserved, and permanent services, as well as connection-oriented and connectionless services. The carriers had big plans to use B-ISDN for services like videotelephony, videoconferencing, electronic newspapers, and TV distribution. Now, B-ISDN is rarely discussed. All you hear about is ATM.

SONET is the physical transport backbone of B-ISDN. It is a fibre-optic-based networking standard that defines a hierarchy of transmission rates and data-framing formats. It is used as a transmission medium to interconnect carrier-switching offices worldwide, and so forms the structure of the communications network. SONET is now used as the medium between carrier-switching offices and customers. SONET transmission rates start at 51.4 Mbits/sec and increase in 52-Mbit/sec building blocks.

ATM is the switching technology for B-ISDN and provides B-ISDN users access to the SONET fibre-optic network. Information received at the ATM layer is placed in fixed-length cells, addressed, and transmitted over the SONET network. ATM provides very high-speed switching of these packets between the links attached to the SONET network. ATM takes full advantage of the transmission speeds available on fibre-optic cable.

ISDN

DEFINITION

ISDN, which stands for Integrated Services Digital Network, is a system of digital phone connections which has been available for over a decade. This system allows voice and data to be transmitted simultaneously across the world using end-to-end digital connectivity. With ISDN, voice and data are carried by bearer channels (B channels) occupying a bandwidth of 64 kb/s (bits per second). Some switches limit B channels to a capacity of 56 kb/s. A data channel (D channel) handles signaling at 16 kb/s or 64 kb/s, depending on the service type. Note that, in ISDN terminology, "k" means 1000 (10^3), not 1024 (2^{10}) as in many computer applications (the designator "K" is sometimes used to represent this value); therefore, a 64 kb/s channel carries data at a rate of 64000 b/s.

A new set of standard prefixes has recently been created to handle this. Under this scheme, "k" (kilo-) means 1000 (10^3), "M" (mega-) means 1000000 (10^6), and so on, and "Ki" (kibi-) means 1024 (2^{10}), "Mi" (mebi-) means 1048576 (2^{20}), and so on. (An alert reader pointed out some inconsistencies in my use of unit terminology throughout this Tutorial. He also referred me to a definitive web site. As a result, I have made every effort to both conform to standard terminology, and to use it consistently. I appreciate helpful user input like this!)

There are two basic types of ISDN service: Basic Rate Interface (BRI) and Primary Rate Interface (PRI). BRI consists of two 64 kb/s B channels and one 16 kb/s D channel for a total of 144 kb/s. This basic service is intended to meet the needs of most individual users. PRI is intended for users with greater capacity requirements. Typically the channel structure is 23 B channels plus one 64 kb/s D channel for a total of 1536 kb/s. In Europe, PRI consists of 30 B channels plus one 64 kb/s D channel for a total of 1984 kb/s. It is also possible to support multiple PRI lines with one 64 kb/s D channel using Non-Facility Associated Signaling (NFAS).

H channels provide a way to aggregate B channels. They are implemented as:

- H0=384 kb/s (6 B channels)
- H10=1472 kb/s (23 B channels)
- H11=1536 kb/s (24 B channels)
- H12=1920 kb/s (30 B channels)-International (E1) only

To access BRI service, it is necessary to subscribe to an ISDN phone line. Customer must be within 18000 feet (about 3.4 miles or 5.5 km) of the telephone company central office for BRI service; beyond that, expensive repeater devices are required, or ISDN service may not be available at all. Customers will also need special equipment to communicate with the phone company switch and with other ISDN devices. These devices include ISDN Terminal Adapters (sometimes called, incorrectly, "ISDN Modems") and ISDN Routers.

ISDN (Integrated Services Digital Network) is a set of CCITT/ ITUstandards for digital transmission over ordinary telephone copper wire as well as over other media. Home and business users who install an ISDNadapter (in place of a telephone modem) receive Web pages at up to 128Kbps compared with the maximum 56 Kbps rate of a modem connection. ISDN requires adapters at both ends of the transmission so your access provider also needs an ISDN adapter.

ISDN is generally available from your phone company in most urban areas in the United States and Europe. In many areas where DSL and cable modem service are now offered, ISDN is no longer as popular an option as it was formerly. There are two levels of service: the Basic Rate Interface (BRI), intended for the home and small enterprise, and the Primary Rate Interface (PRI), for larger users. Both rates include a number of B-channels and a D-channels. Each B-channel carries data, voice, and other services. Each D-channelcarries control and signaling information.

The Basic Rate Interface consists of two 64 Kbps B-channels and one 16 Kbps D- channel. Thus, a Basic Rate user can have up to 128 Kbps service. The Primary Rate consists of 23 B-channels and one 64 Kpbs D-channel in the United States or 30 B-channels and 1 D-channel in Europe. ISDN in concept is the integration of both analog or voice data together with digital data over the same network. Although the ISDN you can install is integrating these on a medium designed for analog transmission, broadbandISDN (BISDN) is intended to extend the integration of both services throughout the rest of the end-to-end path using fibre optic and radio media.

Broadband ISDN encompasses frame relay service for high-speed data that can be sent in large bursts, the Fibre Distributed-Data Interface (FDDI), and the Synchronous Opical Network (SONET). BISDN is intended to support transmission from 2 Mbps up to much higher, but as yet unspecified, rates.

BENEFITS OF ISDN

- Single connection can support both voice and data.
- High quality services being digital right from subs, premises (End to End).
- Eight terminals can be connected on a single line.
- High speed data transfer from PC to PC is possible-64 Kbps against existing 9.6 Kbps (6 times faster).
- Two calls can be established simultaneously on a single pair of wires.

- The call set time is very short (1-2 seconds).
- A number of supplementary services are supported like in pots.

Calling Line Identification, Call Forwarding, Call Forwarding on busy signal, Call Forwarding on no reply, Call Forwarding unconditional, Advice of Charge, Terminal Portability, Multiple Subscriber Number, Closed User Group.

BENEFITS OF ISDN FOR NETWORK OPERATORS

- Avoidance of separate networks for different services.
- Economical use of the equipment of the digitalised telephone network, especially the copper
  pair of the subscriber line.
- Reduction in costs due to simplified operation and maintenance procedures.

ISDN LINE SUPERIOR TO THE PHONE LINE

- The signal on the ISDN line-voice or data, is sent in digital mode.
- The signal level at subscriber's terminal equipment is independent on
  line length.
- An ISDN subscriber can establish two simultaneous independent calls which could be voice, data, image or combination of any two whereas only one call is possible on ordinary telephone lines.
- The call set-up time between two ISDN subscribers is extremely short.

Access to Internet

ISDN subscribers can have access to Internet with a higher bandwidth of 64/128 Kbps.

SERVICES OFFERED BY ISDN

The following services are offered on a dial-up basis between any two ISDN subscribers:

- Photo-Telephone-Calling where called party can see each other's pictures on screen.
- Desk Top Video Conferencing on dial-up basis using a single ISDN line at 128 Kbps.
- High Quality Video Conferencing on dial-up basis between any two ISDN subscribers by using three ISDN lines at 384 Kbps.
- Teleconferencing which facilitates the transmission of pictures, documents and drawings etc., apart from voice & video images of the participants, white board sharing & document sharing is also possible.
- High speed data transmission at 128 Kbps.

- Very high quality in digital mode on account of very high immunity from the noise.
- High speed facsimile. Time taken to send FAX messages reduced to 1/4th.
- All other services which a conventional old telephone line provides. Subscriber can see his metering pulses at his premises.
- ISDN supports all Phone-Plus services available to conventional old telephone line. In addition the following additional facilities are available.

5

Internet: The Communication System and Technology

The Internet is a communication system that allows computers around the world to communicate and to exchange of the data with each other. This also allows to access their resources, such as files, services, or other people. Each of the fellowing pages explains one of the *services* that are possible thanks to the Internet. You already know and use some of them. Here's a short list. The word internet is used to describe a network of networks which incorporate a very large and complicated set of equipment. To understand the internet, there are three areas of discussion which are very helpful. These include the various services provided across the internet, the functions that enable the internet to work, and the various organizations that are part of the internet.

INTERNET SERVICES

The main services used on the internet include:

- *Web browsing*: Supported by the HTTP protocol, this functions allows users to view web pages using a web browser.
- *E-mail*: Allows people to send and receive electronic messages.

Other lesser used services include telnet (allows remote login to computers), FTP (Allows quick file transmission to remote computers), and gopher (An early form of text based form of reading internet documents which is rarely used today).

INTERNET FUNCTIONS

The internet provides for the following two functions which support communications. Without the communications support mentioned below, the internet could not function.

These two functions are provided by internet service providers listed below under the "Internet Organizations" header.

- Physical lines that data is sent across.

Routing of data: There are special machines on the internet called routers, that determine where data needs to go to get from the sender of the data to the receiver of the data.

INTERNET ORGANIZATIONS

- *ISPs (Internet Service Providers)*: They provide the connection to the internet for users and also provide routers that direct internet traffic.
- *Corporations or Web hosting providers with mail servers and web servers*: They provide the information posted on the internet and virtual data connections to other mail servers.

There are also other organizations that regulate the internet, providing communication standards and designing new communication standards for improvements. These communication standards are also known as protocols.

ACCESSING THE INTERNET

People use an internet browser to access web pages that are available across the internet. Internet browsers include Microsoft Internet Explorer, Netscape Navigator, Mozilla, and others. Web pages are created in a marked up form of text file called HTML (Hyper-Text Markup Language). The markup within the text indicates document structure showing where paragraphs begin and end, what items are in a list, headers, tables and other document structure. When people are browsing of surfing the internet, they usually go from place to place by clicking on links.

These links are locations for specific pages and indicate the three things:

- Protocol being used such as http or ftp
- The domain that the web page is found on. This will point to a specific organization's or company's web server.
- The location of the page on the server including the directory path and file name.

The Internet has become such an integral part of our lives, with such powerful capabilities, that it is easy to forget that this technological marvel was created by the long, hard, dedicated efforts of human beings—folks who had a vision of what universal networking could become and worked to make it happen. The key people, projects, and organizations that helped create the Internet are described below, first in a top-level summary and then in sections in roughly chronological order.

WORKING OF INTERNET

The Internet workings include a technical design and a management structure. The management structure consists of a generally democratic collection of loosely-coupled organizations and working groups with mostly non-overlapping responsibilities. The technical design is founded on a complex, interlocking set of hierarchical tree-like structures like Internet

Protocol addresses and domain names, mixed with networked structures like packet switching and routing protocols, all tied together with millions of lines of sophisticated software that continues to get better all the time.

So far this combination of management and technical structures has worked well, providing the reliable, powerful communication platform on which the rest of the complexity of the Internet is built. The following sections provide more information.

DEFINITION OF INTERNET

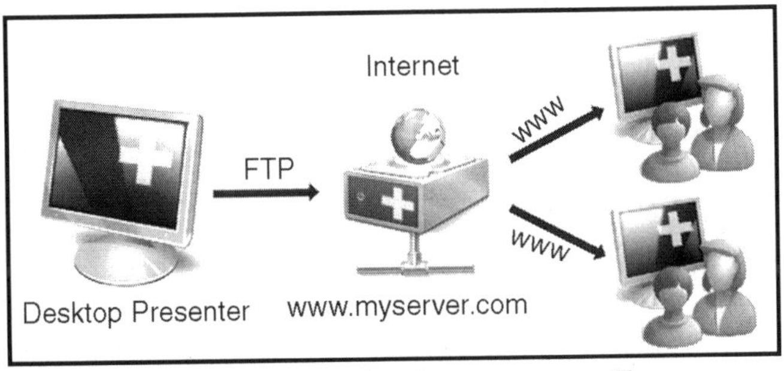

The Internet is a global network of computers. Every computer that is connected to the Internet is considered a part of that network. This means even your home computer. It's all a matter of degrees, you connect to your ISP's network, then your ISP connects to a larger network and so on. At the top of the tree is the high-capacity backbones, all of these interconnect at 'Network Access Points' 'NAPs' at important regions around the world. The entire Internet is based on agreements between these backbone providers who set in place all the fibre optics lines and other technical aspects of the Internet. The first high speed backbone was created by the 'National Science Foundation' in 1987.

The Internet was first created by the Advanced Research Projects Agency (ARPA) of the U.S. government in 1960's, and was first known as the ARPANet. At this stage the Internet's first computers were at academic and government institutions. They were mainly used for accessing files and to send email. From 1983 onwards the Internet as we know it today started to form with the introduction of the communication protocol TCP/IP to ARPANet.

Since 1983 the Internet has accommodated alot of changes and continues to keep developing. The last two decades has seen the Internet accommodate such things as network LANs and ATM and frame switched services. The Internet continues to evolve with it becoming available on mobile phones and pagers and possibly on televisions in the future. The actual term "Internet" was finally defined in 1995 by FNC (The Federal Networking Council). The resolution created by the The Federal Networking Council (FNC) agrees that the following language reflects our definition of the term "Internet". "Internet" refers to the global information system that,

THE EVOLUTION OF THE INTERNET

The underpinnings of the Internet are formed by the global interconnection of hundreds of thousands of otherwise independent computers, communications entities and information systems. What makes this interconnection possible is the use of a set of communication standards, procedures and formats in common among the networks and the various devices and computational facilities connected to them. The procedures by which computers communicate with each other are called "protocols." While this infrastructure is steadily evolving to include new capabilities, the protocols initially used by the Internet are called the "TCP/IP" protocols, named after the two protocols that formed the principal basis for Internet operation.

On top of this infrastructure is an emerging set of architectural concepts and data structures for heterogeneous information systems that renders the Internet a truly global information system. In essence, the Internet is an architecture, although many people confuse it with its implementation. When the Internet is looked at as an architecture, it manifests two different abstractions. One abstraction deals with communications connectivity, packet delivery and a variety of end-end communication services. The other abstraction deals with the Internet as an information system, independent of its underlying communications infrastructure, which allows creation, storage and access to a wide range of information resources, including digital objects and related services at various levels of abstraction.

Interconnecting computers is an inherently digital problem. Computers process and exchange digital information, meaning that they use a discrete mathematical "binary" or "two-valued" language of 1s and 0s. For communication purposes, such information is mapped into continuous electrical or optical waveforms. The use of digital signaling allows accurate regeneration and reliable recovery of the underlying bits. We use the terms "computer," "computer resources" and "computation" to mean not only traditional computers, but also devices that can be controlled digitally over a network, information resources such as mobile programs and other computational capabilities.

The telephone network started out with operators who manually connected telephones to each other through "patch panels" that accepted patch cords from each telephone line and electrically connected them to one another through the panel, which operated, in effect, like a switch. The result was called circuit switching, since at its conclusion, an electrical circuit was made between the calling telephone and the called telephone. Conventional circuit switching, which was developed to handle telephone calls, is inappropriate for connecting computers because it makes limited use of the telecommunication facilities and takes too long to set up connections. Although reliable enough for voice communication, the circuit-switched voice network had difficulty delivering digital information without errors.

For digital communications, packet switching is a better choice, because it is far better suited to the typically "burst" communication style of computers. Computers that communicate typically send out brief but intense bursts of data, then remain silent for a while before sending out the next burst. These bursts are communicated as packets, which are very much like electronic postcards. The postcards, in reality packets, are relayed from computer to computer until they reach their destination. The special computers that perform this forwarding function are called variously "packet switches" or "routers" and form the equivalent of many bucket brigades spanning continents and oceans, moving buckets of electronic postcards from one computer to another. Together these routers and the communication links between them form the underpinnings of the Internet.

Without packet switching, the Internet would not exist, as we now know it. Going back to the postcard analogy, postcards can get lost. They can be delivered out of order, and they can be delayed by varying amounts. The same is true of Internet packets, which, on the Internet, can even be duplicated. The Internet Protocol is the postcard layer of the Internet. The next higher layer of protocol, TCP, takes care of re-sending the "postcards" to recover packets that might have been lost, and putting packets back in order if they have become disordered in transit.

Of course, packet switching is about a billion times faster than the postal service or a bucket brigade would be. It also has to operate over many different communications systems, or substrata. The authors designed the basic architecture to be so simple and undemanding that it could work with most communication services. Many organizations, including commercial ones, carried out research using the TCP/IP protocols in the 1970s. Email was steadily used over the nascent Internet during that time and to the present. It was not until 1994 that the general public began to be aware of the Internet by way of the World Wide Web application, particularly after Netscape Communications was formed and released its browser and associated server software.

Thus, the evolution of the Internet was based on two technologies and a research dream. The technologies were packet switching and computer technology, which, in turn, drew upon the underlying technologies of digital communications and semiconductors. The research dream was to share information and computational resources. But that is simply the technical side of the story. Equally important in many ways were the other dimensions that enabled the Internet to come into existence and flourish. This aspect of the story starts with cooperation and far-sightedness in the U.S. Government, which is often derided for lack of foresight but is a real hero in this story.

It leads on to the enthusiasm of private sector interests to build upon the government funded developments to expand the Internet and make it available to the general public. Perhaps most important, it is fueled by the development of the personal computer industry and significant changes in the telecommunications industry in the 1980s, not the least of which was the decision to open the long distance market to competition. The role of workstations, the Unix operating system and local area networking (especially the Ethernet) are themes contributing to the spread of Internet technology in the 1980s into the research and academic community from which the Internet industry eventually emerged.

Many individuals have been involved in the development and evolution of the Internet covering a span of almost four decades if one goes back to the early writings on the subject of computer networking by Kleinrock, Licklider, Baran, Roberts, and Davies. The ARPANET, described below, was the first wide-area computer network. The NSFNET, which followed more than a decade later under the leadership of Erich Bloch, Gordon Bell, Bill Wulf and Steve Wolff, brought computer networking into the mainstream of the research and education communities. It is not our intent here to attempt to attribute credit to all those whose contributions were central to this story, although we mention a few of the key players

ADVANTAGES OF INTERNET

There are many advantages of using the Internet, such as:

GLOBAL AUDIENCE

Content published on the World Wide Web is immediately available to a global audience of users. This makes the World Wide Web a very cost-effective medium to publish information. Reaching more than 190 countries.

Operates 24 Hours and 365 Days

You don't need to wait until resources are available to conduct business. From a consumer's perspective as well as a provider's business can be consummated at any time. The fact that the Internet is operational at all times makes it the most efficient business machine to date.

Relatively Inexpensive

It is relatively inexpensive to publish information on the Internet. At a fraction of the cost to publish information by traditional methods, various organizations and individuals can now distribute information to millions of users. It costs only a few thousand dollars to establish an Internet presence and publish content on the Internet.

Product Advertising

You can use the World Wide Web to advertise various products. Before purchasing a product, customers will be able to look up various product specification sheets and find out additional information. You can use the multimedia capabilities of the World Wide Web to make available not only various product specification sheets but also audio files, images, and even video clips of products in action.

The beauty of the Web is that it allows customers to explore products in as much detail as they desire. If the client just wants a general overview, he or she can look at the advertising information. For those wanting more in depth information, you can provide white papers and product descriptions for download. The Web allows a business to provide timely information, you can simply place the information on the Web page and it is available immediately for your customers.

Distribute Product Catalogs

The World Wide Web is a very effective medium for distributing product catalogs. In the old days, putting together a product catalog used to be very costly in terms of time and money needed to publish and distribute it. The World Wide Web changes all this by allowing content developers to put together a sales catalog and make it available to millions of users immediately. Furthermore, unlike printed product catalogs that are usually updated around once a month, product catalogs on the World Wide Web can be updated as needed to respond to various changing market conditions.

Online Surveys

Traditional methods of performing surveys are often relatively slow and expensive compared to online surveys conducted on the Internet. For example, in order to fill out various needs of customers or what they would like to see in a future product, it's often necessary to compile a list of address and mail a questionnaire to many customers. The success of such an attempt is not always guaranteed and can be very costly in terms of mailing the questionnaires and entering responses to a databases and analyzing it. On the other hand, you can use the World Wide Web to automate the whole process. For example, you can set up a CGI script to conduct online surveys. Results of such a survey can be automatically updated to a database. This database can then be used to keep a pulse on various opinions and needs of customers.

Announcements

With the World Wide Web, you can distribute various announcements to millions of users in a timely manner. Because there is virtually no time lag from the time it takes to publish information to making the information available to users, the Web is an ideal medium to publicize announcements. As more people discover the virtues of the Web and get connected to the Internet, the Web will become the medium of choice for many organizations and individuals to publicize various announcements.

Provide Technical Support

You can also use Web site to provide technical support to users. Because Web pages can be updated immediately with new information, various technical support literature can be immediately modified in light of new findings and developments. This can be accomplished without having to distribute changes to all users affected by any changes using traditional mediums of information distribution, which are often quite costly compared to the World Wide Web.

Create Online Discussion Forums

By using applications such as WebBoard, it's possible to set up online discussion forums on the Web.

Obtain Customer Feedback

The interactive nature of the World Wide Web is ideal for obtaining customer feedback. You can easily set up a CGI script to obtain customer feedback about a product or service. Because customer feedback submitted by customers can be read immediately, it's possible to respond to various customer concerns in a timely manner, increasing customer satisfaction and quality of customer service.

Immediate Distribution of Information

When information is added to a Web site, it's immediately available for browsing by millions of Internet users. The World Wide Web is an ideal medium of information distribution because it takes away the time lag associated with publishing content and actually making it available to users

Easy Integration with Internal Information Systems

Internet information systems deployed on the Internet can be easily integrated with internal information systems managed with office productivity applications such as Microsoft Office.

Powerful Content Publishing Tools

A new breed of Internet aware applications will start emerging in software stores by the time you read this. These applications will enable users to develop content for the World Wide Web by simply saving as an HTML file. In addition to software developers making existing applications Internet aware, various new, powerful, and easy-to use Internet content publishing applications are also being developed. These applications will make the task of publishing content on the Internet even easier. Most of these applications are developed for Windows users.

Multimedia

The capability to incorporate multimedia into Web pages is a major advantage of using World Wide Web to publish information. For example, many Web sites use sounds and video clips to make the content easier and more interesting to browse.

Formatting Capabilities

Content published on the World Wide Web can be richly formatted by using various HTML tags and graphic formats. The capability to do this is a major reason for the success of the World Wide Web. In addition to using HTML tags and various multimedia formats in Web pages, various interactive controls can also be added to a web page. This capability allows Web site content developers to create "active" Web sites.

For example, before a user sends some information to a Web server for processing, a VBScript or JavaScript subroutine can be used to verify information typed in by the user. Various formatting capabilities, along with technologies such as Java and VBScript, make the World Wide Web a richly interactive medium that you can use to distribute information to millions of users.

DISADVANTAGES OF INTERNET

Many fear the Internet because of its disadvantages. They claim to not use the Internet because they are afraid of the possible consequences or are simply not interested. People who have yet connected to the Internet claim they are not missing anything. Today's technological society must realise, it is up to them to protect themselves on the Internet. Children using the Internet has become a big concern. Most parents do not realise the dangers involved when their children log onto the Internet. When children are online, they can easily be lured into something dangerous. When children talk to others online, they do not realise they could actually be talking to a harmful person. In addition, children may also receive pornography online by mistake; therefore, causing concern among parents everywhere. Whether surfing the Web, reading newsgroups, or using email, children can be exposed to extremely inappropriate material. Pornographic sites tend to make sure they are the first sites to be listed in any search area. Some critics say that parents are responsible for their own children on the Internet because there are available services to protect children. To keep children safe, parents and teachers must be aware of the dangers. They must actively guide and guard their children online.There are a number of tools available today that may help keep the Internet environment safer for children.

Musicians are also concerned with disadvantages to the Net such as, accessibility and freedom. They are upset because the Internet provides their music online at no charge to consumers. File-sharing software, such Kazaa, Emule and may others provides copyrighted songs to all Internet users. The main concern is - the music is free! Musicians feel "they are not getting paid for their work". It is almost impossible to close down all file-sharing services; there are too many of them to count.

Another major disadvantage of the Internet is privacy. Electronic messages sent over the Internet can be easily snooped and tracked, revealing who is talking to whom and what they are talking about. As people surf the Internet, they are constantly giving information to web sites. People should become aware that the collection, selling, or sharing of the information they provide online increases the chances that their information will fall into the wrong hands. When giving personal information on the Internet, people should make sure the Web site is protected with a recognizable security symbol. On the other hand, this does not mean they are fully protected because anyone may obtain a user's information.

Today, not only are humans getting viruses, but computers are also. Computers are mainly getting these viruses from the Internet; yet, viruses may also be transmitted through floppy disks. However, people should mainly be concerned about receiving viruses from the Internet. Some of these dangerous viruses destroy the computer's entire hard drive, meaning that the user can no longer access the computer. Virus protection is highly recommended. In conclusion, today's society is in the middle of a technological boom. People can either choose to take advantage of this era, or simply let it pass them by. The Internet is a very powerful tool. It has many advantages; however, people need to be extremely aware of the disadvantages as well.

RUNNING OF INTERNET

DOMAIN NAME SYSTEM

The Internet evolved as an experimental system during the 1970s and early 1980s. It then flourished after the TCP/IP protocols were made mandatory on the ARPANET and other networks in January 1983; these protocols thus became the standard for many other networks as well. Indeed, the Internet grew so rapidly that the existing mechanisms for associating the names of host computers (*e.g.* UCLA, USC-ISI) to Internet addresses (known as IP addresses) were about to be stretched beyond acceptable engineering limits. Most of the applications in the Internet referred to the target computers by name. These names had to be translated into Internet addresses before the lower level protocols could be activated to support the application. For a time, a group at SRI International in Menlo Park, CA, called the Network Information Centre (NIC), maintained a simple, machine-readable list of names and associated Internet addresses which was made available on the net. Hosts on the Internet would simply copy this list, usually daily, so as to maintain a local copy of the table.

This list was called the "host.txt" file (since it was simply a text file). The list served the function in the Internet that directory services (*e.g.* 411 or 703-555-1212) do in the US telephone system-the translation of a name into an address. As the Internet grew, it became harder and harder for the NIC to keep the list current. Anticipating that this problem would only get worse as the network expanded, researchers at USC Information Sciences Institute launched an effort to design a more distributed way of providing this same information. The end result was the Domain Name System (DNS) which allowed hundreds of thousands of "name servers" to maintain small portions of a global database of information associating IP addresses with the names of computers on the Internet. The naming structure was hierarchical in character. For example, all host computers associated with educational institutions would have names like "stanford.edu" or "ucla.edu".

Specific hosts would have names like "cs.ucla.edu" to refer to a computer in the computer science department of UCLA, for example. A special set of computers called "root servers" maintained information about the names and addresses of other servers that contained more detailed name/address associations.

The designers of the DNS also developed seven generic "top level" domains, as follows:

- *Education*: EDU
- *Government*: GOV
- *Military*: MIL
- *International*: INT
- *Network*: NET
- *Organization*: ORG
- *Commercial*: COM

Under this system, for example, the host name "UCLA" became "UCLA.EDU" because it was operated by an educational institution, while the host computer for "BBN" became "BBN.COM" because it was a commercial organization. Top-level domain names also were created for every country: United Kingdom names would end in ".UK," while the ending ".FR" was created for the names of France.

The Domain Name System (DNS) was and continues to be a major element of the Internet architecture, which contributes to its scalability. It also contributes to controversy over trademarks and general rules for the creation and use of domain names, creation of new top-level domains and the like. At the same time, other resolution schemes exist as well. One of the authors (Kahn) has been involved in the development of a different kind of standard identification and resolution scheme that, for example, is being used as the base technology by book publishers to identify books on the Internet by adapting various identification schemes for use in the Internet environment.

For example, International Standard Book Numbers (ISBNs) can be used as part of the identifiers. The identifiers then resolve to state information about the referenced books, such as location information (*e.g.* multiple sites) on the Internet that is used to access the books or to order them. These developments are taking place in parallel with the more traditional means of managing Internet resources. They offer an alternative to the existing Domain Name System with enhanced functionality. The growth of Web servers and users of the Web has been remarkable, but some people are confused about the relationship between the World Wide Web and the Internet. The Internet is the global information system that includes communication capabilities and many high level applications.

The Web is one such application. The existing connectivity of the Internet made it possible for users and servers all over the world to participate in this activity. Electronic mail is another important application. As of today, over 60 million computers take part in the Internet and about 3.6 million web sites were estimated to be accessible on the net. Virtually every user of the net has access to electronic mail and web browsing capability. E-mail remains a critically important application for most users of the Internet, and these two functions largely dominate the use of the Internet for most users.

INTERNET STANDARDS PROCESS

Internet standards were once the output of research activity sponsored by DARPA. The principal investigators on the internetting research effort essentially determined what technical features of the TCP/IP protocols would become common. The initial work in this area started with the joint effort of the two authors, continued in Cerf's group at Stanford, and soon thereafter was joined by engineers and scientists at BBN and University College London. This informal arrangement has changed with time and details can be found elsewhere. At present, the standards efforts for Internet are carried out primarily under the auspices of the Internet Society (ISOC). The Internet Engineering Task Force (IETF) operates under the leadership of its Internet Engineering Steering Group (IESG), which is populated by appointees approved by the Internet Architecture Board (IAB) which is, itself, now part of the Internet Society.

The IETF comprises over one hundred working groups categorized and managed by Area Directors specializing in specific categories. There are other bodies with considerable interest in Internet standards or in standards that must interwork with the Internet. Examples include the International Telecommunications Union Telecommunications standards group (ITU-T), the International Institute of Electrical and Electronic Engineers (IEEE) local area network standards group (IEEE 801), the Organization for International Standardization (ISO), the American National Standards Institute (ANSI), the World Wide Web Consortium (W3C), and many others.

As Internet access and services are provided by existing media such as telephone, cable and broadcast, interactions with standards bodies and legal structures formed to deal with these media will become an increasingly complex matter. The intertwining of interests is simultaneously fascinating and complicated, and has increased the need for thoughtful cooperation among many interested parties.

MANAGING THE INTERNET

Perhaps the least understood aspect of the Internet is its management. In recent years, this subject has become the subject of intense commercial and international interest, involving multiple governments and commercial organizations, and recently congressional hearings. At issue is how the Internet will be managed in the future, and, in the process, what oversight mechanisms will insure that the public interest is adequately served.

In the 1970s, managing the Internet was easy. Since few people knew about the Internet, decisions about almost everything of real policy concern were made in the offices of DARPA. It became clear in the late 1970s, however, that more community involvement in the decision-making processes was essential. In 1979, DARPA formed the Internet Configuration Control Board (ICCB) to insure that knowledgeable members of the technical community discussed critical issues, educated people outside of DARPA about the issues, and helped others to implement the TCP/IP protocols and gateway functions. At the time, there were no companies that offered turnkey solutions to getting on the Internet.

It would be another five years or so before companies like Cisco Systems were formed, and while there were no PCs yet, the only workstations available were specially built and their software was not generally configured for use with external networks; they were certainly considered expensive at the time. In 1983, the small group of roughly twelve ICCB members was reconstituted (with some substitutions) as the Internet Activities Board (IAB), and about ten "Task Forces" were established under it to address issues in specific technical areas.

The attendees at Internet Working Group meetings were invited to become members of as many of the task forces as they wished. The management of the Domain Name System offers a kind of microcosm of issues now frequently associated with overall management of the Internet's operation and evolution. Someone had to take responsibility for overseeing the system's general operation. In particular, top-level domain names had to be selected, along with persons or organizations to manage each of them. Rules for the allocation of Internet addresses had to be established.

DARPA had previously asked the late Jon Postel of the USC Information Sciences Institute to take on numerous functions related to administration of names, addresses and protocol related matters. With time, Postel assumed further responsibilities in this general area on his own, and DARPA, which was supporting the effort, gave its tacit approval. This activity was generally referred to as the Internet Assigned Numbers Authority (IANA). In time, Postel became the arbitrator of all controversial matters concerning names and addresses until his untimely death in October 1998.

It is helpful to consider separately the problem of managing the domain name space and the Internet address space. These two vital elements of the Internet architecture have rather different characteristics that colour the management problems they generate. Domain names have semantics that numbers may not imply; and thus a means of determining who can use what names is needed. As a result, speculators on Internet names often claim large numbers of them without intent to use them other than to resell them later. Alternate resolution mechanisms, if widely adopted, could significantly change the landscape here.

The rapid growth of the Internet has triggered the design of a new and larger address space (the so-called IP version 6 address space); today's Internet uses IP version 4. However, little momentum has yet developed to deploy IPv6 widely. Despite concerns to the contrary, the IPv4 address space will not be depleted for some time. Further, the use of Dynamic Host Configuration Protocol (DHCP) to dynamically assign IP addresses has also cut down on demand for dedicated IP addresses.

Nevertheless, there is growing recognition in the Internet technical community that expansion of the address space is needed, as is the development of transition schemes that allow interoperation between IPv4 and IPv6 while migrating to IPv6. In 1998, the Internet Corporation for Assigned Names and Numbers (ICANN) was formed as a private sector, non-profit, organization to oversee the orderly progression in use of Internet names and numbers, as well as certain protocol related matters that required oversight. The birth of this organization, which was selected by the Department of Commerce for this function, has been difficult, embodying as it does many of the inherent conflicts in resolving discrepancies in this arena. However, there is a clear need for an oversight mechanism for Internet domain names and numbers, separate from their day-to-day management. Many questions about Internet management remain. They may also prove difficult to resolve quickly. Of specific concern is what role the government and indeed governments around the world need to play in its continuing operation and evolution.

WORLD WIDE WEB

World Wide Web (WWW or W3), collection of globally distributed text and multimedia documents and files and other network services linked in such a way as to create an immense electronic library from which information can be retrieved quickly by intuitive searches. The Web represents the application of hypertext technology and a graphical interface to the Internet to retrieve information that is contained in specially formatted documents that may reside in the same computer or be distributed across many computers around the world. It consists of three main elements.

The Hypertext Markup Language (HTML) comprises the programming codes, or tags, that define fonts, layouts, embedded graphics, and links (hyperlinks) to other documents accessible via the Web. The HyperText Transfer Protocol (HTTP) defines a set of standards for transmitting Web pages across the Internet. The Universal Resource Locator (URL) is a standardized naming convention for identifying a Web document or file, in a sense the address of a link. The result is called the Web because it is made up of many sites, all linked together, with users traveling from one site to the next by clicking a computer's pointing device on a hyperlink.

Web sites, also called Web pages, are really Internet sites that all use the same techniques and HTML tags to create multimedia documents with hypertext links. Each Web page can contain many screens or printed pages of text, graphics, audio, and even video, and the starting point for any Web site is called its home page. Although each page is an Internet site, it must be accessed via a special programme called a Web browser, which can translate the HTML into the graphical images, text, and hypertext links intended by the creator of the page.

Interactive television is a generic term that encompasses a variety of Web-related television technologies and products. Typically, a home television receiver and a telephone line are connected through a small appliance that accesses the Internet through the telephone line and converts the downloaded Web pages into a form that can be displayed on the receiver. A remote control interface allows the user to navigate through the Web and select the information to be displayed.

Ted Nelson, an American computer consultant, had promoted the idea of linking documents via hypertext during the 1960s, but the technology required was not to be available for another 20 years. The foundation of what we now think of as the Web originated with work done on the retrieval of information from distributed systems by Tim Berners-Lee at CERN during the 1980s.

This culminated in the introduction of a text-only interface, or browser, to the scientific community in 1990 and to the public in 1991. Because of the difficulty of using this version, acceptance outside the scientific and academic communities was slow. Marc Andreessen, an undergraduate student working at the National Centre for Supercomputing Applications (NCSA), developed a graphical browser for the Web, introducing a UNIX version in 1993. Versions for the Windows and Macintosh operating systems followed in 1994, and acceptance of the World Wide Web blossomed quickly. In the late 1990s the development of improved browsers with greater multimedia functionality, security, and privacy, as well as more powerful search engines capable of indexing the ever greater information on the Web, led to the commercialization of the Internet.

STRUCTURE OF COURSE WEBSITE

Perhaps the most important and difficult part of developing a web-based course is creating the online content which begins with translating the basic lecture materials to the web and integrating media such as sound, images and even video.

The lecture homepage is divided into:

- *Title*: Lecture number, chapter number, and subject.
- *Lesson*: The main part of the page, which uses multimedia for illustration.
- *Example*: Links for any examples illustrating the lesson (problem statement, given data, required items, solution steps).
- *Pages references*: List of all information resources used to construct the lecture.
- *Assignments*: Link for the lesson assignment and due date.
- Related Links and Extra Readings.
- *Help tools*: Link to calculator, unit converter, and list of tables needed for solving the example.

COMMUNICATION TOOLS

Computer-mediated communication (CMC) is communication accomplished through the use of computer and networking technologies among faculty and students. It can be person-to-person (such as e-mail) or among a group (for example, a 'listserv' or newsgroup). Although the quantity of interaction may not be as great as it is in a standard classroom, users of CMC often find that the quality of the correspondence is better and the rate of learning is higher.

CMC uses include:

- Students use e-mail to ask questions of faculty or teaching assistants at times other than class periods or office hours and even when faculty is away at professional meetings. Answers to frequently asked questions (FAQ) might be posted to a shared location.
- Faculty asks a critical question prior to class so students are better prepared for in-class discussion.

- Students share their papers, outlines, homework problems and project plans to receive feedback from other students.
- Posting important announcements.
- Creating groups and having group discussions on a specific topic.
- Posting lecture notes, sample exam questions, or study tips.
- Requiring discussion questions or homework to be turned in electronically.
- Having an on-line help desk supervised by the professor or teaching assistant.

Computer-mediated communication can be synchronous or asynchronous. Synchronous communication is the exchange of messages among correspondents who are on-line at the same time. One form of synchronous communication is online text-based chat and conferencing. Educational uses include virtual office hours and small group meetings. On the other hand, asynchronous communication is the exchange of messages among correspondents who are not on-line at the same time. The most common forms include e-mail, newsgroups (Usenet), mailing list servers, group project collaboration and course discussion groups.

Whether the type of communication is synchronous or asynchronous, it can be on a whole range of levels. These different levels were implemented in the developed web-based courses.

- *One-alone*: *e.g.* one person accesses on-line resources such as on-line databases or journals, remotely executes software programmes stored on a remote computer, or downloads application software via Internet File Transfer Protocol (FTP).
- *One-to-one*: *e.g.* two people send messages back and forth via e-mail such as a student corresponding with a teacher or two students communicating.
- *One-to-many*: *e.g.* learning materials can be posted to a website by a teacher, forming an electronic lecture which any number of students can view.
- *Many-to-many*: *e.g.* any number of participants (students or teachers) interacts via chatting, a computer conferencing system. Debates, discussion groups and brainstorming can take place.

The following communication components were implemented in the developed web courses:

- *E-mail*: E-mail between faculty and students can be integrated into the web environment. The web page allows e-mail to be sent to faculty and classmates, and a pop mail system can be integrated for reading e-mail messages. In both cases, e-mail can include attachments of any binary file (*e.g.* word processing files, spreadsheets, graphic images, and even sound and video files). The mailing services included in the course website were provided from

Zap Zone Network. Students can access the mail login page. With this service, an instructor can monitor his or her students, send e-mail to all of them at the same time informing them about any changes in the course, or reminding them of any important dates.

- *Message board/discussion group*: A message board for communication among all course participants is a wonderful resource allowing for course discussions, questions regarding course material and assignments, and course announcements. Its advantages are tremendous including greatly enhanced student inclusion and participation in the course. Another communication facility is the discussion group that sets up a forum for site visitors to communicate with each other. A discussion group allows site visitors to post articles and reply to them. The easiest way to create a discussion group with FrontPage 2000 is by using the Discussion Web Wizard. The wizard asks for the desired features, then creates a web and sets up the pages for you. After the web is created, you can open the pages and customise them. Another way to create a message board is by using on-line free board services like inside the web service.
- *Real-time chat facility*: Allows for the holding of real-time typed conversations. Office hours can take place this way without the need for instructor, students or teaching assistants (TAs) to travel to campus. A multichat service was used in the course web page. MultiChat is a Java chat client applet service that enables you to place a chat room on your own site.
- *Feedback form*: Provides the instructor with the student's response and comments. The user should first choose the comment kind from the following: Complaint, problem, suggestion, or praise. Then he should use the pull-down menu to select the item he wants to comment about (website, class, lab, instructor, TA, technical help, or other). The last step is to write the comment in the provided field and his contact information.
- *Announcements*: Effective announcements need to be read; for that to happen the students need to know when a new announcement has been posted. Alert boxes or running footers (using JavaScript) or a blinking link added to a page can let students know of new announcements. Such announce-ments are implemented in the web course site to remind students of exam dates, assignments due date, etc. Announcements are created with FrontPage 2000 using Marquee option from the Insert menu.
- *Yellow Shared Board*: A tool to assist chatting sessions. It lets the instructor illustrate his or her ideas to students as in the same way

as with pen and paper. Meanwhile the student could participate in the illustration. NetWriter, a free shared Yellow Pad on-line service provided by ParaGraph/Vademto, was used in the course website to implement the yellow-shared board. With NetWriter the instructor can reserve the session ahead of time and send e-mails to students to inform them with the session time and number.

EMAIL

DEFINITION

Email is simply the shortened form of electronic mail, a protocol for receiving, sending and storing electronic messages. Email has gained popularity with the spread of the Internet. In many cases, email has become the preferred method of communication.

Email is shothand term meaning Electronic Mail. Email much the same as a letter, only that it is exchanged in a different way. Computers use the TCP/IP protocol suite to send email messages in the form of packets. The first thing you need to send and recieve emails is an email address. When you create an account with a Internet Service Provider you are usually given an email address to send from and recieve emails. If this isn't the case you can create an email address/account at web sites such as yahoo, hotmail and lycos.

HOW DOES E-MAIL WORK?

Billions of electronic mail (e-mail) messages move across the Internet every year. Sending electronic letters, pictures and data files, either across a building or across the globe, has grown so popular that it has started to replace some postal mail and telephone calls. This universal medium is no longer restricted to exchange of simple text messages and is now regularly used to deliver voice mail, facsimiles and documents that may include images, sound and video.

Typically, a message becomes available to the recipient within seconds after it is sent—one reason why Internet mail has transformed the way that we are able to communicate.

MESSAGE SENDER

Uses mail software, called a client, to compose a document, possibly including attachments such as tables, photographs or even a voice or video recording. System software, called Transmission Control Protocol (TCP), divides the message into packets and adds information about how each packet should be handled-for instance, in what order packets were transmitted from the sender. Packets are sent to a mail submission server, a computer on the internal network of a company or an Internet service provider.

Internet Mail Addresses

Attached to each message are in the form "mailbox@domainname" - one specific example being "webmaster@seniorindian.com." The multipart domain name in the above example denotes a top-level domain (".com") following the second-level domain ("seniorindian"). A message is delivered to an individual or a group by the mailbox name ("webmaster").

Mail Submission Server

Converts the domain name of the recipient's mail address into a numeric Internet Protocol (IP) address. It does this by querying domain name servers interspersed throughout the Internet. For example, the mail submission server can first request from the "root" name server the whereabouts of other servers that store information about ".com" domains,

- It can then interrogate the ".com" name server for the location of the specific "sciam.com" name server
- A final request to the "sciam.com" name server provides the IP address for the computer that receives the mail for sciam.com, which is then attached to each message packet

ROUTERS

Dispersed throughout the Internet read the IP address on a packet and relay it toward its destination by the most efficient path. (Because of fluctuating traffic over data lines, trying to transmit a packet directly to its destination is not always the fastest way.) The packets of a single message may travel along different routes, shuttling through 10 or so routers before their journey's end.

Destination Mail Server

Places the packets in their original order, according to the instructions contained in each packet, and stores the message in the recipient's mailbox. The recipient's client software can then display the message.

SEARCH ENGINES

INTRODUCTION

Search engine as: 'a programme designed to help find information stored on a computer system such as the World Wide Web, or a personal computer. The search engine allows one to ask for content meeting specific criteria (typically those containing a given word or phrase) and retrieving a list of references that match those criteria. Search engines use regularly updated indexes to operate quickly and efficiently.'

In other words, a search engine is a sophisticated piece of software, accessed through a page on a website that allows you to search the web by entering search queries into a search box. The search engine then attempts to match your search query with the content of web pages that is has stored, or cached, and indexed on its powerful servers in advance of your search.

Search engines are special tools that anyone can use. They are a database of web sites that contain information that is catalogued and indexed for easy reference. The secret of effective searching in knowing how to state what you want to search for.>

Most search engines allow you to use a group of words that narrow the search for you. If you use a general term like "history" for instance, you may get a listing of 3 or 4 MILLION web sites. It is important to use as many descriptive words as you can think of in order to limit your results to several hundred sites or less.

There are special words that some search engines use that allow you to be even more specific. They are called Boolean Operators. These words include "and", "or", and "not". For example you could specify "history and revolution OR war not french" to search for all revolutions or wars in history that do not include the term French in the description. This would still be a broad search, but you can see how these special words can allow you to become very specific about your interests.

Note: many search engines allow you to search for things other than text: for example, images. However, for the purpose of this course, we will focus on text-based searches. As we pointed out in the last unit, SEO methods are largely (but not exclusively) centred upon text as they involve matching key parts of the text in your web pages with the keywords or key phrases that people actually type into search engines when looking for something on the internet.

There are two main types of search indexes we access when searching the web:

- Directories
- Crawler-based search engines

Directories

Unlike search engines, which use special software to locate and index sites, directories are compiled and maintained by humans. Directories often consist of a categorized list of links to other sites to which you can add your own site. Editors sometimes review your site to see if it is fit for inclusion in the directory.

Crawler-based Search Engines

Crawler-based search engines differ from directories in that they are not compiled and maintained by humans. Instead, crawler-based search engines use sophisticated pieces of software called spiders or robots to search and index web pages. These spiders are constantly at work, crawling around the web, locating pages, and taking snapshots of those pages to be cached or stored on the search engine's servers. They are so sophisticated that they can follow links from one page to another and from one site to another.

Google is a prominent example of a crawler-based search engine. Some search systems are 'hybrid' systems as they combine both forms of index. Yahoo, for example, features both directories and search engines. As we will see later in this course, the SEO process often involves optimizing your site in such a way that it allows search engine spiders to locate every page on your site quickly and easily.

Spidering vs Submitting your Site Manually

If you browse the web, you will notice that many companies will offer to submit your site to search engines for inclusion in their listings. The services these companies offer are largely unnecessary and can prove to be a waste of time and money. It is important to remember that search engine spiders are constantly crawling the web, following links and indexing pages. Because spiders automatically index your pages when they find them, there is absolutely no need to submit your site manually to the major search engines.

INTRANET

DEFINITION

An Intranet is merely a network of computers that can share data with each other using existing standardized WWW protocols. By storing information on an Internal Web Server and providing each computer on the network with browser software such as Internet Explorer, and a network data access application, anyone on the network can view information located on the Intranet Server. This allows for easy and inexpensive distribution of internal corporate information, an essential ingredient in today's fast-moving competitive environment.

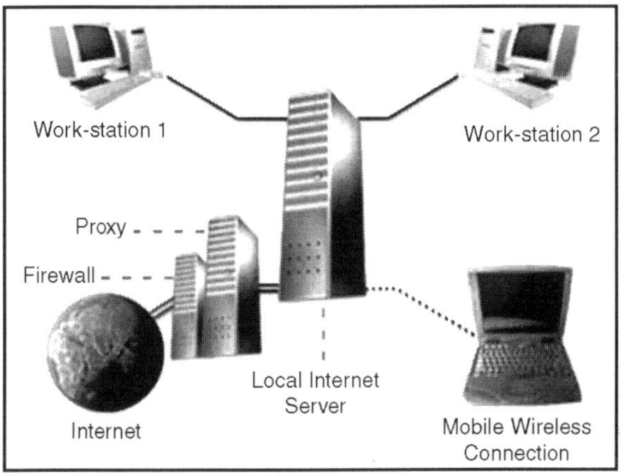

Fig. Intranet Basics

Think of an intranet as your company's own private information network. An intranet is a private communications system built on the infrastructure of the Internet that can increase employee productivity, build stronger ties with your customers and encourage more profitable relationships with vendors. Whether you run a small business or a multi-national corporation, an intranet can serve your company's specific information requirements. It can streamline information access and dissemination.

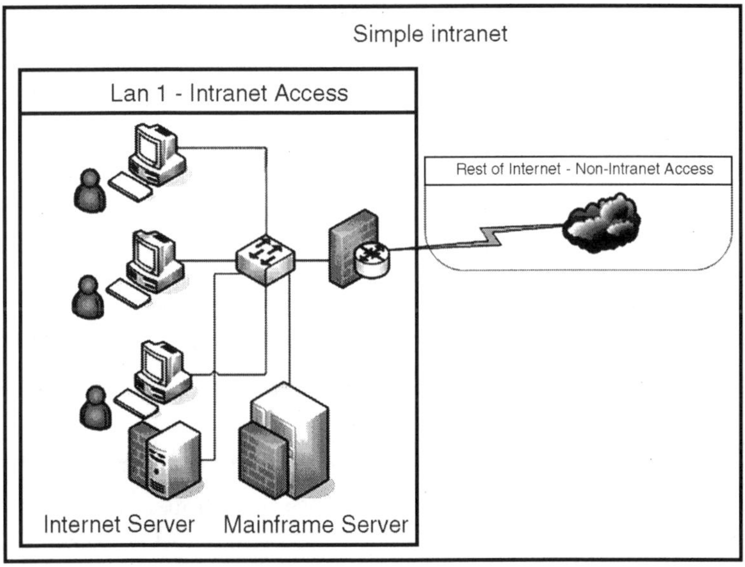

In short, an intranet is a technology tool that can save you time and money. Intranets are widely used across the world as means of sharing information among employees in businesses and/or development teams. Basically, an Intranet is a website running inside a company's LAN or WAN. They can be setup many different ways according to individual needs and budgets. The image below shows a diagram of a simple Intranet.

USING YOUR INTRANET

Your company executives, department heads, and staff will decide how the corporate intranet will be used. However, as the systems administrator, it is your job to implement these decisions. Part of the value an IS manager or systems administrator can add is to recommend to management which end-user intranet applications make sense today based on the functionality and technical aspects of the application and which ones you will want to expand toward in the future.

For example, you obviously wouldn't want to implement an application now that has a Year 2000 problem; you'd replace it with a different application or make the fix before you go through the trouble of loading the programme onto the intranet. Sun's Meske says that a careful examination of how you will use the intranet and what kind of content you intend to put onto it is very important.

At the top of Meske's list of priorities is determining what functions you want to distribute, how you deploy Web servers in your company, and how you deploy proxy servers to minimize the impact on the network. Wise use of intranet servers, Meske adds, will minimize "sneaker net," resulting from foot traffic incurred when the intranet is overloaded. Common uses of corporate intranets include numerous human resource applications (such as policy and benefit manuals, OSHA documentation, staff directories, and online job postings), collaborative computing applications, multimedia, as well as applications linked to sales and marketing applications (like success stories), engineering and design departments, and customer service, among many others. At Sun, Meske says, virtually every corporate function is available to Sun's 19,000 intranet users. These Sun intranet users take advantage of such applications as human resources data, Sun's internal library, sales and marketing, accounts payable, career services, corporate security, education, corporate affairs, and so on.

EXTRANET

INTRODUCTION

A company LAN, or local area network, can house a private Internet-like environment called an *intranet*. The intranet is basically a set of HTML pages relating to internal company business, for employee's eyes only, and is not available to the Internet. If access to or from the Internet is provided, it will be through a firewall gateway that will require a username and password. In this case the intranet becomes an extranet. In short, an extranet is the extension of an intranet to include public access.

An extranet can allow public access to employees, customers, clients or partners. The extranet uses Internet protocols so users can navigate with a browser, but resides on the company's private server rather than on a public Internet server. Extranet access from the Internet can be controlled through various architectures that are password or username specific. In other words, areas of the extranet will be available according to password credentials. This limits users to extranet pages relevant to the business they might be conducting, while keeping other areas of the extranet private and secure.

One very valuable application for an extranet is customer service. Online patches, upgrades, downloads, knowledge bases, and an interactive *Help Desk* are just a few examples of ways to serve a client base using an extranet. Extranet chat boards where customers help each other with company products can also build customer confidence and brand loyalty, while saving valuable human resources. Chat boards are also a rich source for potential future product and support development.

Another resource an extranet can provide is the ability to create secure areas for interaction between an organization and its partners or resellers. Development, dissemination of marketing information and tools, data sharing, research, sales reports and more are all possible using an extranet environment. An extranet can also connect to other extranets through the common language of Internet protocols. This makes it invaluable to organizations involved in collaborative efforts and opens the door to greater creative opportunities. In the past, geography was a significant hindrance to collaboration, but extranet technology bridges that gap effortlessly and virtually cost-free.

Extranets can revolutionize the way a company does business, improve the bottom line, enrich the customer base, and create opportunities that remain out of reach without an extranet. If interested in finding out more about what an extranet can do for your business, consult an extranet site developer. The Internet popularized instant communications with far-flung computers via the simple click of a mouse. Anyone with a Web browser can follow links and hop from site to site, gleaning information that companies and people have decided to publish. That same point and click access can be used to speed communication and enhance collaboration between a company and its partners and customers. But what happens when a company needs to share information that is confidential? That's where the "extranet" comes in.

EXPLANATION

An extranet has the appearance and feel of a website, but adds levels of security to prevent unwanted viewers from clicking through to private data.

Similar to an intranet—a private Internet for people inside a company—an extranet widens the circle to privileged outsiders. An extranet can streamline the sharing of information, as well as applications and services. For example, a public relations agency may want to review marketing materials with a client.

Rather than e-mail a large file, or fax it, or send it via costly overnight mail, the agency could put the materials on a private website. An extranet. The agency might also want to use this extranet to collaborate with clients, sharing calendars, project management tools, and other applications. "An extranet allows the organization to have a closer, interactive relationship with its customers, partners, etc., without the need for complete management of the users or their IT environment," says Ray Wagner, research vice president with Gartner Inc., of Stamford, Conn. An extranet is similar to an intranet but it is made accessible to selected external partners such as business partners, suppliers, key customers, etc, for exchanging data and applications and sharing information.

As with an intranet, an extranet can also provide remote access to corporate systems for staff who spend lots of time out of the office, for instance those in sales or customer support, or home workers. Extranet users should be a well-defined group and access must be protected by rigorous identification routines and security features. An Extranet is similar to an Intranet but it is made accessible to selected external partners such as business partners, suppliers, key customers etc, for exchanging data and applications and sharing information. As with an Intranet, an Extranet can also provide remote access to corporate and organisational systems for staff who spend lots of time out of the office, for instance those in sales, customer support, or home workers.

Extranets offer a cost effective and efficient way for businesses to connect with their trading partners. It also means that your business partners and suppliers can access the information they need 24 hours a day. The ability of the extranet to automate the trading tasks between you and your trading partners can lead to enhanced business relationships and help to integrate your business firmly within their supply chain. Within the tourism industry we have delivered customised extranet solutions that are now helping run day-today business processes on a worldwide level.

Businesses of all sizes are under increasing pressure to use online ordering, electronic order tracking and inventory management. At the same time small businesses are keen to meet the demands of larger companies in terms of working flexibly, adopting new technologies and enabling the exchange of business information and transactions. An Extranet can offer a range of benefits to your organisation or business from lowering costs, to producing faster results and improving the quality of service to customers.

ADVANTAGES

- Improved business relationships with key trading partners because of the close collaborative working that extranets support
- Improved customer service by giving customers direct access to information and enabling them to resolve their own queries
- A single user interface between you and your business partners
- Improving the security of communications between you and your business partners, since exchanges can take place under a controlled and secure environment
- Shared news of product development exclusively with partner companies
- Flexible working for your own staff, as an extranet allows remote and mobile staff to access core business information 24 hours a day, irrespective of location
- More integrated supply chains through the use of online ordering, order tracking and inventory management
- Reduced costs by making manuals and technical documentation available online to trading partners and customers
- More effective collaboration between business partners-perhaps members of a project team-by enabling them to work online on common documentation

USING EXTRANET

Businesses of all sizes are under increasing pressure to use online ordering, electronic order tracking and inventory management. At the same time small businesses are keen to meet the demands of larger companies in terms of working flexibly, adopting new technologies and enabling the exchange of business information and transactions.

Extranets offer a cheap and efficient way for businesses to connect with their trading partners. It also means that your business partners and suppliers can access the information they need 24 hours a day. The ability of the extranet to automate the trading tasks between you and your trading partners can lead to enhanced business relationships and help to integrate your business firmly within their supply chain.

WORKING

Extranet functionality comes in different forms. A public website is a simple extranet, Wagner says. "If it has interactivity, it's a little more complex. If it has a limited user base that's controlled by the organization in some way, it's even more complex," Wagner says. "If it has real applications that allow business transactions, collaboration, or sharing of corporate intellectual property to occur, it's very complex and requires significant resource outlay, planning, and security." Extranets also require measures to ensure privacy and security of information. Some of the security methods that can protect extranets from unauthorized access include the use of virtual private networks (VPNs), firewalls, user authentication and/or encryption.

Extranets for Small Business

One way for a small business to provide an extranet is through hosted applications, like WebEx's Web Office, Trichys' Work Zone, and Microsoft SharePoint Services. In addition, Microsoft plans to release Microsoft Office Live, a hosted version of the Office application suite that allows groups to collaborate.

Sharing information via a hosted workspace is often easier on the bottom line, which is important to the small or fast-growing business, says Karen Leavitt, vice president of WebEx. "It's far more cost effective to put information into a hosted workspace, a shared repository on the Web to exchange information in real time with your clients," Leavitt says. Hosted applications are great for small businesses without an IT department, she says. "There is no setup at all," she says. "Everything is hosted on the Web."

Besides saving a company the cost of running a more expensive server-based application, like Microsoft Exchange, such collaboration services help a company to accelerate revenues. "If a sales guy can literally meet with six different prospects in a day by conducting Web meetings with them, rather than getting on a plane and doing one or two, they have more opportunities to close business for the company," Leavitt says.

USES

Understand what the Internet is and know some of its main uses.

Some of its main uses are to:

- Integrate the operations of multinational corporations.
- Provide access to and share information and databases.
- Transfer and share files between computers.
- Facilitate business transactions.
- Share resources.
- Promote scientific co-operation between research institutions.
- Provide a communications channel for the military.

6

Computer Algorithms and Data Structure

COMPUTER ALGORITHMS

In computer systems, an algorithm is basically an instance of logic written in software by software developers to be effective for the intended "target" computer(s), in order for the software on the target machines to *do something*. For instance, if a person is writing software that is supposed to print out a PDF document located at the operating system folder "/My Documents" at computer drive "D:" every Friday, they will write an algorithm that specifies the following actions: "If today's date (computer time) is 'Friday,' open the document at 'D:/My Documents' and call the 'print' function".

While this simple algorithm does not look into whether the printer has enough paper or whether the document has been moved into a different location, one can make this algorithm more robust and anticipate these problems by rewriting it as a formal CASE statement or as a (carefully crafted) sequence of IF-THEN-ELSE statements. For example the CASE statement might appear as follows (there are other possibilities):

- *Case* 1: IF today's date is NOT Friday THEN *exit this CASE instruction* ELSE
- *Case* 2: IF today's date is Friday AND the document is located at 'D:/My Documents' AND there is paper in the printer THEN print the document (and *exit this CASE instruction*) ELSE
- *Case* 3: IF today's date is Friday AND the document is NOT located at 'D:/My Documents' THEN display 'document not found' error message (and *exit this CASE instruction*) ELSE
- *Case* 4: IF today's date is Friday AND the document is located at 'D:/My Documents' AND there is NO paper in the printer THEN, (i) display 'out of paper' error message (ii) *exit*. Note that CASE 3 includes two possibilities: (i) the document is NOT located at 'D:/My Documents' AND there's paper in the printer OR (ii) the document is NOT located at 'D:/My Documents' AND there's NO paper in the printer.

The sequence of IF-THEN-ELSE tests might look like this:

- *Test* 1: IF today's date is NOT Friday THEN *done* ELSE TEST 2:
- *Test* 2: IF the document is NOT located at 'D:/My Documents' THEN display 'document not found' error message ELSE TEST 3:
- *Test* 3: IF there is NO paper in the printer THEN display 'out of paper' error message ELSE print the document.

These examples' logic grants precedence to the instance of "NO document at 'D:/My Documents' ".

ALGORITHMS

In mathematics, computing, and related subjects, an algorithm is an effective method for solving a problem using a finite sequence of instructions.

Each algorithm is a list of well-defined instructions for completing a task. Starting from an initial state, the instructions describe a computation that proceeds through a well-defined series of successive states, eventually terminating in a final ending state. The transition from one state to the next is not necessarily deterministic; some algorithms, known as randomized algorithms, incorporate randomness.

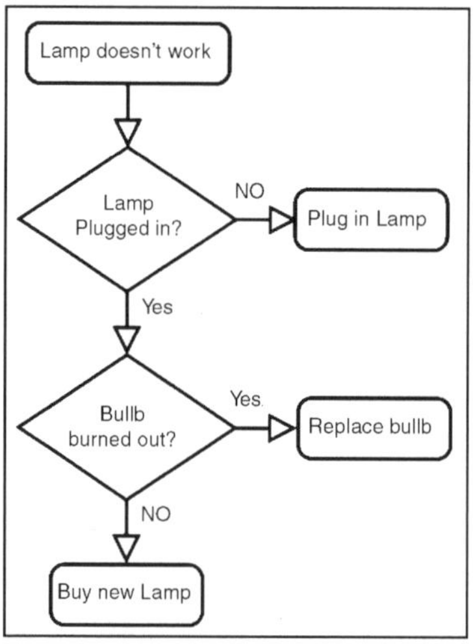

While there is no generally accepted *formal* definition of "algorithm", an informal definition could be "a process that performs some sequence of operations." For some people, a Programme is only an algorithm if it stops eventually. For others, a Programme is only an algorithm if it stops before a given number of calculation steps.

A prototypical example of an algorithm is Euclid's algorithm to determine the maximum common divisor of two integers. We can derive clues to the issues involved and an informal meaning of the word from the following quotation from Boolos & Jeffrey:

No human being can write fast enough, or long enough, or small enough† (†"smaller and smaller without limit...you'd be trying to write on molecules, on atoms, on electrons") to list all members of an enumerably infinite set by writing out their No human being can write fast enough, or long enough,names, one after another, in some notation.

But humans can do something equally useful, in the case of certain enumerably infinite sets: They can give explicit instructions for determining the *n*th member of the set, for arbitrary finite *n*. Such instructions are to be given quite explicitly, in a form in which they could be followed by a computing machine, or by a human who is capable of carrying out only very elementary operations on symbols

FORMALIZATION

Algorithms are essential to the way computers process information. Many computer Programmes contain algorithms that specify the specific instructions a computer should perform (in a specific order) to carry out a specified task, such as calculating employees' paychecks or printing students' report cards. Thus, an algorithm can be considered to be any sequence of operations that can be simulated by a Turing-completesystem.

Typically, when an algorithm is associated with processing information, data is read from an input source, written to an output device, and/or stored for further processing. Stored data is regarded as part of the internal state of the entity performing the algorithm. In practice, the state is stored in one or more data structures.

For any such computational process, the algorithm must be rigorously defined: specified in the way it applies in all possible circumstances that could arise. That is, any conditional steps must be systematically dealt with, case-by-case; the criteria for each case must be clear (and computable). Because an algorithm is a precise list of precise steps, the order of computation will always be critical to the functioning of the algorithm. Instructions are usually assumed to be listed explicitly, and are described as starting "from the top" and going "down to the bottom", an idea that is described more formally by *flow of control*.

So far, this discussion of the formalization of an algorithm has assumed the premises of imperative Programmeming. This is the most common conception, and it attempts to describe a task in discrete, "mechanical" means. Unique to this conception of formalized algorithms is the assignment, setting the value of a variable. It derives from the intuition of "memory" as a scratchpad. There is an example below of such an assignment.

TERMINATION

But if the length of the process isn't known in advance, then "trying" it may not be decisive, because if the process does go on forever — then at no time will we ever be sure of the answer.

As it happens, no other method can do any better, as was shown by Alan Turing with his celebrated result on the undesirability of the so-called halting. There is no algorithmic procedure for determining of arbitrary algorithms whether or not they terminate from given starting states. The analysis of algorithms for their likelihood of termination is called termination analysis.

The examples of (im-)"proper" subtraction at partial function for more about what can happen when an algorithm fails for certain of its input numbers — e.g.,

- Non-termination,
- Production of "junk" (output in the wrong format to be considered a number) or no number(s) at all (halt ends the computation with no output),
- Wrong number(s),
- A combination of these.

Kleene proposed that the production of "junk" or failure to produce a number is solved by having the algorithm detect these instances and produce e.g., an error message (he suggested "0"), or preferably, force the algorithm into an endless loop.

AUGMENTING-PATH ALGORITHMS

The neat part of the Ford-Fulkerson algorithm described above is that it gets the correct result no matter how we solve (correctly!!) the sub-problem of finding an augmenting path. However, every new path may increase the flow by only 1, hence the number of iterations of the algorithm could be very large if we carelessly choose the augmenting path algorithm to use. The function *max_flow* will look like this, regardless of the actual method we use for finding augmenting paths:

```
  int max_flow()
    result = 0
      while (true)
   // the function find_path returns the path
capacity of the
   augmenting path found
   path_capacity = find_path()
   // no augmenting path found
   if (d = 0) exit while
   else result += path_capacity
end while
return result
```

To keep it simple, we will use a 2-dimensional array for storing the capacities of the residual network that we are left with after each step in the algorithm. Initially the residual network is just the original network. We will not store the flows along the edges explicitly, but it's easy to figure out how to find them upon the termination of the algorithm: for each edge x-y in the original network the flow is given by the capacity of the backward edge y-x in the residual network. Be careful though; if the reversed arc y-x also exists in the original network, this will fail, and it is recommended that the initial capacity of each arc be stored somewhere, and then the flow along the edge is the difference between the initial and the residual capacity.

We now require an implementation for the function *find_path*. The first approach that comes to mind is to use a depth-first search (DFS), as it probably is the easiest to implement. Unfortunately, its performance is very poor on some networks, and normally is less preferred to the ones discussed next.

The next best thing in the matter of simplicity is a breadth-first search (BFS). Recall that this search usually yields the shortest path in an un-weighted graph. Indeed, this also applies here to get the shortest augmenting path from the source to the sink. In the following pseudocode we will basically: find a shortest path from the source to the sink and compute the minimum capacity of an edge (that could be a forward or a backward edge) along the path - the path capacity. Then, for each edge along the path we reduce its capacity and increase the capacity of the reversed edge with the path capacity.

```
    int bfs()
      queue Q
       push source to Q
       mark source as visited
       keep an array from with the
  semnification: from[x] is the
       previous vertex visited in the shortest
     path from the source to x;
       initialize from with -1 (or any other
    sentinel value)
        while Q is not empty
          where = pop from Q
        for each vertex next adjacent to where
        if next is not visited and
    capacity[where][next] > 0
          push next to Q
          mark next as visited
          from[next] = where
          if next = sink
            exit while loop
      end for
  end while
  // we compute the path capacity
  where = sink, path_cap = infinity
  while from[where] > -1
```

```
      prev = from[where]// the previous vertex
      path_cap = min(path_cap,
  capacity[prev][where])
      where = prev
    end while
      // we update the residual network; if no
    path is found the while
      loop will not be entered
      where = sink
        while from[where] > -1
          prev = from[where]
          capacity[prev][where] -= path_capacity
            capacity[where][prev] +=
         path_capacity
      where = prev
    end while
    // if no path is found, path_cap is infinity
    if path_cap = infinity
      return 0
    else return path_cap
```

As we can see, this is pretty easy to implement. As for its performance, it is guaranteed that this takes at most $N * M/2$ steps, where N is the number of vertices and M is the number of edges in the network. This number may seem very large, but it is over-estimated for most networks. For example, in the network we considered 3 augmenting paths are needed which is significantly less than the upper bound of 28. Due to the $O(M)$ running time of BFS (implemented with adjacency lists) the worst-case running time of the shortest-augmenting path max-flow algorithm is $O(N * M^2)$, but usually the algorithm performs much better than this.

Next we will consider an approach that uses a priority-first search (PFS), that is very similar to the Dijkstra heap method explained here. In this method the augmenting path with a maximum path capacity is preferred. Intuitively this would lead to a faster algorithm, since at each step we increase the flow with the maximum possible amount. However, things are not always so, and the BFS implementation has better running times on some networks.

We assign as a priority to each vertex the minimum capacity of a path (in the residual network) from the source to that vertex. We process vertices in a greedy manner, as in Dijkstra's algorithm, in decreasing order of priorities. When we get to the sink, we are done, since a path with a maximum capacity is found. We would like to implement this with a data structure that allows us to efficiently find the vertex with the highest priority and increase the priority of a vertex (when a new better path is found) - this suggests the use of a heap which has a space complexity proportional to the number of vertices.

In TopCoder matches we may find it faster and easier to implement this with a priority queue or some other data structure that approximates one, even though the space required might grow to being proportional with the number of edges. This is how the following pseudocode is implemented. We also define a structure node that has the members vertex and prioritywith the above significance. Another field from is needed to store the previous vertex on the path.

```
    int pfs()
     priority queue PQ
     push node(source, infinity, -1) to PQ
     keep the array from as in bfs()
     // if no augmenting path is found, path_cap
   will remain 0
     path_cap = 0
     while PQ is not empty
        node aux = pop from PQ
        where = aux.vertex, cost = aux.priority
        if we already visited where continue
        from[where] = aux.from
        if where = sink
          path_cap = cost
          exit while loop
         mark where as visited
         for each vertex next adjacent to where
           if capacity[where][next] > 0
             new_cost = min(cost,
         capacity[where][next])
             push node(next, new_cost, where) to
           PQ
        end for
      end while
      // update the residual network
      where = sink
      while from[where] > -1
        prev = from[where]
        capacity[prev][where] -= path_cap
        capacity[where][prev] += path_cap
        where = prev
      end while
        return path_cap
```

The analysis of its performance is pretty complicated, but it may prove worthwhile to remember that with PFS at most $2M1gU$ steps are required, where U is the maximum capacity of an edge in the network.

As with BFS, this number is a lot larger than the actual number of steps for most networks. Combine this with the $O(M \lg M)$complexity of the search to get the worst-case running time of this algorithm. Now that we know what these methods are all about, which of them do we choose when we are confronted with a max-flow problem? The PFS approach seems to have a better worst-case performance, but in practice their performance is pretty much the same. So, the method that one is more familiar with may prove more adequate. Personally, I prefer the shortest-path method, as I find it easier to implement during a contest and less error prone.

MAXIMUM FLOW PROBLEM

The maximum flow problem is again structured on a network; but here the arc capacities, or upper bounds, are the only relevant parameters. The problem is to find the maximum flow possible from some given source node to a given sink node. A network model is in Fig. All arc costs are zero, but the cost on the arc leaving the sink is set to -1. Since the goal of the optimization is to minimize cost, the maximum flow possible is delivered to the sink node.

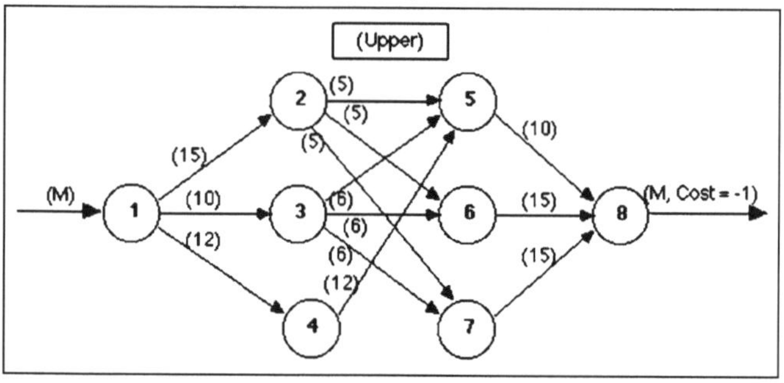

Fig. Network Model for the Maximum Flow Problem.

The solution to the example is in Fig. The maximum flow from node 1 to node 8 is 30 and the flows that yield this flow are shown on the figure. The heavy arcs on the figure are called the minimal cut. These arcs are the bottlenecks that are restricting the maximum flow. The fact that the sum of the capacities of the arcs on the minimal cut equals the maximum flow is a famous theorem of network theory called the max flow min cut theorem. The arcs on the minimum cut can be identified using sensitivity analysis.

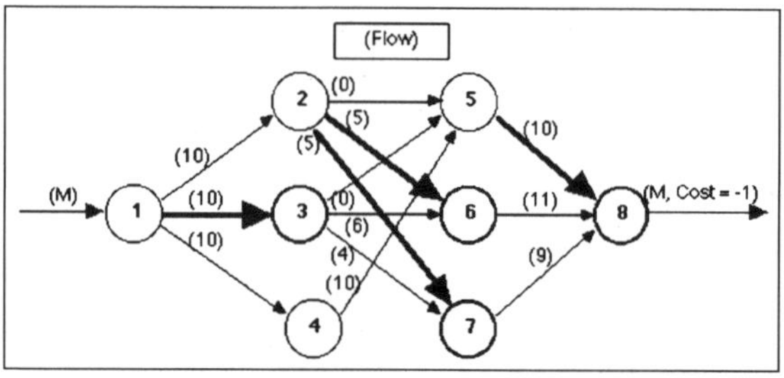

MAX-FLOW/MIN-CUT RELATED PROBLEMS

How to recognize max-flow problems? Often they are hard to detect and usually boil down to maximizing the movement of something from a location to another. We need to look at the constraints when we think we have a working solution based on maximum flow - they should suggest at least an $O(N^3)$ approach. If the number of locations is large, another algorithm (such as dynamic Programmeming or greedy), is more appropriate.

The problem description might suggest multiple sources and/or sinks. For example, in the sample statement in the beginning of this article, the company might own more than one factory and multiple distribution Centres. How can we deal with this? We should try to convert this to a network that has a unique source and sink.

In order to accomplish this we will add two "dummy" vertices to our original network - we will refer to them as super-source and super-sink. In addition to this we will add an edge from the super-source to every ordinary source (a factory). As we don't have restrictions on the number of trucks that each factory can send, we should assign to each edge an infinite capacity.

Note that if we had such restrictions, we should have assigned to each edge a capacity equal to the number of trucks each factory could send. Likewise, we add an edge from every ordinary sink (distribution Centres) to the super-sink with infinite capacity.

A maximum flow in this new-built network is the solution to the problem - the sources now become ordinary vertices, and they are subject to the entering-flow equals leaving-flow property. You may want to keep this in your bag of tricks, as it may prove useful to most problems.

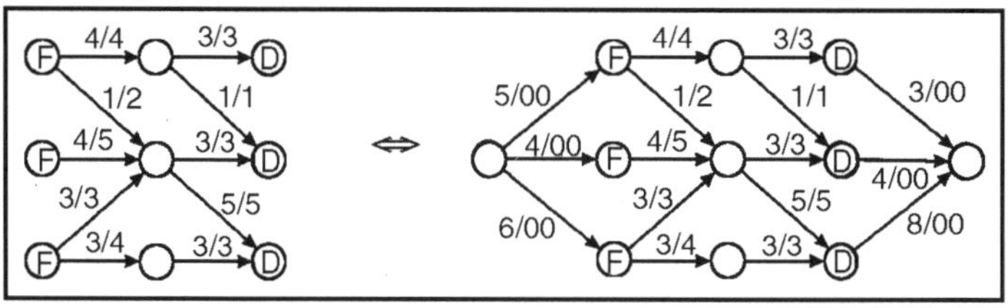

Fig. Reduction of a Multiple-source/
Muitiple-sink Max-flow Proble

What if we are also given the maximum number of trucks that can drive through each of the cities in the country (other than the cities where the factory and the distribution Centre are located)? In other words we have to deal with vertex-capacities too. Intuitively, we should be able to reduce this to maximum-flow, but we must find a way to take the capacities from vertices and put them back on edges, where they belong.

Another nice trick comes into play. We will build a network that has two times more vertices than the initial one. For each vertex we will have two nodes: an in-vertex and an out-vertex, and we will direct each edge x-y from the out-vertex of x to the in-vertex of y. We can assign them the capacities from the problem statement. Additionally we can add an edge for each vertex from the in to the out-vertex. The capacity this edge will be assigned is obviously the vertex-capacity. Now we just run max-flow on this network and compute the result.

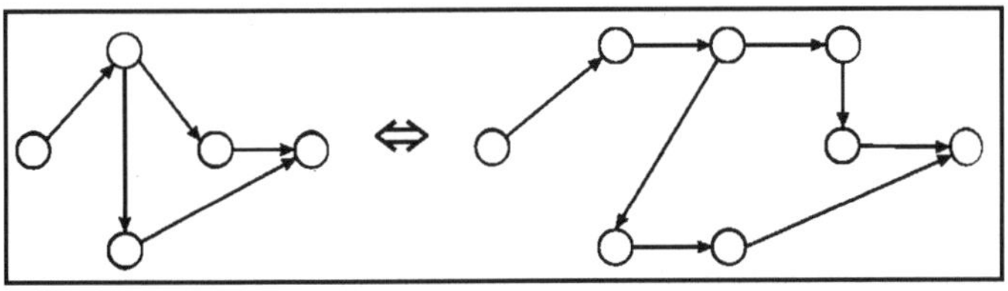

Fig. Eliminating Vertex-Capacities

Maximum flow problems may appear out of nowhere. Let's take this problem for instance:"You are given the in and out degrees of the vertices of a directed graph. Your task is to find the edges (assuming that no edge can appear more than once)." First, notice that we can perform this simple test at the beginning.

We can compute the number M of edges by summing the out-degrees or the in-degrees of the vertices. If these numbers are not equal, clearly there is no graph that could be built. This doesn't solve our problem, though. There are some greedy approaches that come to mind, but none of them work.

We will combine the tricks discussed above to give a max-flow algorithm that solves this problem. First, build a network that has 2 (in/out) vertices for each initial vertex. Now draw an edge from every out vertex to every in vertex. Next, add a super-source and draw an edge from it to every out-vertex. Add a super-sink and draw an edge from every in vertex to it. We now need some capacities for this to be a flow network. It should be pretty obvious what the intent with this approach is, so we will assign the following capacities: for each edge drawn from the super-source we assign a capacity equal to the out-degree of the vertex it points to.

As there may be only one arc from a vertex to another, we assign a 1 capacity to each of the edges that go from the outs to the ins. As you can guess, the capacities of the edges that enter the super-sink will be equal to the in-degrees of the vertices. If the maximum flow in this network equals M - the number of edges, we have a solution, and for each edge between the out and in vertices that has a flow along it (which is maximum 1, as the capacity is 1) we can draw an edge between corresponding vertices in our graph.

Note that both x-y and y-x edges may appear in the solution. This is very similar to the maximum matching in a bipartite graph that we will discuss later. An example is given below where the out-degrees are (2, 1, 1, 1) and the in-degrees (1, 2, 1, 1).

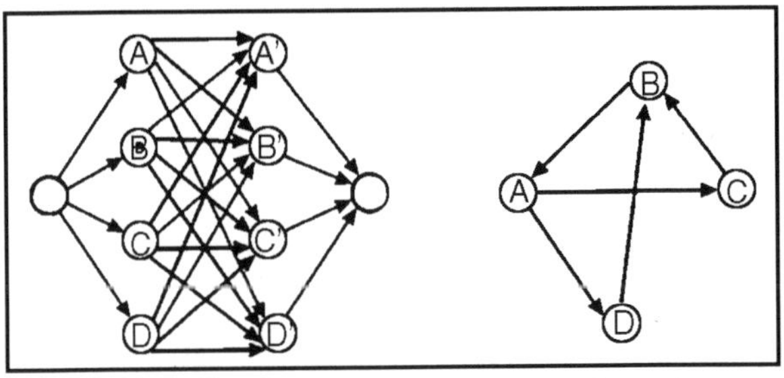

Some other problems may ask to separate two locations minimally. Some of these problems usually can be reduced to minimum-cut in a network. Two examples will be discussed here, but first let's take the standard min-cut problem and make it sound more like a TopCoder problem. We learned earlier how to find the value of the min-cut and how to find an arbitrary min-cut. In addition to this we will now like to have a minimum-cut with the minimum number of edges. An idea would be to try to modify the original network in such a way that the minimum cut here is the minimum cut with the minimum edges in the original one.

Notice what happens if we multiply each edge capacity with a constant T. Clearly, the value of the maximum flow is multiplied by T, thus the value of the minimum cut is T times bigger than the original. A minimum cut in the original network is a minimum cut in the modified one as well. Now suppose we add 1 to the capacity of each edge. Is a minimum cut in the original network a minimum cut in this one? The answer is no, as we can see in Figure shown below, if we take T = 2.

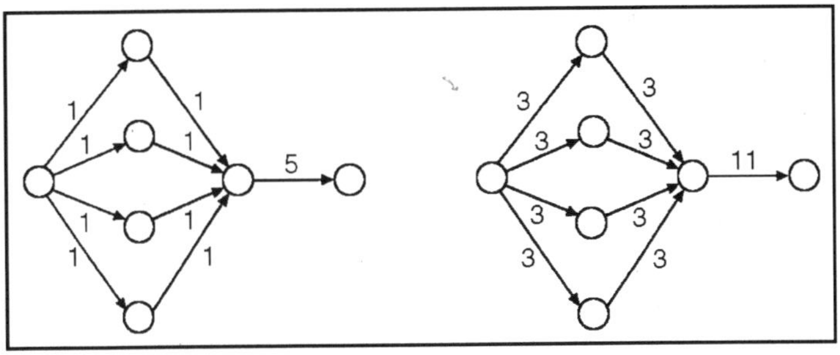

Fig. The Minnimum-cut Before/After

Why did this happen? Take an arbitrary cut. The value of the cut will be T times the original value of the cut, plus the number of edges in it. Thus, a non-minimum cut in the first place could become minimum if it contains just a few edges. This is because the constant might not have been chosen properly in the beginning, as is the case in the example above. We can fix this by choosing T large enough to neutralize the difference in the number of edges between cuts in the network. In the above example T = 4 would be enough, but to generalize, we take T = 10, one more than the number of edges in the original network, and one more than the number of edges that could possibly be in a minimum-cut. It is now true that a minimum-cut in the new network is minimum in the original network as well. However the converse is not true, and it is to our advantage. Notice how the difference between minimum cuts is now made by the number of edges in the cut. So we just find the min-cut in this new network to solve the problem correctly.

Let's illustrate some more the min-cut pattern: "An undirected graph is given. What is the minimum number of edges that should be removed in order to disconnect the graph?" In other words the problem asks us to remove some edges in order for two nodes to be separated. This should ring a bell - a minimum cut approach might work. So far we have only seen maximum flow in directed graphs, but now we are facing an undirected one. This should not be a very big problem though, as we can direct the graph by replacing every (undirected) edge x-y with two arcs: x-y and y-x. In this case the value of the min-cut is the number of edges in it, so we assign a 1 capacity to each of them. We are not asked to separate two given vertices, but rather to disconnect optimally any two vertices, so we must take every pair of vertices and treat them as the source and the sink and keep the best one from these minimum-cuts. An improvement can be made, however. Take one vertex, let's say vertex numbered 1. Because the graph should be disconnected, there must be another vertex unreachable from it. So it suffices to treat vertex 1 as the source and iterate through every other vertex and treat it as the sink.

What if instead of edges we now have to remove a minimum number of vertices to disconnect the graph? Now we are asked for a different min-cut, composed of vertices. We must somehow convert the vertices to edges though. Recall the problem above where we converted vertex-capacities to edge-capacities. The same trick works here. First "un-direct" the graph as in the previous example. Next double the number of vertices and deal edges the same way: an edge x-y is directed from the out-x vertex to in-y. Then convert the vertex to an edge by adding a 1-capacity arc from the in-vertex to the out-vertex. Now for each two vertices we must solve the sub-problem of minimally separating them. So, just like before take each pair of vertices and treat the out-vertex of one of them as the source and the in-vertex of the other one as the sink (this is because the only arc leaving the in-vertex is the one that goes to the out-vertex) and take the lowest value of the maximum flow. This time we can't improve in the quadratic number of steps needed, because the first vertex may be in an optimum solution and by always considering it as the source we lose such a case.

OVERVIEW OF DESIGNING ALGORITHMS

At first glance, the algorithms move-until-out and quick-sort have little in common. One processes structures; the other processes lists. One creates a new structure for the generative step; the other splits up a list into three pieces and recurs on two of them. In short, a comparison of the two examples of generative recursion suggests that the design of algorithms is an ad hoc activity and that it is impossible to come up with a general design recipe. A closer look, however, suggests a different picture.

First, even though we speak of algorithms as processes that solve problems, they are still functions that consume and produce data. In other words, we still choose data to represent a problem, and we must definitely understand the nature of our data if we wish to understand the process. Second, we describe the processes in terms of data, for example, "creating a new structure" or "partitioning a list of numbers."

Third, we always distinguish between input data for which it is trivial to produce a solution and those for which it is not. Fourth, the generation of problems is the key to the design of algorithms. Although the idea of how to generate a new problem might be independent of a data representation, it must certainly be implemented for whatever form of representation we choose for our problem. Finally, once the generated problems have been solved, the solutions must be combined with other values.

Let us examine the six general stages of our structural design recipe in light of our discussion:

Data Analysis and Design

The choice of a data representation for a problem often affects our thinking about the process. Sometimes the description of a process dictates a particular choice of representation. On other occasions, it is possible and worthwhile to explore alternatives. In any case, we must Analyse and define our data collections.

Contract, Purpose, Header

We also need a contract, a definition header, and a purpose statement. Since the generative step has no connection to the structure of the data definition, the purpose statement should not only specify what the function does but should also include a comment that explains in general terms how it works.

Function Examples

In our previous design recipes, the function examples merely specified which output the function should produce for some given input. For algorithms, examples should illustrate how the algorithm proceeds for some given input. This helps us to design, and readers to understand, the algorithm. For functions such as move-until-out the process is trivial and doesn't need more than a few words.

Template

Our discussion suggests a general template for algorithms:

```
  (define (generative-recursive-fun problem)
   cond
   [(trivially-solvable? problem)
   (determine-solution problem)]
   [else
   (combine-solutions
   ... problem...
     (generative-recursive-fun (generate-problem-
    1 problem))
      (generative-recursive-fun (generate-
problem-n problem)))]))
```

Definition

This chapter is only a suggestive blueprint, not a definitive shape. Each function in the template is to remind us that we need to think about the following four questions:

- What is a trivially solvable problem?
- What is a corresponding solution?
- How do we generate new problems that are more easily solvable than the original problem? Is there one new problem that we generate or are there several?
- Is the solution of the given problem the same as the solution of (one of) the new problems? Or, do we need to combine the solutions to create a solution for the original problem? And, if so, do we need anything from the original problem data?

To define the algorithm, we must express the answers to these four questions in terms of our chosen data representation.

Test

Once we have a complete function, we must also test it. As before, the goal of testing is to discover bugs and to eliminate them. Remember that testing cannot validate that the function works correctly for all possible inputs.

Termination

Unfortunately, the standard recipe is not good enough for the design of algorithms. Up to now, a function has always produced an output for any legitimate input. That is, the evaluation has always stopped. After all, by the nature of our recipe, each natural recursion consumes an immediate piece of the input, not the input itself. Because data is constructed in a hierarchical manner, this means that the input shrinks at every stage. Hence the function sooner or later consumes an atomic piece of data and stops.

With functions based on generative recursion, this is no longer true. The internal recursions don't consume an immediate component of the input but some new piece of data, which is generated from the input.

In addition, even the slightest mistake in translating the process description into a function definition may cause an infinite loop. The problem is most easily understood with an example. Consider the following definition of smaller-items, one of the two "problem generators" for quick-sort:

```
;; smaller-items: (listof number) number →       (listof
number)
;; to create a list with all those numbers on
alon
;; that are smaller than or equal to threshold
(define (smaller-items alon threshold)
  (cond
   [(empty? alon) empty]
   [else (if (⇐ (first alon) threshold)
         (cons (first alon) (smaller-items (rest
      alon) threshold))
         smaller-items (rest alon)
   threshold))]))
```

Instead of < it employs ⇐ to compare numbers. As a result, this function produces (list 5) when applied to (list 5) and 5.

The lesson from this example is that the design of algorithms requires one more step in our design recipe: a TERMINATION ARGUMENT, which explains why the process produces an output for every input and how the function implements this idea; or a warning, which explains when the process may not terminate.

For quick-sort, the argument might look like this:

At each step, quick-sort partitions the list into two sublists using smaller-items and larger-items. Each function produces a list that is smaller than the input (the second argument), even if the threshold (the first argument) is an item on the list. Hence each recursive application of quick-sortconsumes a strictly shorter list than the given one. Eventually, quick-sort receives and returns empty.

Without such an argument an algorithm must be considered incomplete. A good termination argument may on occasion also reveal additional termination cases. For example, (smaller-items N (list N)) and (larger-items N(list N)) always produce empty for any N. Therefore we know that quick-sort's answer for (list N) is (list N). To add this knowledge to quick-sort, we simply add a cond-clause:

```
(define (quick-sort alon)
(cond
```

```
[(empty? alon) empty]
[(empty? (rest alon)) alon]
[else (append
      (quick-sort (smaller-items alon (first
     alon)))
       (list (first alon))
       (quick-sort (larger-items alon (first
      alon))))]))
```

The condition (empty? (rest alon)) is one way to ask whether alon contains one item.

Example

Define the function tabulate-div, which accepts a number n and tabulates the list of all of its divisors, starting with 1 and ending in n. A number d is a divisior of a number n if the remainder of dividing n by d is 0, that is, (= (remainder n d) 0) is true. The smallest divisior of any number is 1; the largest one is the number itself.

Exercise

Develop the function merge-sort, which sorts a list of numbers in ascending order, using the following two auxiliary functions:

- The first one, make-singles, constructs a list of one-item lists from the given list of numbers. For example,
- (equal? (make-singles (list 2 5 9 3))
- (list (list 2) (list 5) (list 9) (list 3)))
- The second one, merge-all-Neighbours, merges pairs of Neighbouring lists. More specifically, it consumes a list of lists (of numbers) and merges Neighbours. For example,
- (equal? (merge-all-Neighbours (list (list 2) (list 5) (list 9) (list 3)))
- (list (list 2 5) (list 3 9)))
- (equal? (merge-all-Neighbours (list (list 2 5) (list 3 9)))
- (list (list 2 3 5 9)))

In general, this function yields a list that is approximately half as long as the input. Why is the output not always half as long as the input?

Structural Versus Generative Recursion

The template for algorithms is so general that it even covers functions based on structural recursion. Consider the version with one termination clause and one generation step:

```
(define (generative-recursive-fun problem)
  (cond
   [(trivially-solvable? problem)
   (determine-solution problem)]
```

```
    [else
      (combine-solutions
        problem
          (generative-recursive-fun (generate-
        problem problem)))]))
```

If we replace trivially-solvable? with empty? and generate-problem with rest, the outline is a template for a list-processing function:

```
(define (generative-recursive-fun problem)
  (cond
    [(empty? problem) (determine-solution
  problem)]
    [else
     (combine-solutions
      problem
       (generative-recursive-fun (rest
    problem)))]))
```

PROGRAMMES ANALYSIS OF COMPUTER ALGORITHMS

When analyzing a Programme in terms of efficiency, we want to look at questions such as, "How long does it take for the Programme to run?" and "Is there another approach that will get the answer more quickly?" Efficiency will always be less important than correctness; if you don't care whether a Programme works correctly, you can make it run very quickly indeed, but no one will think it's much of an achievement! On the other hand, a Programme that gives a correct answer after ten thousand years isn't very useful either, so efficiency is often an important issue. The term "efficiency" can refer to efficient use of almost any resource, including time, computer memory, disk space, or network bandwidth. In this section, however, we will deal exclusively with time efficiency, and the major question that we want to ask about a Programme is, how long does it take to perform its task?

It really makes little sense to classify an individual Programme as being "efficient" or "inefficient." It makes more sense to compare two (correct) Programmes that perform the same task and ask which one of the two is "more efficient," that is, which one performs the task more quickly. However, even here there are difficulties. The running time of a Programme is not well-defined. The run time can be different depending on the number and speed of the processors in the computer on which it is run and, in the case of Java, on the design of the Java Virtual Machine which is used to interpret the Programme. It can depend on details of the compiler which is used to translate the Programme from high-level language to machine language. Furthermore, the run time of a Programme depends on the size of the problem which the Programme has to solve. It takes a sorting Programme longer to sort 10000 items than it takes it to sort 100 items. When the run times of two Programmes are compared, it often happens that Programme A solves small problems faster than Programme B, while Programme B solves large problems faster than Programme A, so that it is simply not the case that one Programme is faster than the other in all cases. In spite of these difficulties, there is a field of computer science dedicated to analyzing the efficiency of Programmes. The field is known as Analysis of Algorithms. The focus is on algorithms, rather than on Programmes as such, to avoid having to deal with multiple implementations of the same algorithm written in different languages, compiled with different compilers, and running on different computers. Analysis of Algorithms is a mathematical field that abstracts away from these down-and-dirty details.

Still, even though it is a theoretical field, every working Programmemer should be aware of some of its techniques and results. This section is a very brief introduction to some of those techniques and results. Because this is not a mathematics book, the treatment will be rather informal. One of the main techniques of analysis of algorithms is asymptotic analysis. The term "asymptotic" here means basically "the tendency in the long run." An asymptotic analysis of an algorithm's run time looks at the question of how the run time depends on the size of the problem.

The analysis is asymptotic because it only considers what happens to the run time as the size of the problem increases without limit; it is not concerned with what happens for problems of small size or, in fact, for problems of any fixed finite size. Only what happens in the long run, as the problem size increases without limit, is important. Showing that Algorithm A is asymptotically faster than Algorithm B doesn't necessarily mean that Algorithm A will run faster than Algorithm B for problems of size 10 or size 1000 or even size 1000000 — it only means that if you keep increasing the problem size, you will eventually come to a point where Algorithm A is faster than Algorithm B. An asymptotic analysis is only a first approximation, but in practice it often gives important and useful information.

Using this notation, we might say, for example, that an algorithm has a running time that is $O(n^2)$ or $O(n)$ or $O(\log(n))$. These notations are read "Big-Oh of n squared," "Big-Oh of n," and "Big-Oh of log n" (where log is a logarithm function). More generally, we can refer to $O(f(n))$ ("Big-Oh of f of n"), where $f(n)$ is some function that assigns a positive real number to every positive integer n. The "n" in this notation refers to the size of the problem. Before you can even begin an asymptotic analysis, you need some way to measure problem size. Usually, this is not a big issue. For example, if the problem is to sort a list of items, then the problem size can be taken to be the number of items in the list. When the input to an algorithm is an integer, as in the case of an algorithm that checks whether a given positive integer is prime, the usual measure of the size of a problem is the number of bits in the input integer rather than the integer itself. More generally, the number of bits in the input to a problem is often a good measure of the size of the problem. To say that the running time of an algorithm is O(f(n)) means that for large values of the problem size, n, the running time of the algorithm is no bigger than some constant times f(n). (More rigorously, there is a number C and a positive integer M such that whenever n is greater than M, the run time is less than or equal to C*f(n).) The constant takes into account details such as the speed of the computer on which the algorithm is run; if you use a slower computer, you might have to use a bigger constant in the formula, but changing the constant won't change the basic fact that the run time is O(f(n)). The constant also makes it unnecessary to say whether we are measuring time in seconds, years, CPU cycles, or any other unit of measure; a change from one unit of measure to another is just multiplication by a constant. Note also that O(f(n)) doesn't depend at all on what happens for small problem sizes, only on what happens in the long run as the problem size increases without limit. To look at a simple example, consider the problem of adding up all the numbers in an array. The problem size, n, is the length of the array. Using A as the name of the array, the algorithm can be expressed in Java as:

```
total = 0;
for (int i = 0; i < n; i++)
total = total + A[i];
```

This algorithm performs the same operation, total = total + A[i], n times. The total time spent on this operation is a*n, where a is the time it takes to perform the operation once. Now, this is not the only thing that is done in the algorithm. The value of i is incremented and is compared to n each time through the loop.

This adds an additional time of b*n to the run time, for some constant b. Furthermore, i and total both have to be initialized to zero; this adds some constant amount c to the running time.

The exact running time would then be (a+b)*n+c, where the constants a, b, and c depend on factors such as how the code is compiled and what computer it is run on. Using the fact that c is less than or equal to c*n for any positive integer n, we can say that the run time is less than or equal to (a+b+c)*n. That is, the run time is less than or equal to a constant times n. By definition, this means that the run time for this algorithm is O(n).

If this explanation is too mathematical for you, we can just note that for large values of n, the c in the formula (a+b)*n+c is insignificant compared to the other term, (a+b)*n. We say that c is a "lower order term." When doing asymptotic analysis, lower order terms can be discarded. A rough, but correct, asymptotic analysis of the algorithm would go something like this: Each iteration of the for loop takes a certain constant amount of time. There are n iterations of the loop, so the total run time is a constant times n, plus lower order terms (to account for the initialization). Disregarding lower order terms, we see that the run time is O(n). Note that to say that an algorithm has run time O(f(n)) is to say that its run time is no bigger than some constant times f(n) (for large values of n). O(f(n)) puts an upper limit on the run time. However, the run time could be smaller, even much smaller. For example, if the run time is O(n), it would also be correct to say that the run time is $O(n^2)$ or even $O(n^{10})$. If the run time is less than a constant times n, then it is certainly less than the same constant times n^2 or n^{10}.

Of course, sometimes it's useful to have a lower limit on the run time. That is, we want to be able to say that the run time is greater than or equal to some constant times f(n) (for large values of n). The notation for this is Ω(f(n)), read "Omega of f of n." "Omega" is the name of a letter in the Greek alphabet, and Ω is the upper case version of that letter. (To be technical, saying that the run time of an algorithm is Ω(f(n)) means that there is a positive number C and a positive integer M such that whenever n is greater than M, the run time is greater than or equal to C*f(n).) O(f(n)) tells you something about the maximum amount of time that you might have to wait for an algorithm to finish; Ω(f(n)) tells you something about the minimum time. The algorithm for adding up the numbers in an array has a run time that is Ω(n) as well as O(n). When an algorithm has a run time that is both Ω(f(n)) and O(f(n)), its run time is said to be Θ(f(n)), read "Theta of f of n." (Theta is another letter from the Greek alphabet.) To say that the run time of an algorithm is Θ(f(n)) means that for large values of n, the run time is between a*f(n) and b*f(n), where a and b are constants (with b greater than a, and both greater than 0).

Let's look at another example. Consider the algorithm that can be expressed in Java in the following method:

```
  /**
  * Sorts the n array elements A[0], A[1]...,      A[n-1]
into increasing order.
  */
  public static simpleBubbleSort(int[] A, int      n) {
   for (int i = 0; i < n; i++) {
  // Do n passes through the array...
   for (int j = 0; j < n-1; j++) {
    if (A[j] > A[j+1]) {
  // A[j] and A[j+1] are out of order, so swap
them
      int temp = A[j];
      A[j] = A[j+1];
      A[j+1] = temp;
    }
   }
  }
}
```

Here, the parameter n represents the problem size. The outer for loop in the method is executed n times. Each time the outer for loop is executed, the inner for loop is exectued n-1 times, so the if statement is executed n*(n-1) times. This is n^2-n, but since lower order terms are not significant in an asymptotic analysis, it's good enough to say that the if statement is executed about n^2 times. In particular, the test A[j] > A[j+1] is executed about n^2times, and this fact by itself is enough to say that the run time of the algorithm is W(n^2), that is, the run time is at least some constant times n^2. Furthermore, if we look at other operations — the assignment statements, incrementing i and j, etc. — none of them are executed more than n^2 times, so the run time is also O(n^2), that is, the run time is no more than some constant times n^2. Since it is both W(n^2) and O(n^2), the run time of the simpleBubbleSort algorithm is Q(n^2). You should be aware that some people use the notation O(f(n)) as if it meant Θ(f(n)).

That is, when they say that the run time of an algorithm is O(f(n)), they mean to say that the run time is about equal to a constant times f(n). For that, they should use Θ(f(n)). Properly speaking, O(f(n)) means that the run time is less than a constant times f(n), possibly much less. So far, the analysis has ignored an important detail. We have looked at how run time depends on the problem size, but in fact the run time usually depends not just on the size of the problem but on the specific data that has to be processed. For example, the run time of a sorting algorithm can depend on the initial order of the items that are to be sorted, and not just on the number of items.

To account for this dependency, we can consider either the worst case run time analysis or the average case run time analysis of an algorithm. For a worst case run time analysis, we consider all possible problems of size n and look at the longest possible run time for all such problems. For an average case analysis, we consider all possible problems of size n and look at the average of the run times for all such problems. Usually, the average case analysis assumes that all problems of size n are equally likely to be encountered, although this is not always realistic — or even possible in the case where there is an infinite number of different problems of a given size. In many cases, the average and the worst case run times are the same to within a constant multiple. This means that as far as asymptotic analysis is concerned, they are the same. That is, if the average case run time is O(f(n)) or Θ(f(n)), then so is the worst case. However, later in the book, we will encounter a few cases where the average and worst case asymptotic analyses differ.

So, what do you really have to know about analysis of algorithms to read the rest of this book? We will not do any rigorous mathematical analysis, but you should be able to follow informal discussion of simple cases such as the examples that we have looked at in this section. Most important, though, you should have a feeling for exactly what it means to say that the running time of an algorithm is O(f(n)) or Θ(f(n)) for some common functions f(n). The main point is that these notations do not tell you anything about the actual numerical value of the running time of the algorithm for any particular case. They do not tell you anything at all about the running time for small values of n. What they do tell you is something about the rate of growth of the running time as the size of the problem increases. Suppose you compare two algorithms that solve the same problem. The run time of one algorithm is $\Theta(n^2)$, while the run time of the second algorithm is $\Theta(n^3)$. What does this tell you? If you want to know which algorithm will be faster for some particular problem of size, say, 100, nothing is certain. As far as you can tell just from the asymptotic analysis, either algorithm could be faster for that particular case — or in any particular case. But what you can say for sure is that if you look at larger and larger problems, you will come to a point where the $\Theta(n^2)$ algorithm is faster than the $\Theta(n^3)$ algorithm.

Furthermore, as you continue to increase the problem size, the relative advantage of the $\Theta(n^2)$ algorithm will continue to grow. There will be values of n for which the $\Theta(n^2)$ algorithm is a thousand times faster, a million times faster, a billion times faster, and so on. This is because for any positive constants a and b, the function $a*n^3$ grows faster than the function $b*n^2$ as n gets larger. (Mathematically, the limit of the ratio of $a*n^3$ to $b*n^2$ is infinite as n approaches infinity.)

This means that for "large" problems, a $\Theta(n^2)$ algorithm will definitely be faster than a $\Theta(n^3)$ algorithm. You just don't know — based on the asymptotic analysis alone — exactly how large "large" has to be. In practice, in fact, it is likely that the $\Theta(n^2)$ algorithm will be faster even for fairly small values of n, and absent other information you would generally prefer a $\Theta(n^2)$ algorithm to a $\Theta(n^3)$ algorithm. So, to understand and apply asymptotic analysis, it is essential to have some idea of the rates of growth of some common functions. For the power functions n, n^2, n^3, n^4..., the larger the exponent, the greater the rate of growth of the function.

Exponential functions such as 2^n and 10^n, where the n is in the exponent, have a growth rate that is faster than that of any power function. In fact, exponential functions grow so quickly that an algorithm whose run time grows exponentially is almost certainly impractical even for relatively modest values of n, because the running time is just too long. Another function that often turns up in asymptotic analysis is the logarithm function, log(n). There are actually many different logarithm functions, but the one that is usually used in computer science is the so-called logarithm to the base two, which is defined by the fact that $\log(2^x) = x$ for any number x. (Usually, this function is written $\log_2(n)$, but I will leave out the subscript 2, since I will only use the base-two logarithm in this book.) The logarithm function grows very slowly. The growth rate of log(n) is much smaller than the growth rate of n. The growth rate of n*log(n) is a little larger than the growth rate of n, but much smaller than the growth rate of n^2.

IMPORTANT FACTORS OF COMPARING THE ALGORITHMS

There are two important factors when measuring the performance of a sorting algorithm. The algorithms have to compare the magnitude of different elements and they have to move the different elements around. So counting the number of comparisons and the number of exchanges or moves made by an algorithm offer useful performance measures. When sorting large record structures, the number of exchanges made may be the principal performance criterion, since exchanging two records will involve a lot of work. When sorting a simple array of integers, then the number of comparisons will be more important.

It has been said that the only thing going for the bubble (exchange) sort is its catchy name. The logic of the algorithm is simple to understand and it is fairly easy to Programme. It can also be Programmemed to detect when it has finished sorting. The selection sort, by comparison, always goes through the same amount of work regardless of the data and the quick sort performs particularly badly with ordered data. However, in general the bubble sort is a very inefficient algorithm.

The insertion sort is a little better and whilst it cannot detect that it has finished sorting, the logic of the algorithm means that it comes to a rapid conclusion when dealing with sorted data. The selection sort is a good one to use with students. It is intuitive and very simple to Programme. It offers quite good performance, its particular strength being the small number of exchanges needed. For a given number of data items, the selection sort always goes through a set number of comparisons and exchanges, so its performance is predictable.

The first three algorithms all offer O(n2) performance, that is sorting times increase with the square of the number of elements being sorted. That means that if you double the number of elements being sorted, then there will be a four-fold increase in the time taken. Ten times more elements increases the time taken by a factor of 100!

This is not a problem with small data sets, but with hundreds or thousands of elements, this becomes very significant. With most large data sets, the quick sort is a vastly superior algorithm (although as you might expect, it is much more complex), as the table below shows.

RANDOM DATA SET: NUMBER

Sort/Elements	50	100	200	300	400	500
Selection Sort	1225	4950	19900	44850	79800	124750
Exchange Sort	1410	5335	20300	45650	79866	126585
Insertion Sort	1391	5399	20473	44449	78779	123715
Quick Sort	399	990	1954	3384	5066	6256

It should be pointed out that the methods above all belong to one family, they are all internal sorting algorithms. This means that they can only be used when the entire data structure to be sorted can be held in the computer's main memory. There will be situations where this is not possible, for example when sorting a very large transaction file which is stored on, say, magnetic tape or disc.

DATA STRUCTURE

The art of Programmeming beyond this simple beginning depends on inventing, or should reinventing, sophisticated data structures. The problem is where to begin and the general consensus is that the stack is where it's at.

A stack is exactly what it sounds like. Make a stack of cards, say, on a table and you have everything you need to know about a stack. What are the basic stack operations – you can put a new card on the top of the stack and you can take a card off the top of the stack. As long are you aren't cheating and dealing from the bottom (that would make it a data structure called a deque) putting something on the top and taking something off the top are the only two stack operations allowed. Usually these two operations are called "push" and "pull" or "push" and "pop" but what you call them doesn't really matter as long as you understand what is going on.

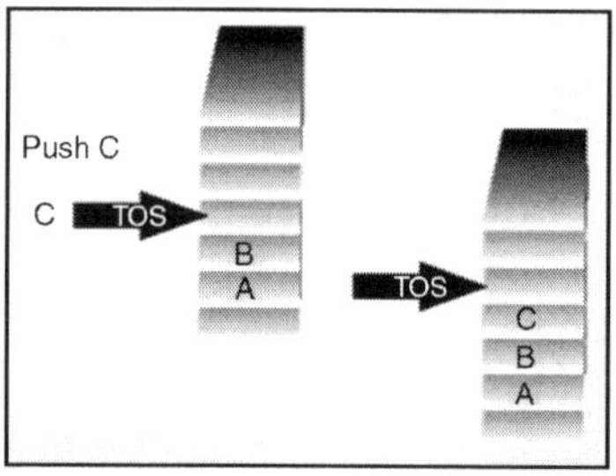

Pushing C onto a stack stores it where the TOS pointer indicates

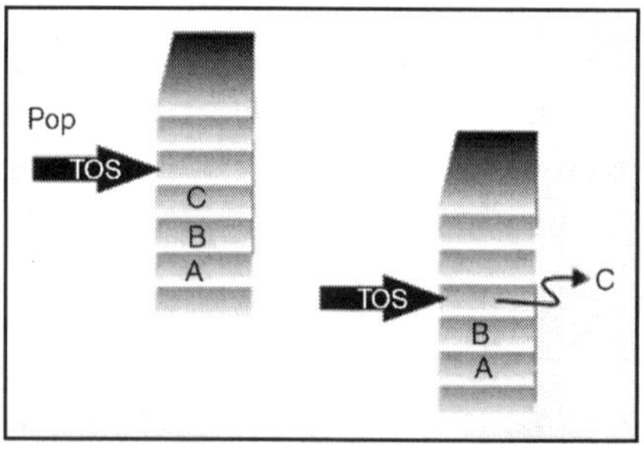

Popping the stack retrieves the top data item and moves the TOS down one

If we have a stack and we do Push A, Push B and Push C what do you think you get if we next do a Pop? If your answer is C you understand how a stack works. Stacks are interesting because they can be used to alter the order of things. You stack A, B and C and you get back C, B and then A. It reverses the order without you having to do anything and this is very useful. This accounts for the other name for a stack – a Last In First Out stack or LIFO stack. In fact this order changing ability is such a powerful property that you can build computers that have no other memory than a stack and no other storage operations than push and pop. You can even create Programmeming languages that have nothing but a stack as their single data structure and all of their commands refer to the stack. Even though you can have stack-oriented languages there are few popular or common languages that have stacks as standard – you have to create your own using whatever they provide. If you know how fine, if not then you have to use something less appropriate.

So, how is it done? All you need is an array and a variable to act as a pointer to the top of stack or TOS as it is usually known. The array simply has to be big enough to hold the maximum number of items. The pointer is simply set initially to the start of the array. You might set up the stack as:

```
Dim Stack(10)
Pointer=1
```

To push something on to the stack the operation is:

```
Stack(Pointer)=something
Pointer=Pointer+1
```

To pop something off the stack the operation is:

```
Pointer=Pointer-1
Something=Stack(Pointer)
```

If you want to get picky about stacks you can argue the point of whether the pointer should point to the item on the top of the stack or to the next free space on the stack. Experts prefer to have the pointer to the item on the top of stack rather than the next free space. About the only thing that can go wrong with a stack is that it runs out of space i.e. the stack pointer goes beyond the end of the array or that it under runs, i.e. the user of the stack attempts to pop something off the stack when there isn't anything to pop.

OBJECTS

Of course the modern view isn't that the stack is a data structure – it's an object. That is, something with methods, i.e. pop and push, and an existence that goes beyond mere data. If "CStack" is a class based implementation of a stack then in an object-oriented language we can create as many stacks as we like:

```
Dim MyStack1 As CStack
Dim MyStack2 As CStack
```

These would be used something like:

```
MyStack1.push "A"
```

or

```
Data=MyStack2.pop
```

where it is assumed that the methods are push and pop.

Notice that the object-based implementation has the advantage that you don't need to ask how the stack works, what's inside the object if you like. This means that the Programmemer can implement the internal working any way that they want and they can even change things without the outside world being any the wiser. Objects are good...

Queue & the Deque

Once you have seen a stack you can invent all of the stack-like objects that have ever been thought of, and some. For example, a queue or a First In First Out (FIFO) stack is simply an array with two pointers – one to the start and one to end of the queue. Anything added to the queue goes to the end anything taken from the queue comes from the front.

In object-oriented terms the queue has two methods, Join and Leave. A queue doesn't change the order that things are stored in and it's mostly useful to slow things down so that they can be processed when the Programme is ready. (Hardware people often call queues "buffers".)

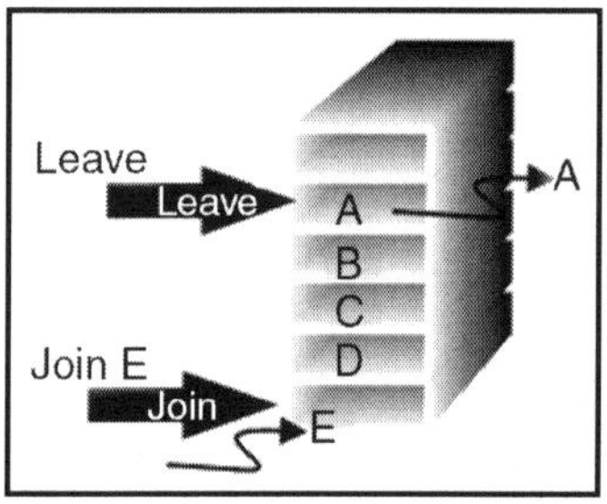

A queue has two pointers – one to the start of the queue and one to the end A deque is a queue that you can join and leave from the front or the back and it has four methods, JoinFront, JoinEnd, LeaveFront and LeaveEnd. You are probably getting the idea by now. This sort of data structure simply has methods that adds new things and methods that retrieve new things according to when they were added.

Trees

The tree is probably the most important of the really advanced data structures and in many ways it's the most complicated and sophisticated. To be abstract for the moment, a tree consists of a set of nodes – the places where the branches do their branching – and the branches that connect the nodes. The idea, or rather the picture, that you should have in your head of a branching tree-like structure is simple enough, actually implementing it in computer terms is not quite as straightforward. To start with the nodes are the things that we work with. A node has space to store the data in the tree, a person's name for example, and it also stores "pointers" to the nodes that are connected to its child nodes. The big problem is how many pointers? In general a tree can have nodes with as many child nodes as you care to imagine and this is difficult to implement. As a result we like trees that have a fixed number of child nodes – 2 say gives us the binary tree. In this case, i.e. a binary tree, we can refer to the "right child node" and the "left child node" or just the "right" and "left" nodes. A tree also has a first or "root node" that everything else grows from.

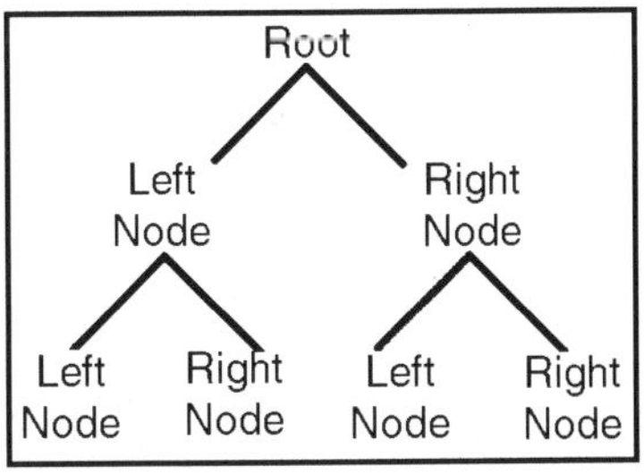

In a binary tree each node has two child nodes – one left and one right.

Now we can invent an object that behaves like a node in a binary tree, i.e. an object with two properties - left and right child nodes, and a single data property, which stores the value at the node.

We can now build a tree by creating a root node:

```
Dim root As New Node
```

and then add extra nodes as required:

```
Root.LeftNode=New Node
Root.RightNode=New Node
```

How do we get at these nodes so that we can grow the tree another level? Easy we just continue the same notation:

```
Root.LeftNode.LeftNode=New Node
  Root.LeftNode.RightNode=New Node
```

and so on.

Of course we are also assuming that nodes have a data property which can be used to store whatever you want at each node. For example,

```
Root.LeftNode.data= "john"
```

would store the indicated name at the first left child node from the root. You should be able to see how to build up a data structure that corresponds to a family tree in which each "node" gives rise to just two offspring.

If you want more, or even a variable number of, offspring at each node then it works in the same sort of way but you need a collection of pointers to the child nodes and this is awkward to write down. There is also the small problem of working with trees. Clearly you can keep on writing out Left Node.Right Node.Right Node. Left Node type names to specify a node of your choice – it's too clumsy. What actually happens in practice is that a pointer to a node is used as the "current" node and this moves its way down the tree by being set to the current nodes left or right child:

```
CurrentNode=CurrentNode.LeftNode
```

And so on. You can generalise this to more than two child nodes and even work out ways of writing Programmes that do standard tasks such as visiting every node in a tree. This is again another area where things can seem complicated because you can ask that every node is visited in a particular order.

For example going down each branch as far as possible before starting again to go down the next branch is called"depth first", while visiting all nodes at the same depth before going deeper, is called"breadth first". The jargon also gets more impressive - we talk of"traversing the tree" and eventually you will encounter the fact that trees and"recursion" go together. Recursion is a whole topic in its own right and the source of the only good computer science joke I know - dictionary definition of recursion"Recursion - see recursion".

What are trees used for? Well, everything from keeping track of where files are stored on a disk drive to analysing natural language and applications in artificial intelligence. It's worth point out that XML is a data language that can only describe tree structures so the idea must be powerful. You can't Programme for long without meeting trees.

DATA STRUCTURES DISJOINT SETS

Many times the efficiency of an algorithm depends on the data structures used in the algorithm. A wise choice in the structure you use in solving a problem can reduce the time of execution, the time to implement the algorithm and the amount of memory used. During SRM competitions we are limited to a time limit of 2 seconds and 64 MB of memory, so the right data structure can help you remain in competition. While some Data Structures have been covered before, in this article we'll focus on data structures for disjoint sets.

THE PROBLEM

Let's consider the following problem: In a room are N persons, and we will define two persons are friends if they are directly or indirectly friends. If A is a friend with B, and B is a friend with C, then A is a friend of C too. A group of friends is a group of persons where any two persons in the group are friends. Given the list of persons that are directly friends find the number of groups of friends and the number of persons in each group. For example N = 5 and the list of friends is: 1-2, 5-4, and 5-1. Here is the figure of the graph that represents the groups of friends. 1 and 2 are friends, then 5 and 4 are friends, and then 5 and 1 are friends, but 1 is friend with 2; therefore 5 and 2 are friends, etc.

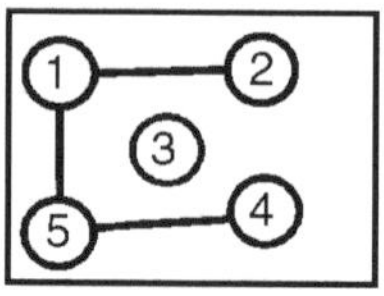

In the end there are 2 groups of friends: one group is {1, 2, 4, 5}, the other is {3}.

The Solution

This problem can be solved using BFS, but let's see how to solve this kind of problem using data structures for disjoint sets. First of all: a disjoint-set data structure is a structure that maintains a collection S_1, S_2, S_3, ..., S_n of dynamic disjoint sets. Two sets are disjoint if their intersection is null. For example set {1, 2, 3} and set {1, 5, 6} aren't disjoint because they have in common {1}, but the sets {1, 2, 3} and {5, 6} are disjoint because their intersection is null. In a data structure of disjoint sets every set contains a representative, which is one member of the set.

Let's see how things will work with sets for the example of the problem. The groups will be represented by sets, and the representative of each group is the person with the biggest index. At the beginning there are 5 groups (sets): {1}, {2}, {3}, {4}, {5}. Nobody is anybody's friend and everyone is the representative of his or her own group.

The next step is that 1 and 2 become friends, this means the group containing 1 and the group with 2 will become one group. This will give us these groups: {1, 2}, {3}, {4}, {5}, and the representative of the first group will become 2. Next, 5 and 4 become friends. The groups will be {1,2}, {3}, {4, 5}. And in the last step 5 and 1 become friends and the groups will be {1, 2, 4, 5}, {3}. The representative of the first group will be 5 and the representative for second group will be 3.

(We will see why we need representatives later). At the end we have 2 sets, the first set with 4 elements and the second with one, and this is the answer for the problem example: 2 groups, 1 group of 4 and one group of one. Perhaps now you are wondering how you can check if 2 persons are in the same group.

This is where the use of the representative elements comes in. Let's say we want to check if 3 and 2 are in the same group, we will know this if the representative of the set that contains 3 is the same as the representative of the set that contains 2. One representative is 5 and the other one is 3; therefore 3 and 2 aren't in same groups of friends.

SOME OPERATIONS

Let's define the following operations:

- *Create-set(x)*: Creates a new set with one element {x}.
- *Merge-sets(x, y)*: Merge into one set the set that contains element x and the set that contains element y (x and y are in different sets). The original sets will be destroyed.
- *Find-set(x)*: Returns the representative or a pointer to the representative of the set that contains element x.

Solution Using these Operations

Let's see the solution for our problem using these operations:

```
Read N;
for (each person x from 1 to N) CREATE-SET(x)
for (each pair of friends (x y)) if (FIND-      SET(x)
!= FIND-SET(y)) MERGE-SETS(x, y)
```

Now if we want to see if 2 persons (x, y) are in same group we check if FIND-SET(x) == FIND-SET(y).

We will Analyse the running time of the disjoint-set data structure in terms of N and M, where N is the number of times that CREATE-SET(x) is called and M is the total number of times that CREATE-SET(x), MERGE-SETS(x, y) and FIND-SET(x) are called.

Since the sets are disjoint, each time MERGE-SETS(x, y) is called one set will be created and two will be destroyed, giving us one less set.

If there are n sets after n-1 calls of MERGE-SETS(x,y) there will remain only one set. That's why the number of MERGE-SETS(x,y) calls is less than or equal to the number of CREATE-SET(x) operations.

IMPLEMENTATION WITH LINKED LISTS

One way to implement disjoint set data structures is to represent each set by a linked list. Each element (object) will be in a linked list and will contain a pointer to the next element in the set and another pointer to the representative of the set.

Here is a figure of how the example of the problem will look like after all operations are made. The blue arrows are the pointers to the representatives and the black arrows are the pointers to the next element in the sets. Representing sets with linked lists we will obtain a complexity of O(1) for CREATE-SET(x) and FIND-SET(x). CREATE-SET(x) will just create a new linked list whose only element (object) is x, the operation FIND-SET(x) just returns the pointer to the representative of the set that contains element (object) x.

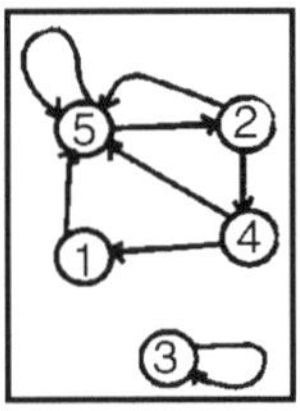

Now let's see how to implement the MERGE-SETS(x, y) operations. The easy way is to append x's list onto the end of y's list. The representative of the new set is the representative of the original set that contained y. We must update the pointer to the representative for each element (object) originally on x's list, which takes linear time in terms of the length of x's list. It's easy to prove that, in the worst case, the complexity of the algorithm will be O(M^2) where M is the number of operations MERGE-SETS(x, y). With this implementation the complexity will average O(N) per operation where N represents the number of elements in all sets.

WEIGHTED UNION HEURISTIC

Let's see how a heuristic will make the algorithm more efficient. The heuristic is called "a weighted-union heuristic." In this case, let's say that the representative of a set contains information about how many objects (elements) are in that set as well. The optimization is to always append the smaller list onto the longer and, in case of ties, append arbitrarily. This will bring the complexity of the algorithm to O(M + NlogN) where M is the number of operations (FIND-SET, MERGE-SETS, CREATE-SETS) and N is the number of operations CREATE-SETS. I will not prove why the complexity is this, but if you are interested you can find the proof in the resources mentioned at the end of the article. So far we reach an algorithm to solve the problem in O(M + NlogN) where N is the number of persons and M is the number of friendships and a memory of O(N). Still the BFS will solve the problem in O(M + N) and memory of O(N + M). We can see that we have optimized the memory but not the execution time.

Next Step: Root Trees

The next step is to see what we can do for a faster implementation of disjoint set data structures. Let's represent sets by rooted trees, with each node containing one element and each tree representing one set. Each element will point only to its parent and the root of each tree is the representative of that set and its own parent. Let's see, in steps, how the trees will look for the example from the problem above.

Step 1: Nobody is anybody friend

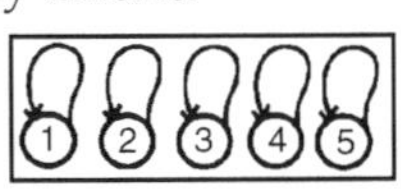

We have 5 trees and each tree has a single element, which is the root and the representative of that tree.

Step 2: 1 and 2 are friends, MERGE-SETS(1, 2):

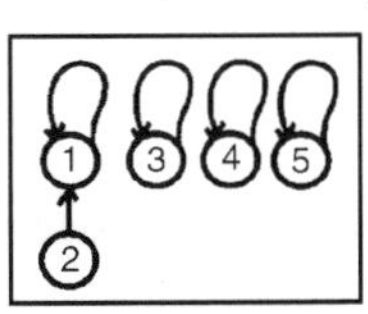

The operation made is MERGE-SETS(1, 2). We have 4 trees one tree contain 2 elements and have the root 1. The other trees have a single element.

Step 3: 5 and 4 are friends, MERGE-SETS(5, 4)

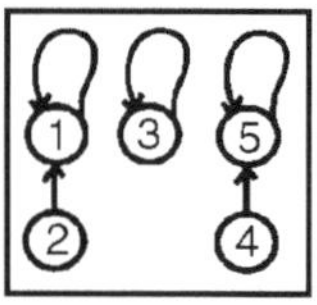

The operation made is MERGE-SETS(5, 4). Now we have 3 trees, 2 trees with 2 elements and one tree with one element.

Step 4: 5 and 1 are friends, MERGE-SETS(5, 1)

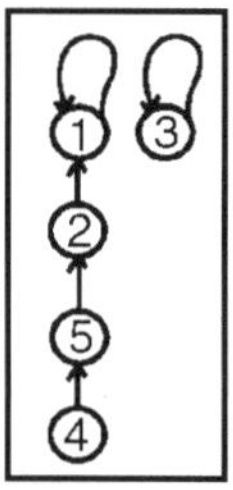

The operation made is MERGE-SETS(5, 1). Now we have 2 trees, one tree has 4 elements and the other one has only one element. As we see so far the algorithm using rooted trees is no faster than the algorithm using linked lists.

Two Heburistics

Next we will see how, by using two heuristics, we will achieve the asymptotically fastest disjoint set data structure known so far, which is almost linear in terms of the number of operations made. These two heuristics are called "union by rank" and "path compression." The idea in the first heuristic "union by rank" is to make the root of the tree with fewer nodes point to the root of the tree with more nodes. For each node, we maintain a rankthat approximates the logarithm of the sub-tree size and is also an upper bound on the height of the node. When MERGE-SETS(x, y) is called, the root with smaller rank is made to point to the root with larger rank. The idea in the second heuristic "path compression," which is used for operation FIND-SET(x), is to make each node on the find path point directly to the root. This will not change any ranks.

To implement a disjoint set forest with these heuristics, we must keep track of ranks. With each node x, we keep the integer value *rank[x],* which is bigger than or equal to the number of edges in the longest path between node x and a sub-leaf. When CREATE-SET(x) is called the initial rank[x] will be 0. When a MERGE-SETS(x, y) operation is made then the root of higher rank will become the parent of the root of lower rank – or, in case of tie, we arbitrarily choose one of the roots as the parent and increment its rank.

Let's see how the algorithm will look.

```
Let P[x] = the parent of node x.
CREATE-SET(x)
```

```
      P[x]  = x
      rank[x]  = 0
      MERGE-SETS(x, y)
      PX = FIND-SET(X)
      PY =FIND-SET(Y)
      If (rank[PX] > rank[PY]) P[PY] = PX
      Else P[PX] = PY
      If (rank[PX] == rank[PY]) rank[PY] =
rank[PY] + 1
```

And the last operation looks like:

```
    FIND-SET(x)
      If (x != P[x]) p[x] = FIND-SET(P[X])
    Return P[X]
```

Now let's see how the heuristics helped the running time. If we use only the first heuristic "union by rank" then we will get the same running time we achieved with the weighted union heuristic when we used lists for representation. When we use both "union by rank" and "path compression," the worst running time is O(m α(m,n)), where α(m,n) is the very slowly growing inverse of Ackermann function. In application α(m,n) ⇐ 4 that why we can say that the running time is linear in terms of m, in practical situations.

Back to the Problem

The problem from the beginning of the article is solvable in O(N + M) and O(N) for memory using disjoint-set data structure. The difference for time execution is not big if the problem is solved with BFS, but we don't need to keep in memory the vertices of the graph. Let's see if the problem was like: In a room are N persons and you had to handle Q queries. A query is of the form "x y 1," meaning that x is friends with y, or "x y 2" meaning that we are asked to output if x and y are in same group of friends at that moment in time. In this case the solution with disjoint-set data structure is the fastest, giving a complexity of O(N + Q).

Practice

Disjoint-set data structures are a helpful tool for use in different algorithms, or even for solving problems in an SRM. They are efficient and use small amount of memory. They are useful in applications like "Computing the shorelines of a terrain," "Classifying a set of atoms into molecules or fragments," "Connected component labeling in image analysis," and others.

To practice what you've learned, try to solve GrafixMask – the Division 1 500 from SRM211. The idea is to keep track of all the blocks and consider each grid point as a node. Next, take all the nodes that aren't blocked and let (x, y) be the coordinate of the left, right, down or up node, and if (x, y) is not blocked then you do the operation MERGE-SETS(node, node2). You should also try to determine how disjoint-set data structures can be used in the solution of RoadReconstruction from SRM 356. Disjoint-set data structures can also be used inTopographicalImage from SRM 210 and PathFinding, from SRM 156.

OPERATIONS ON SETS

Let x be an object. We wish to support the following operations:

- MAKE-SET(x) creates a new set whose only member is pointed by x; Note that x is not in the other sets.
- UNION(x,y) unites two dynamic sets containing objects x and y, say Sx and Sy, into a new set that Sx *" Sy, assuming that Sx)" Sy =";
- FIND-SET(x) returns a pointer to the representative of the set containing x.
- INSERT(a,S) inserts an object a to S, and returns S*"{a}.
- DELETE(a,S) deletes an object a from S, and returns S-{a}.
- SPLIT(a,S) partitions the objects of S into two sets S1 and S2 such that S1 ={bbd"a&b"S}, and S2 =S- S1.
- MINIMUM(S) returns the minimum object in S.

DISJOINT-SET DATA STRUCTURES

Here we show two application examples:

- Connected components (CCs)
- Minimum Spanning Trees (MSTs)

Algorithm for Connected Components

Connected components (G)

```
for each v"V
do MAKE-SET (v)
for every edge (u,v)"E
do if FIND-SET (u) '" FIND-SET (v)
then UNION (u,v)
Same-Components (u,v)
if FIND-SET (u) = FIND-SET (v)
    then return TRUE
return FALSE
```

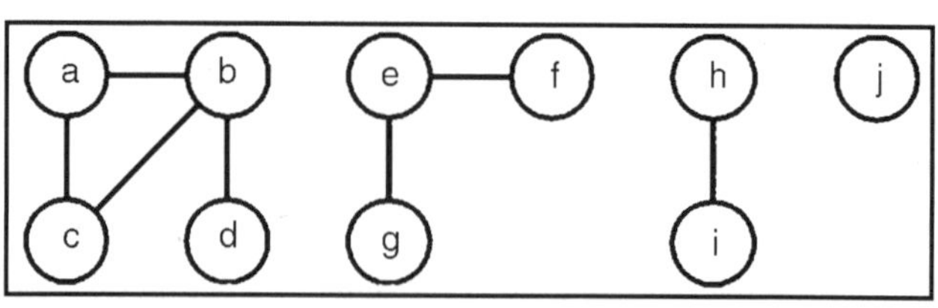

Fig: A Graph with four Connected Components: {a,b,c,d}, {e,f,g}, {h,i}, and {j}.

Table. This Table Shows the State of the Collection of Disjoint Sets as Each Edge is Processed. The Processed Edge is Listed on the Left and the Rest of the Columns show the State of the Collection.

Edge processed	Collection of disjoint sets									
Initial sets	{a}	{b}	{c}	{d}	{e}	{f}	{g}	{h}	{i}	{j}
(b,d)	{a}		{c}		{e}	{f}	{g}	{h}	{i}	{j}
(e,g)	{a}	{b,d}	{c}		{e,g}	{f}		{h}	{i}	{j}
(a,c)	{a,c}	{b,d}			{e,g}	{f}		{h}	{i}	{j}
(h,i)	{a,c}	{b,d}			{e,g}	{f}		{h,i}		{j}
(a,b)	{a,b,c,d}				{e,g}	{f}		{h,i}		{j}
(e,f)	{a,b,c,d}				{e,f,g}			{h,i}		{j}
(b,c)	{a,b,c,d}				{e,f,g}			{h,i}		{j}

DISJOINT SET REPRESENTATION

The Linked-list Representation

A set can be represented by a linked list. In this representation, each node has a pointer to the next node and a pointer to the first node.

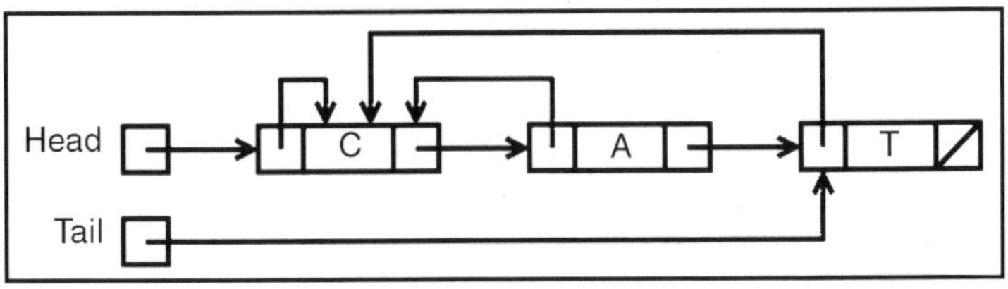

Fig. Linked-list Representation.

Each disjoint set can be represented by a linked-list. Each node has a pointer to the head node and a pointer to the next node.

Consider the following operation sequence:

```
MAKE-SET (x1),
MAKE-SET (x2),
:,
MAKE-SET (xn-1),
MAKE-SET (xn),
UNION (x1, x2),
UNION (x2, x3),:,
UNION (xn-1, xn).
```

What's the total time complexity of the above operations?

A Weighted-union Heuristic

Assume that the representative of each set maintains the number of objects in the set, and always merge the smaller list to the larger list, then

Theorem

Using the linked list representation of disjoint sets and the weighted-union heuristic, a sequence of m MAKE-SET, Union, and Find_Set operations, n of which are MAKE-SET, takes O(m+nlogn) time.

Hint: observe that for any kd"n, after x's representative pointer has been updated #logk# times, the resulting set containing x must have at least k members.

DISJOINT SET FORESTS

A faster implementation of disjoint sets is through the rooted trees, with each node containing one member and each tree representing one set. Each member in the tree has only one parent.

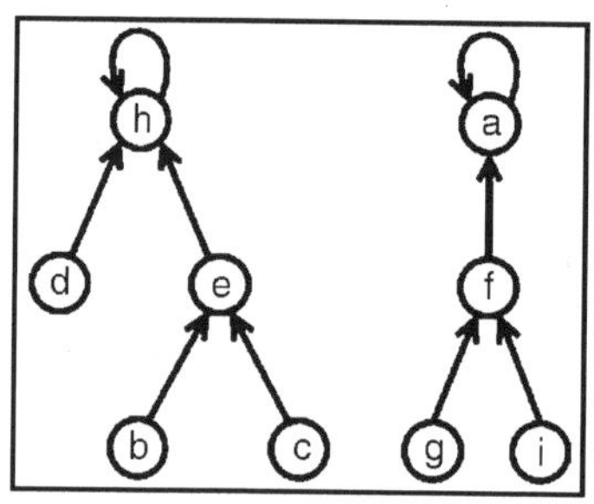

Fig. Rooted Tree Representation of Disjoint Sets.

Each tree has a "representative" h for the left tree and a for the right tree.

Heuristics for Disjoint Set Operations

- Union by rank.
- Path compression

The idea of union by rank is to make the root of the tree with fewer nodes point to the root of the tree with more nodes. Rather than explicitly keeping track of the size of the subtree rooted at each node, for each node we maintain a *rank* that approximates the logarithm of the subtree size and is also an upper bound on the height of the node.

Time complexity: O(mlogn), assuming that there are m union operations. Path compression is quite simple and very effective. We use this approach during FIND-SET operations to make each node on the path point directly to the root. Path compression does not change any ranks.

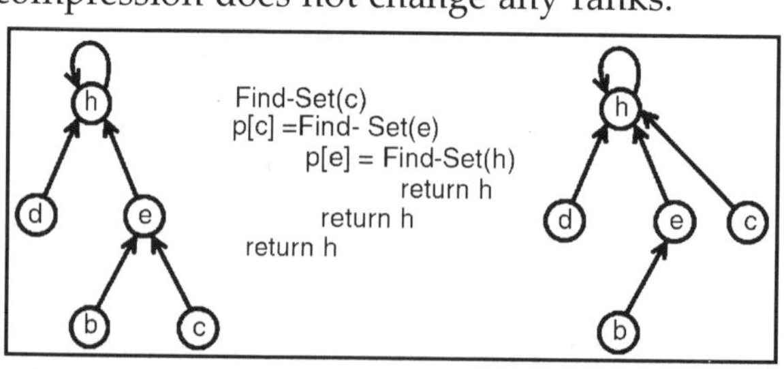

Fig. Path Compression Takes Place During the FIND-SET Operation.

This works by recursing from the given input node up to the root of the tree, forming a *path*. Then the root is returned and assigned as the parent for each node in *path*. The parent of c after FIND-SET (c) is h.

Time complexity: Θ(f log1+f/n) n) if fe"n and Θ(n+flogn) otherwise, assume that there are n MAKE-SET operations and f FIND-SET operations.

```
MAKE-SET (x)
p[x] ← x
rank[x] ← 0
FIND-SET (x)
if x'"p[x]
    then p[x] ← FIND-SET (p[x])
return p[x]
UNION (x,y)
 LINK(FIND-SET (x), FIND-SET (y))
 LINK (x,y)
if rank[x]>rank[y]
    then p[y] ← x
     else p[x] ← y
            if rank[x]=rank[y]
               then rank[y] ← rank[y]+1
```

where rank[x] is the height of x in the tree. If both of the above methods are used together, the time complexity is O(mα(m,n)).

The Rank Properties

- rank[x] ≤ rank[p[x]]
- for any tree root x, size(x) ≥ 2rank[x] (Link operation)
- for any integer r, there are at most n/ 2r nodes of rank r
- each node has rank at most $\lfloor \log n \rfloor$, assuming there are at n objects involved.

METHODOLOGY AUGMENT OF DATA STRUCTURES

There are some Programmeming situations that can be perfectly solved with standard data structures such as a linked lists, hash tables, or binary search trees. Many others require a dash of creativity. Only in rare situations will you need to create an entirely new type of data structure, though. More often, it will suffice to augment (to modify) an existing data structure by storing additional information in it.

You can then Programme new operations for the data structure to support the desired application. Augmenting a data structure is not always straightforward, however, since the added information must be updated and maintained by the ordinary operations on the data structure. Data structure that supports general order-statistic operations on a dynamic set. It's called dynamic order statistics. Any order statistic could be retrieved in O(n) time from an unordered set. How red-black trees can be modified so that any order statistic can be determined in O(lg(n)) time. It presents two algorithms OS-Select(i), which returns i-th smallest item in a dynamic set, and OS-Rank(x), which returns rank (position) of element x in sorted order.

General methodology of how to augment a data structure.

Augmenting a data structure can be broken into four steps:

- Choosing an underlying data structure.
- Determining additional information to be maintained in the underlying data structure.
- Verifying that the additional information can be maintained for the basic modifying operations (insert, delete, rotate, etc.) on the underlying data structure.
- Developing new operations.

The second part of the lecture applies this methodology to construct a data structure called interval trees. This data structure maintains a dynamic set of elements, with each element x containing an interval. Interval is simply pair of numbers (low, high). For example, a time interval from 3 o'clock to 7 o'clock is a pair (3, 7).

Lecture gives an algorithm called Interval-Search(x), which given a query interval x, quickly finds an interval in the set that overlaps it. Time complexity of this algorithm is O(lg(n)).

ABOUT LUCTURE

The lecture is motivated by two things:

- The implementation of ADTs that extend standard ADTs by one or more additional operations;
- Application in which data "live in" various data structures simultaneously.

Augmentation is a process by which one adds fields to the nodes as necessary.

Augmenting a data structure can be broken into four steps:

- choosing an underlying data structure
- determining additional information to be maintained in the underlying data structure
- verifying that the additional information can be efficiently maintained for the basic modifying operations on the underlying data structure
- developing new operations

DYNAMIC ORDER-STATISTIC TREES

ADT: set S; Dictionary operations (*Insert, Delete, Search*) + two additional operations:

- *Rank(S,x)*: Returns rank of node x (smallest rank is 1)
- *Select(S, i)*: Select ith smallest element from set S

Implementation

An *order-statistic tree* T is simply a red-black tree with additional information stored at each node. Besides the usual red-black tree fields *key*[x], *left*[x], *right*[x],*p*[x] and *Colour*[x] in a node *x*, we have another field *size*[*x*]. This field contains the number of internal nodes in the subtree rooted at *x* (including x itself), that is, the size of the subtree.

$$size[x] = size[left[x]] + size[right[x]] + 1$$

The node of the *order-statistic tree* will now look as follows:

figure

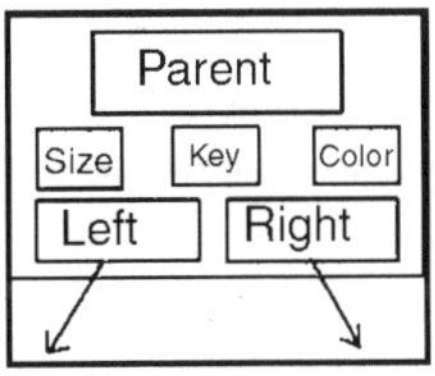

There are couple of things though that we have to worry about:

1. Can *size* be updated in $O(\log_2 n)$ time per operation?
2. *Rank*(x) and *select*(S, i) to be done in $O(\log_2 n)$ time.

Operations on Order-statistic trees

Insert

As we know, insertion into a red-black tree consists of two phases. Phase 1 goes down the path from the root inserting the new node as a child of the existing node. To maintain the subtree sizes we simply increment *size*[*x*] for each node *x* on the path traversed from the root down toward the leaves. The new node added gets size 1. Figure illustrates Phase 1.

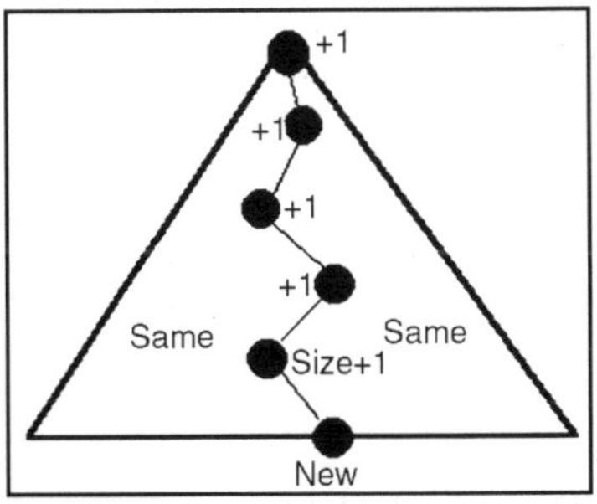

In the Phase 2, the only structural changes to the underlying red-black tree are caused by *rotations*, of which there are at most two. Rotation is a local operation and it invalidates only the two *size* fields in the nodes incident on the link around which the rotation is performed. Figure shows *Left* and *Right*rotations.

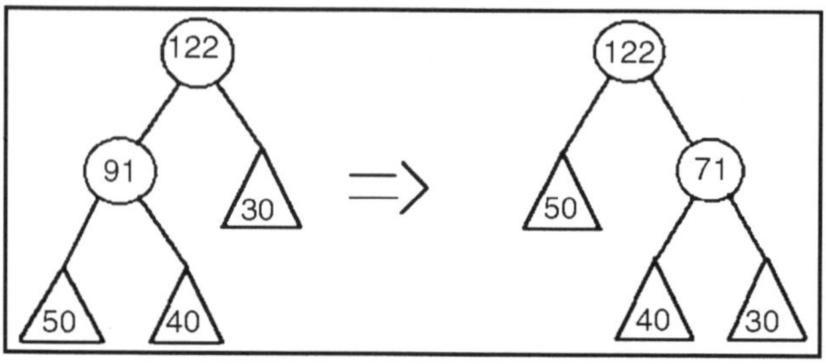

Delete

Phase 1 splices out the node we wish to delete. To update subtree sizes we simply traverse a path from node we wish to delete up to the root, decrementing*size* field for each node on the path.

Figure illustrates this process.

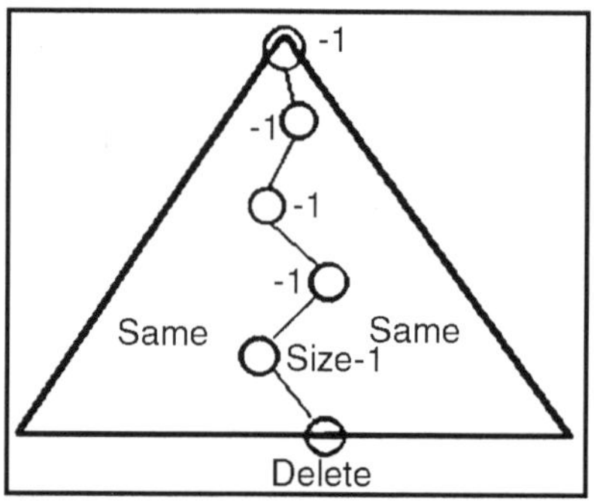

The rotations in the Phase 2 are handled in the same manner as for insertion.

Running time: To maintain tree sizes in the Phase 1 of insertion or deletion we have to increment or decrement *size*[*x*] for each node *x* on the path from the root down toward the leaves. Since there are $O(\log_2 n)$ nodes on the traversed path, the additional cost of maintaining the *size* fields is $O(\log_2 n)$. Moreover, rotation is a local operation and hence only O(1) additional time is spent updating *size* fields in the Phase 2. Thus, both insertion and deletion take $O(\log_2 n)$ time.

Select

The procedure *Select*(*x*, *i*) returns a pointer to the node containing the ith smallest key in the subtree rooted at *x*.

```
Select(x, i)
r (rank of root) = size[left[x]] + 1
case r = i: return x
```

```
case r > i: return Select(left[x], i)
case r < i: return Select(right[x], i)
```

Because each recursive call goes down one level in the order-statistic tree, the total time for *Select* is at worst proportional to the height of the tree. Since the tree is the red-black tree, its height is $O(\log_2 n)$. Thus, the running time of *Select* is $O(\log_2 n)$.

Rank

The procedure *Rank*(*T*, *x*) returns the position of *x* in the linear order determined by an inorder tree walk of *T*. Let *x* is a pointer to the node in the tree.

```
Rank(T, x)
r = size[left[x]] + 1
y = x
while y <> root do
if right[parent[y]] = y
then r += size[left[parent[y]]] + 1
y = parent[y]
return r
```

Since each iteration of the while loop takes O(1) time and *y* goes up one level in the tree with each iteration, the running time of *Rank* is at worst proportional to the height of the tree: $O(\log_2 n)$.

Figure illustrates the *Rank* procedure.

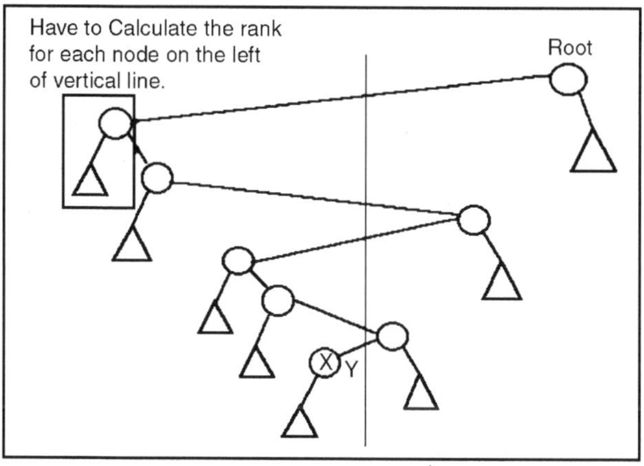

Fig. Link to our Java Applet

BINARY SEARCH TREES FOR BROWSING ADT

Dictionary + Browsing operations:

- MIN
- MAX

- Predecessor
- Successor

Implementation

The underlying data structure is a red-black tree where besides usual red-black tree fields each node is augmented with *Min*[*x*], *Max*[*x*], *Predecessor*[*x*] and*Successor*[*x*]. Figure 6 shows the augmented Red-Black tree on the input {1 2 3 4 5 6 7 8 9 10 11}.

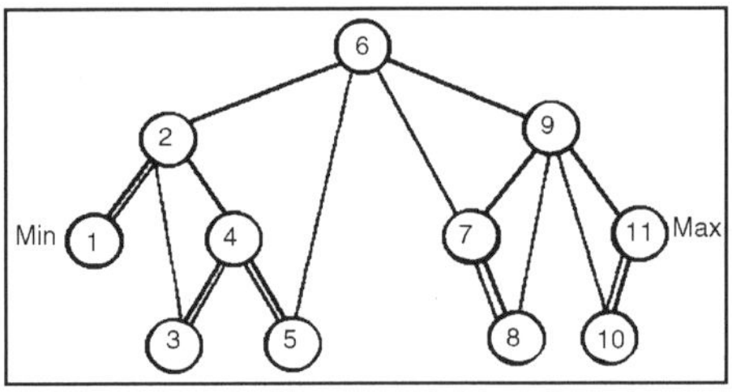

The data structure in Figure 6 can be looked at as a binary search tree or a sorted linked list as shown in Figure 7. In fact, according to Prof. Devroye, it is a smooth "marriage" of both data structures.

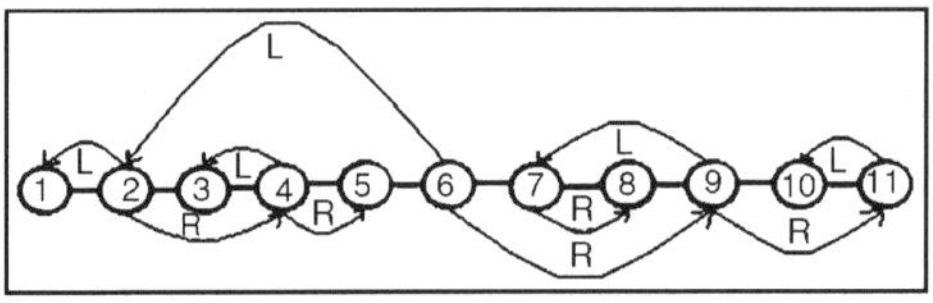

When we insert or delete a node we always have to update *predecessor* and *successor* pointers. In the Figure 8 we have deleted a new node with a *key*value 8. Accordingly we have to update *successor* and *predecessor* pointers. The time it takes to update pointers is equal to O($\log_2 n$), since we either follow a path up the tree or down the tree. Rotation operations take as usual O(1) time, so the running time for insertion or deletion is O($\log_2 n$). In figure the updated pointer.

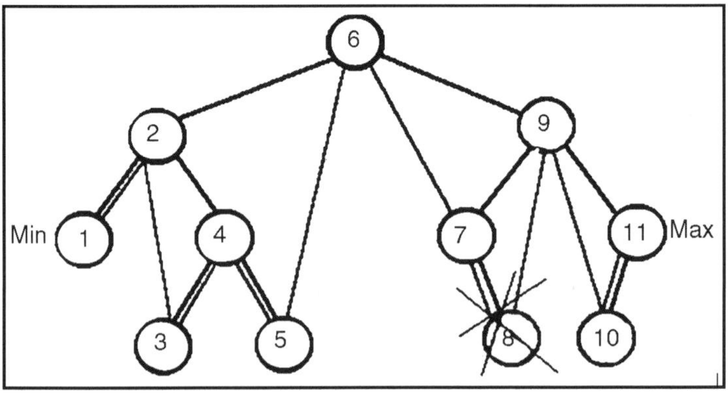

INTERVAL TREES

Interval tree is a binary search tree for intervals which are efficient for the dictionary operations and overlap. *Overlap*(*x*, *i*) for interval *i* and a tree rooted at *x*, returns a pointer to an interval in the collection that overlaps the given interval *i* or returns NIL otherwise.

The underlying data structure is a red-black tree in which each node *x* contains an interval *int*[*x*] and the key of *x* is a low endpoint of interval, *low*[*int*[*x*]].*high*[*x*] is the high endpoint of interval. In addition, each node *x* contains a value *max*[*x*] which is the maximum value of any interval endpoint stored in the subtree rooted at *x*.

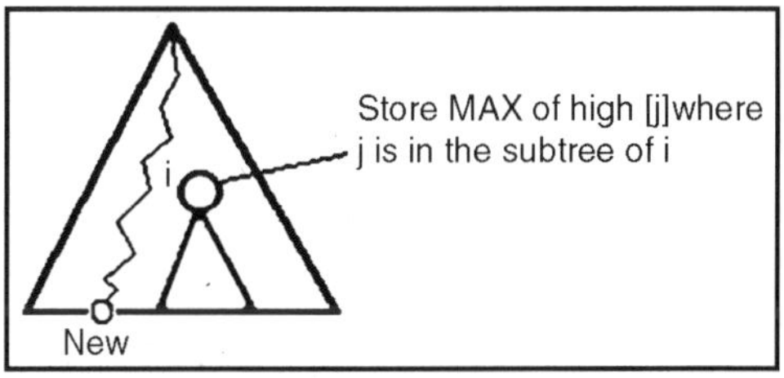

Operations

- Determine overlap with some interval in the tree: return Yes or No
- Dictionary operations (Insert, Delete, Search)

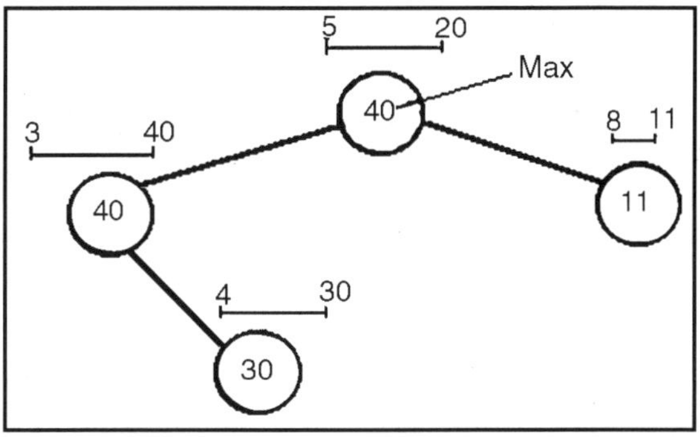

Given interval *i* and pointer to the root *x* Overlap(x, i) returns NIL if no overlap occured or pointer to the node if there is an overlap.

```
Overlap(x, i)
if x = NIL then return NIL
while x <> NIL and i doesn't overlap int[x] do
if left[x] <> NIL and low[i] Ü max[left[x]]
then x = left[x]
else x = right[x]
```

Running Time

The search for the inteval that overlaps *i* starts with *x* at the root of the tree and proceeds downward. It terminates when either overlapping interval is found or x becomes NIL. Since each iteration of the basic loop takes O(1) time, and since the height or the red-black tree is $O(\log_2 n)$ *Overlap*takes $O(\log_2 n)$ time. Insertion of a node x into a tree consists of *two* phases. During the first phase x is inserted as a child of an existing node. The value of $max[x]$ can be computed in O(1) time since it depends only on information in the other fields of x itself and x's children, but x's children are both NIL. Once $max[x]$ is computed, the change propagates up the tree. Thus, total time for the first phase is $O(\log_2 n)$. During second phase the only structural changes are caused by rotations. Since only *two* nodes change in rotation, the total time for updating the *max* fields is $O(\log_2 n)$ per rotation. Since the number of rotations during insertion is at most *two*, the total time for insertion is $O(\log_2 n)$.

In the first phase of deletion, changes occur if the deleted node is replaced by its successor, and then again when either the deleted node or its successor is spliced out. Propagating the updates to *max* caused by these changes costs at most $O(\log_2 n)$ since the changes modify the tree locally. Fixing up the red-black tree during the second phase requires at most *three* rotations, and each rotation requires at most $O(\log_2 n)$ time to propagate the updates to *max*. Thus, like insertion, the total time for deletion is $O(\log_2 n)$.

Problem: Layout of VSLI chips

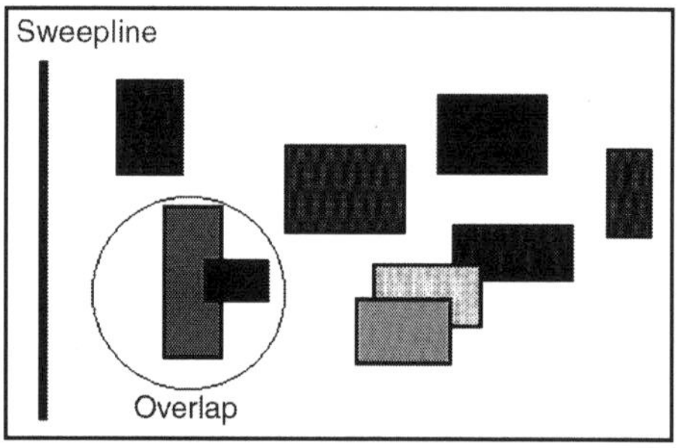

In this section we present a problem which is motivated by automated chip design. The problem is how can we place many printed circuits on one chip without overlapping? To make the problem more amenable to analysis, we assume that all n rectangles to be aligned with horizontal axis. We also assume that we are given a configuration of the rectangles, and our task is merely to check whether there is any overlap between rectangles.

In the naive solution we try to remove overlapped rectangles and place them randomly again. It takes time of Θ (n^2). The more efficient algorithm, which takes $O(n\log_2 n)$ time, uses a technique known as *sweeping*.

In sweeping an imaginary vertical sweep line passes through a given set of geometric objects (rectangles), usually from left to right. Sweeping provides a method for ordering geometric objects, usualy by placing them into dynamic data structure. We sort the rectangles' endpoints by increasing x-coordinate and proceed from left to right. We insert y-direction intervals into an interval tree when its left endpoint is encountered and we delete it from interval tree when its right endpoint is encountered. Whether two segments first become consecutive in the total order, we check if they overlap.

Sweepline (Turning 2-d into 1-d)

- Sort x coordinates of rectangles
- Interval tree for y direction intervals
- for i = 1 to 2n do

If ith point is start then if (a, ß) overlap some interval in interval tree - STOP: Insert((*a*, ß), interval tree) *endpoint* then Delete((*a*, ß), interval tree) *a* is a segment immediately above segment *i* and ß is a segment immediately below segment *i*. Sorting takes $O(n\log_2 n)$ time using mergesort or heapsort.

Since there are $2n$ points the *for* loop iterates at most $2n$ times. Each iteration takes $O(\log_2 n)$ time, since each red-black tree operation takes $O(\log_2 n)$ time. To check if there is an overlap takes O(1) time. Thus the total running time is $O(\log_2 n)$.

7

Computer Graphics System

Today there are very few aspects of our lives not affected by computers. Practically every cash or monetary transaction that takes place daily involves a computer. In many cases, the same is true of computer graphics. Whether you see them on television, in newspapers, in weather reports or while at the doctor's surgery, computer images are all around you.

"A picture is worth a thousand words" is a well-known saying, and highlights the advantages and benefits of the visual presentation of our data. We are able to obtain a comprehensive overall view of our data and also study features and areas of particular interest.

A well-chosen graph is able to transform a complex table of numbers into meaningful results. Such graphs are used to illustrate papers, reports, and theses, as well as providing the basis for presentation material in the form of slides and overhead transparencies. A range of tools and facilities are available to enable users to visualise their data, and this document provides a brief summary and overview. Computer graphics are used in many disciplines and subjects but for the purpose of this document, we will split the topic of computer graphics into the following fields:

CHARTING

One of the prime uses for graphical software at the University is to produce graphs and charts. Everyone has data of one kind or another, whether on paper, in the computer, or just in the mind. We often need to know the significance and properties of the data, or to be able to compare different parts of it against other data sets. One of the simplest aspects of data display is the production of charts. This is where you would want to put your data into a graphical form to show relationships and comparisons between sets of values.

There may be a number of reasons why you would want to put your data into a chart:

- To illustrate differences between different sets of data,
- To show trends between two variables,
- To show patterns of behaviour in one variable.

There are basically two broad areas of graphs:

- Presentation charts and graphs of the kind used to illustrate a few principal points. We see these on news and current affairs programmes on television. A bar chart or a pie chart is used to indicate results of data obtained so far and the general trends. They are often liberally decorated with bright colours to increase their visual appeal and attractiveness to the viewers and to hold their attention. They are used for visual impact and getting a simple point over clearly and effectively.
- Scientific charts and graphs are more concerned with ensuring that the detail in the data is represented accurately and faithfully. We may have some results obtained from experimental measurements and wish to display them. We may want to compare the results from the data measurements with the results we would expect according to a particular theoretical model. We may want to draw a curve through the data points (*i.e.* interpolate the data) and display this along with the original points.

The aims of the two are different, and so the facilities you will want from your charting package will also be different. Presentation charting has more to do with impressive presentation graphics where the aim is to put a salient point across to an audience. As a result the priority with this sort of charting is not always accuracy of representation. You want charts with strong colours, an impressive look and special effects. The effect of a presentation can be enhanced by using 3D graphs, adding pictures to the graph, or using pictograms. These sorts of charts are rarely produced in isolation but as part of a general presentation. Therefore, some presentation packages also have their own charting module for this purpose. Word and PowerPoint use a module called Microsoft Graph and Excel's charting module has some very powerful presentation graphics features. Origin and Gsharp, both dedicated charting packages, also provide professional presentation charting facilities on the PC systems. Gsharp is also available on the UNIX systems.

In scientific charting you want to display data as accurately as possible in order to analyse it graphically or demonstrate clearly your comparisons and results. As this sort of charting is done mainly for analysis, it is rarely an isolated activity but is often done alongside detailed numerical analysis of your data. Two of the most powerful charting packages available are Origin on the PC network and Gsharp on the PC and UNIX systems. Also, many numerical analysis packages have their own charting modules integrated with the rest of the package.

It is clear that your choice of charting programme will depend very much on what purpose you want the chart to fulfil, and also what other programmes you are already using. On the whole, if you are already using a programme that has its own charting module, use that. The table below gives some rough guidelines on your choice of charting PC package, with the packages increasing in facilities and complexity going down the table.

Requirement	*Choice*
Simple bar, column, line or pie charts to integrate in a word processor	Microsoft Graph in Word, Charting Module in Excel
Charts for use in a presentation	Microsoft Graph in Word or PowerPoint, Charting Module in Excel, Origin
Raw data requiring good quality scientific charting	Origin, Gsharp
Data requiring simple mathematical or statistical analysis	Charting Module in Excel, Origin, Gsharp
Complicated statistical analysis and good quality scientific charts	Graphics module in SPSS

PRESENTATIONS

Presentation software is used to create material used in presentations, such as OHP transparencies and 35mm slides. The term is also commonly used when a presentation is given using the output from a computer screen. The use of presentation software is becoming of increasing importance as higher standards become expected in courses and presentations. This will often include making use of colour, graphics and the University logo. Course materials produced using presentation packages can be delivered in a number of ways. The simplest way is to print the material on a laser printer and then use a photocopier to produce overhead projector (OHP) acetates (first making sure that the photocopier can accept acetates). You can also use the output services produced by Information Systems Services and University Media Services to produce colour output or output on 35mm slides. Alternatively you can give a desktop presentation using OHP projection tablets or projection systems to deliver a presentation using the output from a computer system directly. The simplest presentation software is a word processor.

Word processing packages such as Word, which can produce text in a variety of sizes, can be used to create OHP transparencies. Specialist presentation packages, such as PowerPoint, provide a wider range of facilities than word processors and, in general, are easier to use for the production of presentation materials. PowerPoint is a presentation software programme that helps you quickly and easily create professional quality presentations. Presentations can be transferred onto paper, overheads or 35mm slides, or they can be shown on a video screen or computer monitor. PowerPoint's printing options include formats ranging from audience handouts to speaker's notes.

DRAWING, PAINTING AND DESIGN

Drawing and painting software is available on most platforms at the University. However, there are many differences between software intended primarily for drawing and that intended for painting. Drawing software will provide the user with a set of 'entities' used to construct the drawing (an entity is a drawing element such as a line, circle, or text string). Drawing entities can range from simple lines, points and curves in 2D to their equivalents in 3D and may include 3D surfaces. Advanced versions of drawing packages used for design are referred to as Computer Aided Design (CAD) systems. Painting software tends to work on a conceptually lower layer. Whilst it may provide some entities for constructing geometric shapes (these tend to be 2D geometric shapes), a painting package will also provide control over individual pixels in the image, *i.e.* it provides direct control over the bitmap. It is worth remembering that opening any image in a painting package causes it to become pixelated.

The following packages are available on the ISS NT Cluster Desktop:

- Paint Very basic painting programme. Can create simple pictures and edit bitmaps. Only possible to read in and save files in a BMP format.
- Picture Publisher Painting package used to edit and create pictures. Can read in and save files in a number of different formats.
- Paint Shop Pro Recommended as the main painting package on the desktop. Used to edit and create pictures. Can read in and save files in a number of different formats.
- CorelDraw Recommended as the main drawing package on the desktop. Useful for editing vector graphics.Can read in and save files in both vector and bitmap formats.
- Micrografx Designer Drawing package used for technical drawing.

The following drawing and painting software is available on the Suns:

- Island Paint Painting programme that provides tools for creating and editing images formed by monochrome and colour bitmaps. Several painting tools can be used to create geometric and freehand shapes. Scanned images and clip art can also be imported.
- Island Draw 2D drawing package.
- Island Paint General purpose CAD system in use in engineering, and allows 3D solid modelling as well as 2D/3D draughting. An extension, AEC, for architectural and construction applications, is also available.

THE EVOLUTION OF COMPUTER GRAPHICS

CGI was first used in movies in 1973, in the science fiction film, *Westworld*. The film was the story of a society in which humans and robots were integrated, working and living together. Its sequel, *Futureworld* (1976) featured the first use of 3D wireframe imagery. The third film ever to use this technology was *Star Wars* (1977), designing the Death Star and the targeting computers in the X-wings and the Millenium Falcon, Han Solo's ship. Later on, *The Black Hole* (1979) used raster wire-frame model rendering to create a black hole onscreen. That same year, James Cameron's *Alien* used the raster wireframe model to render the image of navigation monitors in the scene where the spaceship follows a beacon for landing guidance. Long before this, computer engineers at MIT and Cornell were in the midst of creating the very basics that eventually enabled these filmmakers to utilize computer animation technology. It all began in 1963.

1960s

- 1963: Ivan Sutherland presented his Ph.D. dissertation, an interactive design on a vector graphics display monitor with a light pen input device called *Sketchpad*. This instance is often credited as the event that marks the beginning of computer graphics.
- Jack Bresenham develops a system of drawing lines and circles on a raster device, and Steve Coons introduces parametric surfaces and computer-aided geometric design concepts.
- Arthur Appel at IBM introduces hidden surface and shadow algorithms.
- The fast Fourier transform was discovered by J. W. Cooley and John Tukey, allowing computer engineers to better understand signals to develop antialiasing techniques.
- Doug Englebart develops the mouse at Xerox PARC.
- Evans & Sutherland Corps. and GE start building flight simulators with raster graphics.

1970s

- Rendering and a reflection model were discovered and developed by H. Gouraud and Bui Tuong Phong at the University of Utah.
- Xerox PARC develops a "paint programme."
- Edward Catmull introduces parametric patch rendering, the z-buffer algorithm and texture mapping.
- Turner Whitted develops recursive ray tracing that would become the standard for photorealism.
- Apple I and Apple II computers were the first commercially successful options for personal computing.
- Arcade games Pong and Pac Man become popular.

1980s

- Microprocessors begin to take off but remain in early stages of development.

- Loren Carpenter begins exploring fractals in computer graphics.
- Adobe formed by John Warnock, who discovers Postscript. Adobe markets Photoshop.
- Steve Cook introduces stochastic sampling.
- Character animation becomes a goal for animators.
- Video arcade games take off.
- C++, C, and MS-DOS programming gain popularity.

1990s

- Shaded raster graphics appear in films.
- Computers have 24-bit raster display and hardware support for Gouraud shading.
- Laser printers and single-frame video recorders become standard.
- Mosaic, the first graphical internet browser is created.
- Dynamical systems that allowed programmers to animate collisions, friction and cause and effects are introduced.
- Handheld computers are invented at Hewlett-Packard and zip drives invented at Iomega.
- Nintendo 64 game console arrives on the market.
- Linux and open source software emerges.
- Pixar is first studio to fully embrace an entirely computer-generated film with *Toy Story*.

2000s

- Graphic software reaches a peak in quality and user accessibility.
- PC displays support real-time texture mapping.
- Flatbed scanners, laser printers, digital video cameras, etc., become commonplace.
- Programme language moves towards Java and C++.
- 3D modeling captures facial expressions, human face, hair, water, and other elements formerly difficult to render.

GRAPHICS SYSTEM

Let us consider the organization of a typical graphics system we might use. As our initial emphasis will be on how the applications programmer sees the system, we shall omit details of the hardware.

The model is general enough to include workstations, personal computers, terminals attached to a central time-shared computer, and sophisticated image-generation systems. In most ways, this block diagram is that of a standard computer. How each element is specialized for computer graphics will characterize this diagram as one of a graphics system, rather than one of a general-purpose computer.

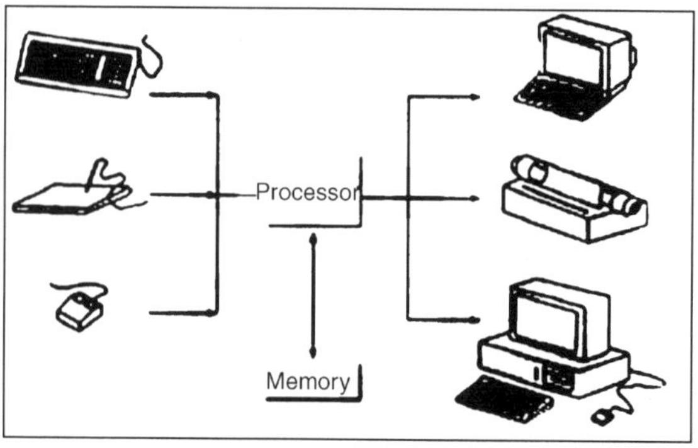

Fig. The Graphic System

THE PROCESSOR

Within the processor box, two types of processing take place. The first is picture formation processing. In this stage, the user programme or commands are processed. The picture is formed from the elements (lines, text) available in the system using the desired attributes. Such as line colour and text font. The user interface is a part of this processing. The picture can be specified in a number of ways, such as through an interactive menu-controlled painting programme or via a C programme using a graphics library. The physical processor used in this stage is often the processor in the workstation or host computer.

The second kind of processing is concerned with the display of the picture. In a raster system, the specified primitives must be scan converted. The screen must be refreshed to avoid flicker. Input from the user might require objects to be repositioned on the display. The kind of processor best suited for these jobs is not the standard type of processor found in most computers. Instead, special boards and chips are often used. As we have already noted, one of the elements that distinguishes real-time graphics systems is their use of display processors. Since we have agreed to stay at the block-diagram level for now, however, we shall not explore these architectures in any detail until later.

MEMORY

There are often two distinct types of memory employed in graphics systems. For the processing of the user programme, the memory is similar to that of a standard computer, as the picture is formed by a standard type of arithmetic processing. Display processing, however, requires high-speed display memory that can be accessed by the display processor, and, in raster systems, memory for the frame buffer. This display memory usually is different in both its physical characteristics and its organization from what is used by the picture processor. At this point, we need not consider details of how memory can be organized. You should be aware that the way the internals of our processor and memory boxes are organized distinguishes a slow system from a real-time picture-generating system, such as a flight simulator. However, from our present perspective, we shall emphasize that all implementations have to do the same kinds of tasks to produce output.

OUTPUT DEVICES

Our basic system has one or more output devices. As raster displays are the dominant type, we shall assume there is a raster-scan CRT on our system. We shall consider the frame buffer to be part of the display memory. In a self-contained system such as a workstation, the display is an integral part of the system, so the transfer of information from the processor to the display will happen rapidly. When the display is separate, such as with a graphics terminal, the speed of the connection is much slower. Terminals with raster displays usually must have their own frame buffers, so the displays can be refreshed locally. In our simple system, we might also have other displays, such as a plotter, to allow us to produce hardcopy.

INPUT DEVICES

A simple system may have only a keyboard to provide whatever input is necessary. Keyboards provide digital codes corresponding to sequences of keystrokes by a user. These sequences are usually interpreted as codes for characters. If individual keystrokes or groups of keystrokes are interpreted as graphical input, the keyborad can be used as a complex input device. For example, the "arrow" keys available on most keyboards can be used to direct the movement of a cursor on the screen. Most graphics systems will provide at least one other input device. The most common are the mouse, the lightpen, the joystick, and the data tablet. Each can provide positional information to the system and each usually is equipped with one or more buttons to provide signals to the processor. From the programmer's perspective, there are numerous important issues with regard to the input and output devices. We must consider how the programme can communicate with these devices. We must decide what kinds of input and output can be produced. We will be interested in how to control multiple devices, so that we can choose a particular device for our input, and can direct our output to some group of the available output devices.

MULTIMEDIA DESIGN

The combination of low-bandwidth considerations and primitive interface options creates interesting design challenges for Web developers who wish to incorporate multimedia elements into their sites. Designers need to inform users when they are entering a high-bandwidth area and give them the tools they need to control their experience once in the area.

INFORM YOUR USERS

One aspect of the Web is that you don't always know where you're going or what you'll find there. For some this uncertainty is exciting. For many, it is annoying, particularly when a long wait is involved. Most frustrating, perhaps, is when you finally receive the requested page only to find that is not what you expected or that it contains materials in a format you are not set up to view.

With content that is as technologically demanding as multimedia, it is especially important to give users enough information to make an informed decision *before they click,* so that they know what to expect and are prepared to receive your materials.

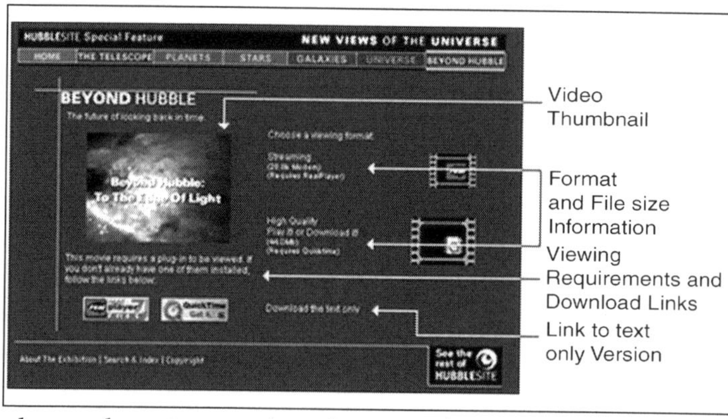

High-demand content such as large multimedia files should not be part of your basic page design. These materials should appear on secondary pages that are described and can be accessed from the main pages of your site. Make the menu page a plain HTML page that loads quickly and does not require special software. Include descriptive information about the materials along with previews such as still shots from the video. Include the run time for time-based media, and include the file size for materials that download. In addition, fully explain any special software requirements for accessing the materials and provide a download link. Your users should have a clear idea of what your materials are before they begin to download. With a menu interface, users can confirm that their systems are properly configured and that they have enough bandwidth, time, and patience to load the materials.

Provide Controls

Be sure to give users status information and controls when you are presenting multimedia materials. The QuickTime controller bar is an extremely effective interface element that provides both controls and status information. It allows users both to adjust the volume control and to play, stop, and scrub through a movie, and it provides information about the movie's download status.

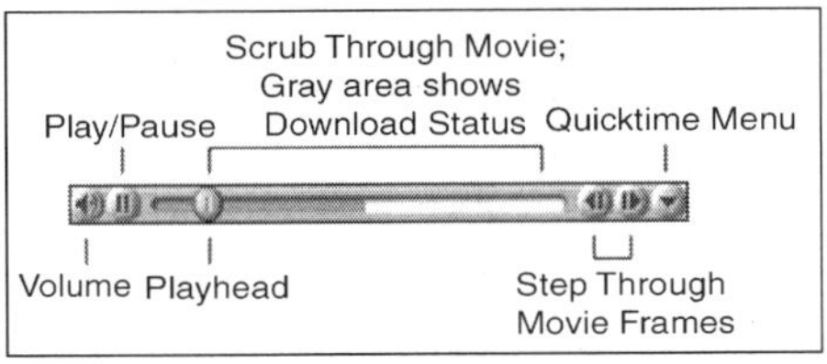

If you don't include controls, users will hit your page with no way to control their viewing environment. For example, if a visitor is looking at your page at a public workstation and you have looping bird calls as a background sound without any control options, the visitor will experience an unsettling (and potentially embarrassing) moment when he or she cannot control interaction with your site. Many users in this situation will simply close the browser window to make the sound stop, which means that they never get to see the page content.

When designing a media interface, let interaction with your media be entirely user-driven. Always include user controls, such as a media controller bar, and make sure that users have a way to turn it off. Avoid prescribed playback options like auto play or looping that take control from the user. With auto play, for example, media files begin playing when a Web page is loaded. If the page has other elements, such as descriptive text, the user who wants just the text will find the video distracting. Design your media interface so that files play only when the user explicitly elects to initiate playback.

MULTIMEDIA USER INTERFACE DESIGN GUIDELINES

Multimedia user interfaces combine several kinds of media to help people use a computer. These media can include text, graphics, animation, images, voice, music, and touch. Multimedia user interfaces are gaining popularity because they are very effective at keeping the interest of their users, improve the amount of information users remember, and can be very cost-effective. Several reports support the value of multimedia. Bethlehem Steel found that multimedia training courses cut training time by 20% to 40%, improved retention rates 20% to 40%, and allowed employees to take training when it was most convenient.

A Department of Defense literature survey concluded that, in higher education, interactive videodisc training roughly improved the performance of students in the 50th percentile to about the 75th percentile of performance. Big 5 Sporting Goods reported that training time for a point-of-sale cashier dropped about 75% to 50%, cashiers made fewer errors at the point of sale, cashiers and sales representatives retained their skills, and the company standardized training. Another study found that the greater the level of interactivity in the course materials, the more students learned. Compared to standard classroom lecture, students who used interactive videodiscs retained

19% more information when tested four weeks after the training period. Successful multimedia designers build their products with primary emphasis on the user. Multimedia designers determine which human sensory system is most efficient at receiving specific information, then use the media that involves that human sensory system. For example, to teach someone how to fix a part on a jet engine it is probably most efficient for the student to watch someone else fixing the part rather than hearing a lecture on how to fix the part. The human visual system is better at receiving this complex information. So, the designer for this multimedia product should probably use video as the medium of communication.

This heavy emphasis on the user's senses, rather than the media, means that we should probably call these product user interfaces "multisensory" rather than "multimedia". The human senses that designers use most frequently in their multimedia products are sight, sound, and touch. Multimedia products often stimulate these senses simultaneously. For example, a user can see and hear a video, and then touch a graphical button to freeze the video image.

Since so many media are available to the multimedia user interface designer, it is very easy to overwhelm and confuse the users of these products. The following guidelines are based on the way people think and perceive information. These guidelines will help you build multimedia user interfaces that are easy and comfortable for people to learn and use.

GENERAL GUIDELINES

Here are some general guidelines.

- Keep the user interface simple — This is the most important guideline to remember when you design multimedia user interfaces. Don't show off what you can do with multimedia technology. Instead, give the users only what they need to do their tasks. One study suggests that you provide only five to nine choices for the user to select at one time. As Thoreau wrote, "Our life is frittered away by detail.... Simplify. Simplify."
- Be consistent — Use similar objects to perform similar functions throughout your product. That way, what users learn in one place they can use in other places. This quality helps users learn your product quickly and builds their confidence.
- Let the user control the interaction — Let the user, rather than the computer, control what happens next. Let the user decide where to go, what to see, and when to leave. For example, when watching a video, let the user cancel the video rather than watching the whole thing before being able to move on. That way, if the user saw the video during an earlier interaction, he or she does not have to see it all over again. This feature is shown in Figure below.

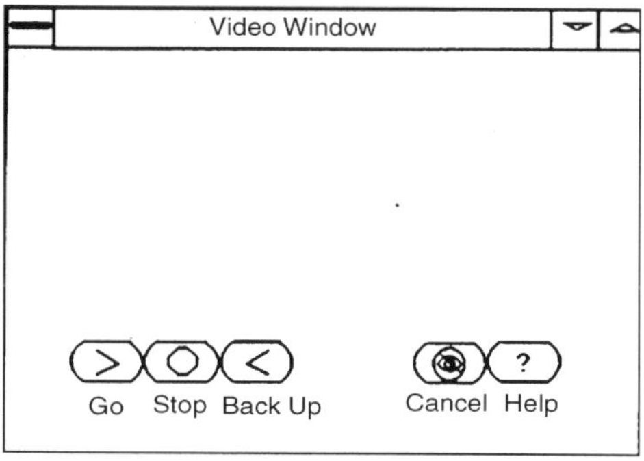

Fig. User Cancels Video by Pressing Cancel Push Button

Exceptions to this suggestion are computer-based training applications that include tasks the user needs to learn in a specific order.

- Give immediate, obvious feedback for every user action — Let the user know that the computer is working and that it received and is responding to the user action. For example, when the user selects a push button, change the button to inverse video, and have the computer emit a short beep and process the action on the push button. This design characteristic will help keep the user interested in using your product.
- Use familiar metaphors — Take advantage of the user's prior learning by using familiar objects and actions. This characteristic improves learning and increases user comfort. For example, if the user needs to dial a telephone number, provide an image of a telephone with a touch-sensitive key pad. The user recognizes the telephone and knows how to make it work. Other familiar metaphors include televisions, video cassette recorders, and calculators.
- Let the user safely explore your product — The user should be able to navigate through your product without worrying about breaking or deleting something. If appropriate, don't provide a delete function. If the user needs to delete objects, design your user interface so the user can confirm or cancel a deletion. Let the user undo actions that are not easy to reverse. Let the user go back to the previous screen from the current screen. Make obvious what the user can do next. These design characteristics help make your user interface inviting and comfortable.

Sight

The medium of sight is helpful when you need to communicate detailed information, such as instructions, that the user may need to refer to later.

Here are some guidelines that involve sight.

- *Use pastel colours* — Except for videos and black and white text, it is generally a good idea to use slightly washed out, desaturated, impure colours. This is most important for the small objects that you put on screens. Scientists believe that these kinds of colours let people focus on small objects better and are less likely to cause objects to appear to float on the display. In your videos, stick with the original colours in which the video was shot. Use high-contrast foreground-background colours for text.

- *Use fonts that have serifs* — Serifs are small lines that finish off the main strokes of a letter and often appear at the top or bottom of a letter. The text you are reading has a serif font. Use fonts with serifs because these fonts may help readers differentiate letters and because readers seem to prefer fonts with serifs.

Sound

The medium of sound is helpful when you need to communicate short, simple information, such as confirmation beeps, that users don't have to refer to later. Here are some guidelines that involve sound.

- *Limit your use of sound* — A product that is constantly buzzing, beeping, chattering, and singing to its users quickly becomes annoying. The user is working with your product to get a job done. Limit your use of sound to those instances where sound informs, rather than simply entertains, the user.
- *Use lower frequency sounds* — High-frequency sounds can be shrill and annoying, especially when the user has to hear them repeatedly. Generally, try to use lower frequency sounds, around 100 hertz to 1000 hertz, in your product.
- *Let the user control sound volume quickly and easily*— The user may want to make the sound louder or softer for personal preference or to avoid disturbing people nearby. Design your product so the user can adjust the sound volume. Make sound controls large and obvious and let the user turn the sound off. These features are shown in Figure below.

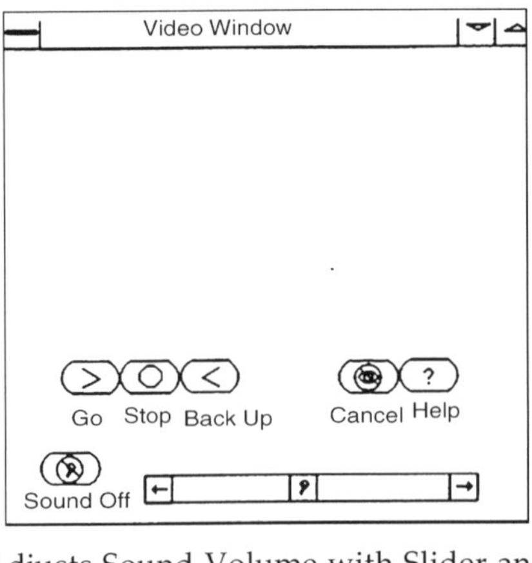

Fig. User Adjusts Sound Volume with Slider and Turns off Sound with Sound off Push Button

Touch

The medium of touch is helpful when you need to ask the user to make simple choices, such as product navigation decisions, without using a keyboard. Here are some guidelines that involve touch.

- *Use large touch areas* — If your product has a touch-sensitive screen, make it easy for the users to activate the touch areas by making those areas fairly large. One study suggests using rectangular touch areas that are 40 mm wide and 36 mm high surrounding smaller visual targets, such as push buttons, that are 27 mm wide and 22 mm high. This is shown in Figure below.

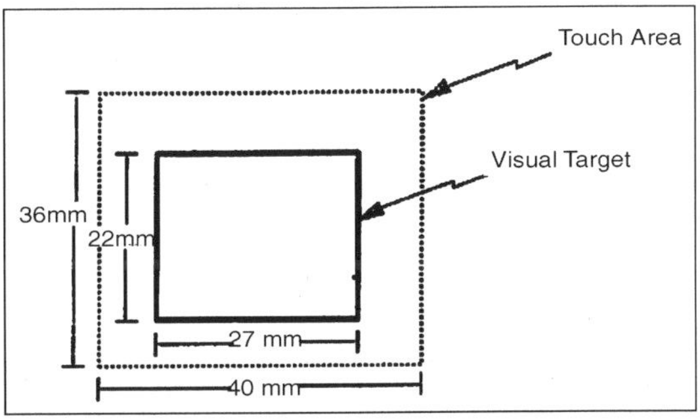

Fig. Suggested Sizes for Touch Areas and Visual Targets

Be sure to separate your touch areas with inactive spaces. Limit the number of touch areas on one screen to about 10 or less.

INTEGRATED MULTIMEDIA PUBLISHING

Multimedia publishing is presenting multimedia works that have been authored and produced by a multimedia artist or video editor. As opposed to multimedia authoring and production, that start the processes from source materials and developed (designed) to a formal work of art, multimedia publishing is outputting the final work to either print format or digital format on discs or on the web.

Integrated media is targeted towards the user as an individual rather than a part of a mass audience. By integrating content from several sources into a database, the user is able to select a unique combination of content particles that fit his/her own interests. Examples of such customised news services are Pointcast (http://www.pointcast.com/), NewsPage (http://www.newspage.com/), and Crayon (http://www.crayon.net/). The publisher may use the integrated database as a source for various publications. In traditional media, integration aggregates the items into a product on a higher level. Text and photos constitute a news story on a newspaper page. The articles and advertisements on the pages constitute a newspaper. The TV channel consists of separate programmes, as a newsstand consists of several publications. However, the integration is static; at the newsstand, the reader is not able to create his/her own paper by adding content from different papers and magazines. The IMU (Integrated publishing in Multimedia Network) system, developed in this work, is a unique attempt to integrate TV news and newspaper sources. The content of six different source publications is automatically collected into the database as separate text and multimedia news stories. In addition to integration, IMU also offers personalisation. A reader may "clip" the papers of this media kiosk and assemble a personal publication or channel - even including video content. Thus, you can set up "Bill Clinton" or "EMU" channels containing what the newspapers and TV have told about these topics. The appearance of the publication can also be personalised and the publication adapts to the user terminal, be it a PC monitor with various resolutions or a TV set.

Personalisation is an efficient way to improve the usability of publications. Personalisation of the content filters out excess information which the user does not need. Personalisation of the appearance presents the content in a form at which best suits the user and the context of use. Personalisation consists of classifying the information, maintaining user models and the actual personalisation. The classification involves analysing the information, dividing it into elements and creating and storing metadata, which describes the information and the elements. The user model contains information about the user which is needed in the personalisation.

Personalisation of the content involves selecting the information on the basis of the metadata and the user model. Personalisation of the appearance modifies the presentation of the content on the basis of the user model, which can be based on ready-made stereotype models, using questionnaires or adaptively. Adaptive systems register, analyse and classify the behaviour of the user and update the user model accordingly. In the IMU system, we use both questionnaires and adaptive personalisation.

THE IMU SYSTEM

The IMU trial system integrates TV news from two Finnish broadcasters (YLE, MTV3) and newspaper content from four Finnish newspapers (Aamulehti, Iltalehti, Turun Sanomat, Keskisuomalainen), and offers the personalised multimedia publications to users over fast Internet connections like cable TV and ADSL.

In the field trial the bi-directional cable TV network of Helsinki Media Corporation was used. Some experiments were also made in the ADSL telephone network maintained by Helsinki Telephone Company, HPY. A stripped IMU version without video can also be used from Internet TV. The core of the system is the active proxy server, which performs the content gathering, combination and interlinking. The proxy collects material both by downloading web content through the Internet and by digitising analogue TV broadcasts. The content flows from the server through a shared 155 Mbit/s ATM fibre link (Unspecified Bit Rate) to the end user distribution networks.

The average machine-to-machine transmission rate through the ATM was measured at over 40 Mbit/s, which allows a transmission of 50 simultaneous 800 kbit/s video streams. The users watch the publication on their PCs with a normal WWW browser that connects to the proxy server. Because of the Java programming, the user does not have to install any other plug-ins in addition to the Xing video player.

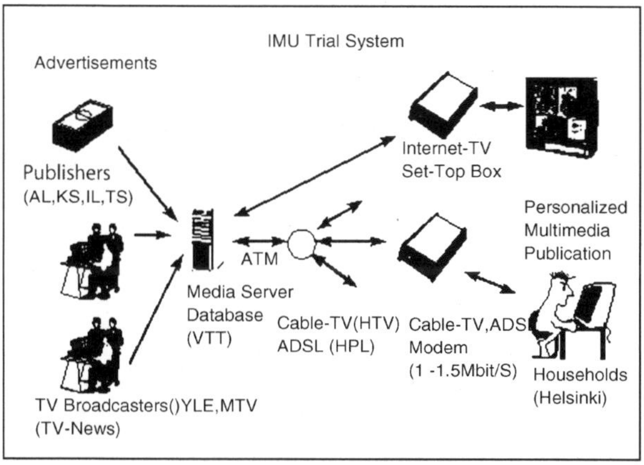

Fig. The IMU Trial Set-up, where the Active Proxy Server at VTT Downloads and Digitises Content from Media Houses for use over Fast Networks or Through the Internet TV.

MULTIMEDIA PRODUCTION

After the invention of the printing press, it is the advent of multimedia that has changed the way we learn and comprehend. Integration of multiple media such as visual imagery, text, audio, video, graphics and animation together multiply the impact of the message. Multimedia differs fundamentally from the conventional media like slides and films. While, conventional media are linear (one event follows another in a sequence), multimedia is non-linear - it has the capacity for branching in different directions and establishing linkages between different sections or components of the programme. The non-linear attribute provides the end-user the luxury of viewing the multimedia presentation at their convenience and pace.

DELIVERING MULTIMEDIA CONTENT THROUGH INTERNET

Websites on internet are making CD-ROMs redundant as a medium for delivering multimedia. This is because of the economies of reach that the Internet offers, coupled with the facility of day to day updation and instant worldwide reach.

The pace at which technological innovation is increasing bandwidth and making instant download of real audio and real video feasible, soon internet will take over CD-ROMs for delivering multimedia content. In the field of Humanities, especially for a country with a rich heritage like India, effective use of multimedia can go a long way in preserving the ancient culture for posterity and disseminating information to sensitise the audience. This chapter is meant as a guide for people who want to accept the challenge of being a part of the multimedia industry. It explores the steps involved in the production of a multimedia application.

INTRODUCTION TO MULTIMEDIA PRODUCTION MANAGEMENT

1968: An auditorium is full of sales managers watching a projected presentation at a large convention centre. The presentation consists of filmstrips, synchronised tape recorders and overlapping slide projectors. The presentation is called multimedia.

1978: Two teenagers are engrossed pulling at an electronic game paddle, which in turn slams a tiny electronic ball across a video playing field, coupled with sounds of boops and beeps. Their game is advertised as multimedia.

1988: A pop music artist is performing a concert in which computers not only generate the music but also control the lighting and accompanying video. The bow of the artist's violin sends digital signals that trigger the computers. The performance is described as multimedia.

1998: A family returns home and the father in his home office plugs digital pictures into a business presentation, while the mother learns a second language from an interactive software programme and the children hook on to internet seeking help with their homework. Multimedia has become part of everyday life.

2008: Virtual reality on the internet, interactive televisions ..., its Nostradamus' guess.

The word multimedia is a very elastic term but broadly it refers to the integration of multiple media - such as visual imagery, text, video, audio, sound and animation - which together can multiply the impact of the message.

THE PROCESS OF PRODUCTION MANAGEMENT

The production of interactive multimedia applications is a complex one, involving multiple steps. This process can be divided into the following phases:

Conceptualisation

The process of making multimedia starts with an "idea" or better described as "the vision" - which is the conceptual starting point. The starting point is ironically the visualisation of the ending point - the multimedia experience that the targeted end-user will have. Conceptualisation involves identifying a relevant theme for the multimedia title. *We, at Magic, prefer choosing themes that are socially important and exciting to work on*. Other criteria like availability of content, how amenable is the content to multimedia treatment and issues like copyright are also to be considered.

Development

Defining project goals and objectives: After a theme has been finalised for a multimedia project, specific goals, objectives and activities matrix must be laid down.

Goals: In multimedia production goals are general statements of anticipated project outcomes, usually more global in scope.

Objectives: Specific statements of anticipated project outcomes.

Activities: These are actions, things done in order to implement an objective. Specific people are responsible for their execution, a cost is related to their implementation and there is a time frame binding their development.

DEFINING THE TARGET AUDIENCE

A very important element that needs to be defined at this stage is the potential target audience of the proposed title since, this will determine how the content needs to be presented.

Preproduction

It is the process of intelligently mapping out a cohesive strategy for the entire multimedia project, including content, technical execution and marketing. Based on the goals and objectives, the three pillars of multimedia *viz*. Hardware, software and user participation are defined. At this stage the multimedia producer begins to assemble the resources and talent required for creating the multimedia application.

The Production Manager undertakes the following activities:

- Development of the budget control system
- Hiring of all specialists involved in the multimedia application process
- Contracting video and audio production crews and recording studios
- Equipment rental, leasing and purchasing
- Software acquisition and installation
- Planning the research work of the content specialists
- Development of the multimedia application outline, logic flow, scripts and video and audio files production scripts and schedules
- Coordination of legal aspects of production.

Production

Once all the preproduction activities have been completed, the multimedia application enters the production phase.

Activities in this phase include:

- Content Research
- Interface Design
- Graphics Development
- Selection of musical background and sound recording
- Development of computer animation
- Production of digital video
- Authoring.

Postproduction

In this phase, the multimedia application enters the alpha and beta testing process. Once the application is tested and revised, it enters the packaging stage. It could be burned into a CD-ROM or published on the Internet as a website.

Developing Documentation

User documentation is a very important feature of high-end multimedia titles. This includes instructions for installing, system requirements, developing acknowledgments, copyrights, technical support and other information important for the user.

ADAPTIVE HYPERMEDIA APPLICATIONS

An *adaptive hypermedia application system* (AHS) is a special kind of hypermedia system, which can adapt the contents and links of an application depending on observed user features. For building an AHS, the author has to provide two (related) parts: first of all the author has to write the actual hypertext; second, the author has to specify some dynamic adaptation control information.

In practice it turns out to be necessary to provide authoring tools that facilitate the specification of both aspects. In existing AHS authoring is often inconvenient, due to the mixture of (textual) content and diverse hints for adaptation. In Interbook the author must write structured, annotated MS-Word files.

In AHA the author must write annotated HTML files. This mixture of content, links and adaptation makes it difficult for authors to maintain a clear picture of how *concepts* relate to each other. This implies that it is hard to adapt to the user on an abstract conceptual level.

In we have presented a reference model for adaptive hypermedia applications, called the AHAM model. In order to separate different authoring aspects, AHAM splits up an adaptive hypermedia application into a *user model* (UM), *domain model* (DM) and *teaching model* (TM). These three parts together form what the Dexter hypermedia reference model [HS90, HS94] calls the *Storage layer*. Apart from this layer Dexter and AHAM also mention (but do not formally define) a Runtime layer which deals with sessions and the actual presentation and interaction on the screen, and a Within-Component layer which deals with implementation dependent representations of content and links.

We address the operations of DM, UM and TM that are needed for creating (authoring) adaptive hypermedia applications. We describe these operations at the conceptual level, not the implementation level. The definition of these operations shows how the tasks of

(1) Creating content,
(2) Combining smaller pieces into composite (abstract) concepts,
(3) Defining relationships between these concepts, and
(4) Defining rules for the adaptation of content and links to each individual user, are separated. The separation of these tasks will make authoring of adaptive hypermedia applications easier than it is today.

The separated tasks together form a description of the functionality of an authoring tool based on the AHAM model. This chapter is organized as follows: We describe the AHAM reference model, with its three parts (domain model, user model, teaching model). We show how authoring is facilitated by adding support functions to these three parts.

AHAM, A DEXTER-BASED REFERENCE MODEL

In hypermedia applications the emphasis is always on the information nodes and on the link structure connecting these nodes. The Dexter model captures this in what it calls the Storage layer.

It represents a *domain model* DM, *i.e.* the author's view on the application domain expressed in terms of concepts. In adaptive hypermedia applications the central role of DM is shared with a *user model* UM. UM represents the relationship between the user and the domain model by keeping track of how much the user knows about each of the concepts in the application domain.

In order to perform adaptation based on DM and UM an authors needs to specify how the user's knowledge influences the presentation of the information from DM. In AHAM this is done by means of a *teaching model* TM consisting of pedagogical rules. An adaptive engine uses those rules to manipulate link anchors from the Dexter model's *anchoring* and to generate what the Dexter model calls the *presentation specifications*. Like the Dexter model, AHAM focuses on the Storage layer, the anchoring and the presentation specifications. The structure of adaptive hypermedia applications in the AHAM model.

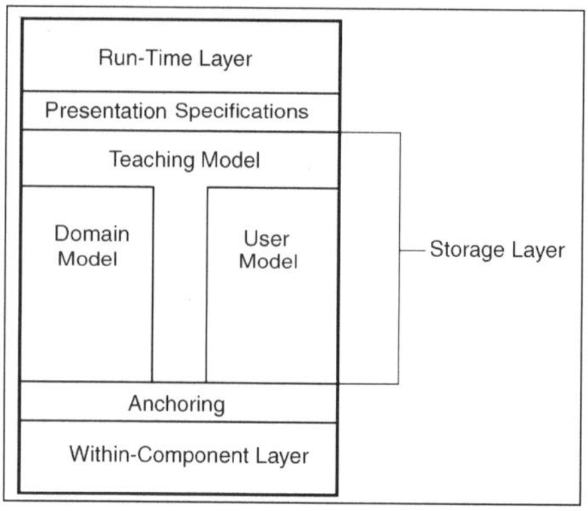

Fig. Global Structure of Adaptive Hypermedia Applications.

In this chapter we present the elements of AHAM that we will use, to illustrate the authoring functionality.

A *component* is an abstract notion in an AHS. It is a pair (uid, cinfo) where uid is a globally unique (object) identifier for the concept, and cinfo represents the component's information.

A component's information consists of:

- A set of attribute-value pairs;
- A sequence of anchors (for attaching links);
- A presentation specification.

A *concept* is a component representing an abstract information item from the application domain. It can be either an *atomic concept* or a *composite concept*. An *atomic concept* corresponds to a fragment of information. It is primitive in the model. Its attribute and anchor values belong to the Within-component layer and are thus implementation dependent and not described in the model.

A composite component has two additional attributes:

- A sequence of children (concepts);
- A constructor function (to denote how the children belong together).

The children of a composite concept are all atomic concepts (then we call it a *page* or in typical hypertext terms a *node*) or all composite concepts. The composite concept component hierarchy must be a DAG (directed acyclic graph). Also, every atomic concept must be included in some composite concept.

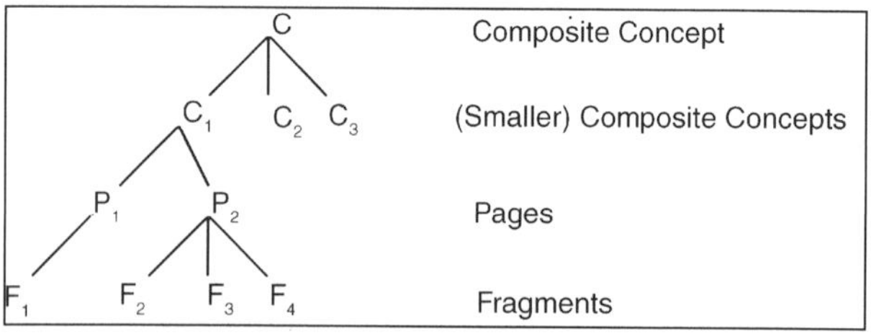

Fig. Example Concept Hierarchy

An *anchor* is a pair (aid, avalue), where aid is a unique (object) identifier for the anchor within the scope of its component and avalue is an arbitrary value that specifies some location, region, item or substructure within a concept component. Anchor values of atomic concepts belong to the (implementation dependent) Within-component layer. Anchor values of composite concepts are identifiers of concepts that belong to that composite.

A *specifier* is a tuple (uid, aid, dir, pres), where uid is the identifier of a concept, aid is the identifier of an anchor, dir is a direction (FROM, TO, BIDIRECT, or NONE), and pres is a presentation specification.

A concept relationship is a component, with two additional attributes:

- A sequence of specifiers;
- A concept relationship type.

The most common type of concept relationship is the type link. This corresponds to the link components in the Dexter model, or links in most hypermedia systems. However, in AHAM we consider other types of relationships as well, which play a role in the adaptation. A common type of concept relationship is prerequisite.

When a concept C_1 is a prerequisite for C_2 it means that the user should read C_1 before C_2. It does not mean that there must be a link from C_1 to C_2. It only means that the system somehow takes into account that reading about C_2 is not desired before some (enough) knowledge about C_1 has been acquired. A small set of (only binary) relationships, both prerequisites and links.

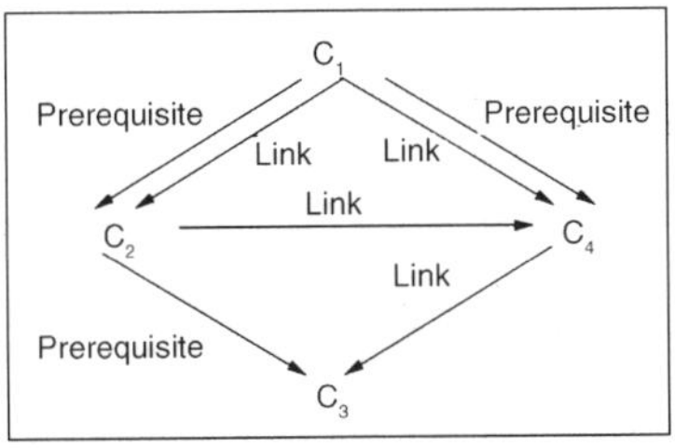

Fig. Example Concept Relationship Structure.

The atomic concepts, composite concepts and concept relationships together form the *domain model* DM of an adaptive hypermedia application. An AHS associates a number of (system or author defined) *user-model attributes* with each concept component of DM. For each user the AHS maintains a *table* in which for each concept the attribute values for that concept are stored. The structure of this table is the *user model scheme.*

The table for a specific user is a *user model instance*. If there is no confusion between scheme and instance we just use the term *user model*. One of the attributes of the user model is the concept's unique identifier. Apart from the concept's identifier (which may be just a name) a typical AHS will store a *knowledge value* for each concept, and possibly also a *read* value which indicates whether (and how much) information about the concept has been read by the user. While the model uses a table representation, implementations of AHS may use different data structures, for instance a logfile for the *read* attributes. The table illustrates the (conceptual) structure of a user model, for a course on hypermedia. (In the example table the concepts Xanadu and KMS were at least partially learnt.

The concept WWW, consisting of two sub-parts, is partially learnt because WWW-page1 has been read but WWW-page2 has not. One can see that WWW must be a composite concept which is not a page because it is already partially learnt while it has not been read at all.)

concept name (uid)	knowledge value	read	...
Xanadu	well learned	true	...
KMS	learned	true	...
WWW-page1	well learned	true	...
WWW-page2	not known	false	...
WWW	learned	false	...
...	...	...	...

A *generic pedagogical rule* is a tuple (R, PH, PR), where R is a "triggered" rule, PH is the "phase" for the execution of the rule and PR is a Boolean "propagate" field which indicates whether this rule may trigger other rules. The "phase" of a rule can have the value pre or post.

The phase pre is executed before and during the generation of the page, while post is executed afterwards. The syntax of the permissible rules depends on the AHS. A *specific pedagogical rule* is a tuple (R, SC, PH, PR) where (in addition to a generic rule) SC is a set of concepts used in the rule. The rule uses and sets user-model attributes and "predicates" over the specific concepts of SC. An AHS may have predefined or implicit generic pedagogical rules. If these rules suffice there is no need for a language in which authors can write new rules.

Author defined rules take precedence over predefined rules. Specific rules take precedence over generic rules, and are thus used to define exceptions to generic rules. The existence of the two execution phases makes it possible to do adaptation based on the "previous" state of the user model, and to update the user model to a "new" state afterwards.

A typical standard pedagogical rule for the pre phase is the rule that says that a link anchor will be *hidden* (or annotated as undesirable) if some prerequisite knowledge for the destination of the link is still not known. A typical standard rule for the post phase is the rule that says that a page-concept becomes *well learned* when the page is accessed and all prerequisite knowledge was present, and it becomes only *learned* when the page is accessed but some prerequisite knowledge was still not acquired. The *teaching model* of an AHS is the set of (generic and specific) pedagogical rules.

An adaptive engine is a software environment that performs the following functions:

- It offers generic page constructors. For each page the author selects a constructor to use for building the adaptive presentation of the page.
- It optionally offers a (very simple programming) language for describing new page constructors.
- It performs adaptation by executing the page constructors. This means selecting fragments, sorting them, maybe presenting them in a specific way, etc. It also means performing adaptation to links by manipulating link anchors depending on the state of the link (like enabled, disabled, hidden, etc.).
- It updates the user model (instance) each time the user visits a page. It does so by triggering the necessary pedagogical rules. The engine will thus set the knowledge value for each atomic concept of displayed fragments of the page to a value which depends on a configurable amount (this could be 1 by default but possibly overridden by the author). It also maintains a log of visited (concepts associated with) pages.

The adaptive engine thus provides the implementation dependent aspects while DM, UM and TM describe the information and adaptation at the conceptual level.

An *adaptive hypermedia application* is a 4-tuple (DM, UM, TM, AE), where DM is a domain model. UM is a user model, TM is a teaching model, and AE is an adaptive engine.

DEFINITION OF THE HYPERTEXT

"Information is linked and cross-referenced in many different ways and is widely available to end users".

"Hypertext means a database in which information (text) has been organised nonlinearly. The database consists of nodes and links between nodes".

Vannever Bush's article "As We May Think": There should be a tool that would enhance human memory and thinking and that allows people to retrieve information from a computer in many of the same ways in which retrieval is accomplished within human memory.

A Hypermedia Timeline

Ted Nelson: Xanadu is Ted Nelson's dream since early '60s: all the world literature in one publicly accessible global online system (analogy: you can today get a telephone link from anywhere to anywhere, so why not from any text to any other?). Every reference to a text will lead to royalties being paid automatically to the author. Includes the use of full versioning (claimed to be horrifyingly complex), "hot links" (called transclusions) and zippered texts (*e.g.* parallel texts like for translations or annotations.). A few of ideas in Xanadu are now implemented in WWW. Dough Englebart: Can be called as The father of the Hypertext. He invented f.ex. mouse and touch screens. He is also creator of one of the first hypermedia systems NLS/Augment.

Definitions of Concepts

A link is defined by source and destination nodes, and by an anchor in the source node. The destination of a link can be a file (so-called string-to-lexia link) or a string in a file (string-to-string link). With a string-to-lexia link it is not possible to reference to a certain part of a file. This kind of link can make hypermedia easily navigable, especially if the destination nodes are "short" documents. String-to-string links would permit the destination to be a string in a file, but this kind of link requires more planning in the design process. String-to-lexia links also support implicit linking. Implicit links are generated by the hypermedia software on runtime, for example referential links from a concept to the definition of the concept. To some extent hypermedia software should generate links from the fluctuated forms of concepts (a link from word "matrix" and "matrices"). In contrast to implicit links, explicit links are generated by the hypermedia author. The nodes and links form a network structure in the database. Hypermedia is a database which contains pictures, digitised videos, sound and animations in addition to text.

DOCUMENT MARKUP LANGUAGES

Why we need a document markup? Bryan defines markup as: "Markup is the term used to describe codes added to electronically prepared text to define the structure of the text or the format in which it is to appear." There can be two types of markups: specific markup and generalized markup. Specific markup describes the format of the document whereas generalized markup describes the structure of the.document (headings, citations etc.). For example, Rich Text Format (RTF) is a specific markup language and TeX, LaTeX, SGML and HTML are general markup languages.

Standard Generalized Markup Language (SGML)

SGML is an international stardard (ISO 8879) for document markup. An SGML document contains a document type definition (DTD) and a set of elements, that are defined in DTD. Each element has a name and it can be used as a tag in SGML document.

HyperText Markup Language (HTML)

HTML is a SGML based markup language for WWW documents. HTML is actually a DTD, a set of definitions of how to interpret HTML tags.

HyTime

HyTime is an international standard for hypermedia documents. It is based on SGML, but it can reference to a data in almost any format. Only the hypertext link information is required to be in SGML format.

TeX and LaTeX

TeX and LaTeX are also general markup languages in the sense that we only describe document structures with LaTeX macros. The definition of the macros can be later changed and the document could be formatted differently.

There is a HyperTeX that has limited hypertext capability by implementing/special keyword so that is supports for example URL's. DVI viewer is then used to display ps files containing URL's. DVI viewer could call WWW browser to follow the URL.

Rich Text Format (RTF)

The difference between SGML and RTF is that SGML describes the structure of a document, whereas RTF describes mainly the physical characteristics of the text (text face, size, etc). However, RTF includes also certain tags that describe document structure. The author can define a set of styles for the document (heading 1, heading 3, abstract, etc.) that are written into the beginning of the RTF file and have a special tag in the RTF markup. An RTF file contains all text formatting, pictures and formulas and it is a standard defined by Microsoft.

OpenMath

OpenMath consortium is an international group of researchers designing a protocol for exchanging mathematical information between applications. For example, a general purpose computer algebra system could call a specific purpose application to execute an algorithm implemented only in this application. OpenMath tries to preserve semantic information in addition to the structural information of the formula. For example, TeX describes only the visual appearance of a formula, not the semantic structure of the formula. Similar visual representation of mathematical formulas has been planned to SGML. MathLink is communications protocol for exchanging Mathematical expressions and data between Mathematical and external applications. The difference between MathLink and OpenMath is that MathLink does not define the semantical information of a formula.

8

Computer Science Education

INTRODUCTION TO COMPUTER

A computer is a machine that manipulates data according to a list of instructions. Although mechanical examples of computers have existed throughout history, the first resembling a modern computer were developed in the mid-20th century (1940–1945). The first electronic computers were the size of a large room, consuming as much power as several hundred modern personal computers (PC).

Modern computers based on tiny integrated circuits are millions to billions of times more capable than the early machines, and occupy a fraction of the space. Simple computers are small enough to fit into a wristwatch, and can be powered by a watch battery. Personal computers in their various forms are icons of the Information Age, what most people think of as a "computer", but the embedded computers found in devices ranging from fighter aircraft to industrial robots, digital cameras, and toys are the most numerous. The ability to store and execute lists of instructions called programmes makes computers extremely versatile, distinguishing them from calculators.

The Church–Turing thesis is a mathematical statement of this versatility: any computer with a certain minimum capability is, in principle, capable of performing the same tasks that any other computer can perform. Therefore computers ranging from a personal digital assistant to a supercomputer are all able to perform the same computational tasks, given enough time and storage capacity.

DEFINITION

A computer is a device that accepts information (in the form of digitalized data) and manipulates it for some result based on a programme or sequence of instructions on how the data is to be processed. Complex computers also include the means for storing data (including the programme, which is also a form of data) for some necessary duration. A programme may be invariable and built into the computer (and called *logic circuitry* as it is on microprocessors) or different programmes may be provided to the computer (loaded into its storage and then started by an administrator or user). Today's computers have both kinds of programming.

Most histories of the modern computer begin with the Analytical Engine envisioned by Charles Babbage following the mathematical ideas of George Boole, the mathematician who first stated the principles of logic inherent in today's digital computer. Babbage's assistant and collaborator, Ada Lovelace, is said to have introduced the ideas of programme loops and subroutines and is sometimes considered the first programmer.

Apart from mechanical calculators, the first really useable computers began with the vacuum tube, accelerated with the invention of the transistor, which then became embedded in large numbers in integrated circuits, ultimately making possible the relatively low-cost personal computer. Modern computers inherently follow the ideas of the stored programme laid out by John von Neumann in 1945. Essentially, the programme is read by the computer one instruction at a time, an operation is performed, and the computer then reads in the next instruction, and so on.

Recently, computers and programmes have been devised that allow multiple programmes (and computers) to work on the same problem at the same time in parallel. With the advent of the Internet and higher bandwidth data transmission, programmes and data that are part of the same overall project can be distributed over a network and embody the Sun Microsystems slogan: "The network is the computer."

MAIN UNITS

Central Processing Unit

A central processing unit (CPU) or processor is an electronic circuit that can execute computer programmes. This broad definition can easily be applied to many early computers that existed long before the term "CPU" ever came into widespread usage. The term itself and its initialism have been in use in the computer industry at least since the early 1960s (Weik 1961). The form, design and implementation of CPUs have changed dramatically since the earliest examples, but their fundamental operation has remained much the same. Early CPUs were custom-designed as a part of a larger, sometimes one-of-a-kind, computer.

However, this costly method of designing custom CPUs for a particular application has largely given way to the development of mass-produced processors that are made for one or many purposes. This standardization trend generally began in the era of discrete transistor mainframes and minicomputers and has rapidly accelerated with the popularization of the integrated circuit (IC). The IC has allowed increasingly complex CPUs to be designed and manufactured to tolerances on the order of nanometers. Both the miniaturization and standardization of CPUs have increased the presence of these digital devices in modern life far beyond the limited application of dedicated computing machines. Modern microprocessors appear in everything from automobiles to cell phones to children's toys.

History of CPU

Prior to the advent of machines that resemble today's CPUs, computers such as the ENIAC had to be physically rewired in order to perform different tasks. These machines are often referred to as "fixed-programme computers," since they had to be physically reconfigured in order to run a different programme. Since the term "CPU" is generally defined as a software (computer programme) execution device, the earliest devices that could rightly be called CPUs came with the advent of the stored-programme computer.

The idea of a stored-programme computer was already present during ENIAC's design, but was initially omitted so the machine could be finished sooner. On June 30, 1945, before ENIAC was even completed, mathematician John von Neumann distributed the paper entitled "First Draft of a Report on the EDVAC." It outlined the design of a stored-programme computer that would eventually be completed in August 1949 (von Neumann 1945). EDVAC was designed to perform a certain number of instructions (or operations) of various types. These instructions could be combined to create useful programmes for the EDVAC to run. Significantly, the programmes written for EDVAC were stored in high-speed computer memory rather than specified by the physical wiring of the computer. This overcame a severe limitation of ENIAC, which was the large amount of time and effort it took to reconfigure the computer to perform a new task. With von Neumann's design, the programme, or software, that EDVAC ran could be changed simply by changing the contents of the computer's memory.

While von Neumann is most often credited with the design of the stored-programme computer because of his design of EDVAC, others before him such as Konrad Zuse had suggested similar ideas. Additionally, the so-called Harvard architecture of the Harvard Mark I, which was completed before EDVAC, also utilized a stored-programme design using punched paper tape rather than electronic memory. The key difference between the von Neumann and Harvard architectures is that the latter separates the storage and treatment of CPU instructions and data, while the former uses the same memory space for both. Most modern CPUs are primarily von Neumann in design, but elements of the Harvard architecture are commonly seen as well.

Being digital devices, all CPUs deal with discrete states and therefore require some kind of switching elements to differentiate between and change these states. Prior to commercial acceptance of the transistor, electrical relays and vacuum tubes (thermionic valves) were commonly used as switching elements. Although these had distinct speed advantages over earlier, purely mechanical designs, they were unreliable for various reasons.

For example, building direct current sequential logic circuits out of relays requires additional hardware to cope with the problem of contact bounce. While vacuum tubes do not suffer from contact bounce, they must heat up before becoming fully operational and eventually stop functioning altogether. Usually, when a tube failed, the CPU would have to be diagnosed to locate the failing component so it could be replaced. Therefore, early electronic (vacuum tube based) computers were generally faster but less reliable than electromechanical (relay based) computers.

Tube computers like EDVAC tended to average eight hours between failures, whereas relay computers like the (slower, but earlier) Harvard Mark I failed very rarely (Weik 1961:238). In the end, tube based CPUs became dominant because the significant speed advantages afforded generally outweighed the reliability problems. Most of these early synchronous CPUs ran at low clock rates compared to modern microelectronic designs (see below for a discussion of clock rate). Clock signal frequencies ranging from 100 kHz to 4 MHz were very common at this time, limited largely by the speed of the switching devices they were built with.

Discrete Transistor and IC CPUs

The design complexity of CPUs increased as various technologies facilitated building smaller and more reliable electronic devices. The first such improvement came with the advent of the transistor. Transistorized CPUs during the 1950s and 1960s no longer had to be built out of bulky, unreliable, and fragile switching elements like vacuum tubes and electrical relays. With this improvement more complex and reliable CPUs were built onto one or several printed circuit boards containing discrete (individual) components.

During this period, a method of manufacturing many transistors in a compact space gained popularity. The integrated circuit (IC) allowed a large number of transistors to be manufactured on a single semiconductor-based die, or "chip." At first only very basic non-specialized digital circuits such as NOR gates were miniaturized into ICs. CPUs based upon these "building block" ICs are generally referred to as "small-scale integration" (SSI) devices.

SSI ICs, such as the ones used in the Apollo guidance computer, usually contained transistor counts numbering in multiples of ten. To build an entire CPU out of SSI ICs required thousands of individual chips, but still consumed much less space and power than earlier discrete transistor designs. As microelectronic technology advanced, an increasing number of transistors were placed on ICs, thus decreasing the quantity of individual ICs needed for a complete CPU. MSI and LSI (medium- and large-scale integration) ICs increased transistor counts to hundreds, and then thousands. In 1964 IBM introduced its System/360 computer architecture which was used in a series of computers that could run the same programmes with different speed and performance. This was significant at a time when most electronic computers were incompatible with one another, even those made by the same manufacturer. To facilitate this improvement, IBM utilized the concept of a microprogram (often called "microcode"), which still sees widespread usage in modern CPUs (Amdahl *et al.* 1964). The System/360 architecture was so popular that it dominated the mainframe computer market for the decades and left a legacy that is still continued by similar modern computers like the IBM zSeries. In the same year (1964), Digital Equipment Corporation (DEC) introduced another influential computer aimed at the scientific and research markets, the PDP-8.

DEC would later introduce the extremely popular PDP-11 line that originally was built with SSI ICs but was eventually implemented with LSI components once these became practical. In stark contrast with its SSI and MSI predecessors, the first LSI implementation of the PDP-11 contained a CPU composed of only four LSI integrated circuits (Digital Equipment Corporation 1975).

Transistor-based computers had several distinct advantages over their predecessors. Aside from facilitating increased reliability and lower power consumption, transistors also allowed CPUs to operate at much higher speeds because of the short switching time of a transistor in comparison to a tube or relay. Thanks to both the increased reliability as well as the dramatically increased speed of the switching elements (which were almost exclusively transistors by this time), CPU clock rates in the tens of megahertz were obtained during this period. Additionally while discrete transistor and IC CPUs were in heavy usage, new high-performance designs like SIMD (Single Instruction Multiple Data) vector processors began to appear. These early experimental designs later gave rise to the era of specialized supercomputers like those made by Cray Inc.

Microprocessors

The introduction of the microprocessor in the 1970s significantly affected the design and implementation of CPUs. Since the introduction of the first microprocessor (the Intel 4004) in 1970 and the first widely used microprocessor (the Intel 8080) in 1974, this class of CPUs has almost completely overtaken all other central processing unit implementation methods. Mainframe and minicomputer manufacturers of the time launched proprietary IC development programmes to upgrade their older computer architectures, and eventually produced instruction set compatible microprocessors that were backward-compatible with their older hardware and software. Combined with the advent and eventual vast success of the now ubiquitous personal computer, the term "CPU" is now applied almost exclusively to microprocessors. Previous generations of CPUs were implemented as discrete components and numerous small integrated circuits (ICs) on one or more circuit boards. Microprocessors, on the other hand, are CPUs manufactured on a very small number of ICs; usually just one. The overall smaller CPU size as a result of being implemented on a single die means faster switching time because of physical factors like decreased gate parasitic capacitance. This has allowed synchronous microprocessors to have clock rates ranging from tens of megahertz to several gigahertz. Additionally, as the ability to construct exceedingly small transistors on an IC has increased, the complexity and number of transistors in a single CPU has increased dramatically. This widely observed trend is described by Moore's law, which has proven to be a fairly accurate predictor of the growth of CPU (and other IC) complexity to date.

While the complexity, size, construction, and general form of CPUs have changed drastically over the past sixty years, it is notable that the basic design and function has not changed much at all. Almost all common CPUs today can be very accurately described as von Neumann stored-programme machines. As the aforementioned Moore's law continues to hold true, concerns have arisen about the limits of integrated circuit transistor technology. Extreme miniaturization of electronic gates is causing the effects of phenomena like electromigration and subthreshold leakage to become much more significant. These newer concerns are among the many factors causing researchers to investigate new methods of computing such as the quantum computer, as well as to expand the usage of parallelism and other methods that extend the usefulness of the classical von Neumann model.

CPU Operation

The fundamental operation of most CPUs, regardless of the physical form they take, is to execute a sequence of stored instructions called a programme. The programme is represented by a series of numbers that are kept in some kind of computer memory. There are four steps that nearly all CPUs use in their operation: fetch, decode, execute, and writeback.

The first step, fetch, involves retrieving an instruction (which is represented by a number or sequence of numbers) from programme memory. The location in programme memory is determined by a programme counter (PC), which stores a number that identifies the current position in the programme. In other words, the programme counter keeps track of the CPU's place in the current programme. After an instruction is fetched, the PC is incremented by the length of the instruction word in terms of memory units. Often the instruction to be fetched must be retrieved from relatively slow memory, causing the CPU to stall while waiting for the instruction to be returned. This issue is largely addressed in modern processors by caches and pipeline architectures.

The instruction that the CPU fetches from memory is used to determine what the CPU is to do. In the decode step, the instruction is broken up into parts that have significance to other portions of the CPU. The way in which the numerical instruction value is interpreted is defined by the CPU's instruction set architecture (ISA). Often, one group of numbers in the instruction, called the opcode, indicates which operation to perform.

The remaining parts of the number usually provide information required for that instruction, such as operands for an addition operation. Such operands may be given as a constant value (called an immediate value), or as a place to locate a value: a register or a memory address, as determined by some addressing mode. In older designs the portions of the CPU responsible for instruction decoding were unchangeable hardware devices. However, in more abstract and complicated CPUs and ISAs, a microprogram is often used to assist in translating instructions into various configuration signals for the CPU. This microprogram is sometimes rewritable so that it can be modified to change the way the CPU decodes instructions even after it has been manufactured.

After the fetch and decode steps, the execute step is performed. During this step, various portions of the CPU are connected so they can perform the desired operation. If, for instance, an addition operation was requested, an arithmetic logic unit (ALU) will be connected to a set of inputs and a set of outputs. The inputs provide the numbers to be added, and the outputs will contain the final sum. The ALU contains the circuitry to perform simple arithmetic and logical operations on the inputs (like addition and bitwise operations). If the addition operation produces a result too large for the CPU to handle, an arithmetic overflow flag in a flags register may also be set. The final step, writeback, simply "writes back" the results of the execute step to some form of memory.

Very often the results are written to some internal CPU register for quick access by subsequent instructions. In other cases results may be written to slower, but cheaper and larger, main memory. Some types of instructions manipulate the programme counter rather than directly produce result data. These are generally called "jumps" and facilitate behavior like loops, conditional programme execution (through the use of a conditional jump), and functions in programmes. Many instructions will also change the state of digits in a "flags" register. These flags can be used to influence how a programme behaves, since they often indicate the outcome of various operations.

For example, one type of "compare" instruction considers two values and sets a number in the flags register according to which one is greater. This flag could then be used by a later jump instruction to determine programme flow. After the execution of the instruction and writeback of the resulting data, the entire process repeats, with the next instruction cycle normally fetching the next-in-sequence instruction because of the incremented value in the programme counter. If the completed instruction was a jump, the programme counter will be modified to contain the address of the instruction that was jumped to, and programme execution continues normally. In more complex CPUs than the one described here, multiple instructions can be fetched, decoded, and executed simultaneously. This section describes what is generally referred to as the "Classic RISC pipeline," which in fact is quite common among the simple CPUs used in many electronic devices (often called microcontroller). It largely ignores the important role of CPU cache, and therefore the access stage of the pipeline.

IMPORTANCE OF THE COMPUTER SCIENCES

Study of Computer Sciences has been given due place in our school education programme by being made as a compulsory subject. Not only that more and more emphasis is now being paid over the scientific and technical education. By doing so infect a right step has been taken to push our country forward and to enable us to complete with other progressive nations. It has necessitated top to lay due emphasis on the Computer Science Education & Teaching right from the primary stage. Realizing such need Kothari Communizing has very rightly remarked in their recommendations as follows:

"Science and Mathematics should be taught on compulsory basis of all pupils as a part of general education during the first ten years of schooling".

PLACE IN THE SCHOOL CURRICULUM

The question here may arise that why the subject science including Computer Science has been given so much weight as to be taught compulsorily during the ten years of one's school life. The answer may be satisfactorily discovered in its various uses, applications and advantages in the following pages.

UTILITARIAN VALUE OF DAY-TO-DAY USE

Modern age is science age. We see a network of scientific gadgets based on latest scientific inventions all around us in the field of Computer Science. There was a time in olden age when we used to burn an earth ware oil lamp for light but today, we have electrical bulbs, tube lights illuminating as bright as sun. Olden ways of transport on horses and camels have given way to electric trains, cars and aeroplanes.

We have newspapers, radios televisions, cinemas applications in their places. On looking at the Moon, we used to wonder what that old woman is doing with that spinning wheel. Today man has reached the moon, stepped on it and is busy in exploring it for further details. There is a miraculous change labour saving gadgets and machines. They have made all our complicated work not only easy but also these are done much faster. Science has revolutionized our way of living. Now our lives depend on scientifically invented gadgets so much that we cannot do without them. It is now imperative for everyone not only to understand science but also to master it from all angles Herbert Spencer has rightly said, "The knowledge gained through science is much useful in guiding our life style than gained through other sources".

INTELLECTUAL VALUE

The study of Computer Science provides us the opportunity of developing our mental faculties of reasoning, imagination, memory, observation, concentration, analysis, and originality and of systematic thinking. Science gives us the insight, which enables us to search the truth and the reality of nature around us. We are able to do useful except anything which we cannot prove by actual observation, reasoning and experimentations. The queries like 'why' and 'how' of all problems and phenomena can be satisfactorily answered only by the wisdom of science. A mature scientist can solve all problems with his shape intelligence and wisdom.

DISCIPLINARY VALUE

Study of Computer Sciences develops our personality as a whole. It inculcate spirit of enquiry, seriousness and systematic thinking. It brings about total transformation of one's viewpoint and makes thought process more organized. These sciences make us think seriously and help to observe the real nature of the problem. It helps us to judge all the good and bad points together, with the gain and loss likely to be incurred in the plan of action contemplated.

These sciences also check one to take a hasty action prompted by one's sentiments and influenced by the biased opinions of others, which are against the principles of science. Study of Computer Sciences promotes interest in study, concentration on habit of hard and systematic work. It also inculcates the habit of viewing a problem impartially with an alert mind. This helps to lead one's daily life successfully in well-organized and systematic way.

CULTURAL VALUE

Before we discuss the cultural value of Computer Sciences let us try to understand what is culture. According to the great Indian poet Dinkar, "Culture is the way of life which has been handed over to society from one generation to another in the form of accumulated customs, habits and mode of living. The mode and style of living is different from one society to another and therefore their culture is also not the same". According to the above definition of culture, our activities like way of life, our food, customs, our views, our art and craft, scientific interests, social and economic conditions, all determine our standard of life. From time immemorial man has been trying to maintain and preserve their way of life and standard through the use of science. But somehow our way of life has been changing with the passage of time and progress of science. This change in our life-style is due to the inventions of computer science. The development of culture is the history of science.

We can judge the progress of civilization and culture of a nation by its progress in science. Therefore study of Computer Sciences not only develops our culture but also helps in preserving it. We are constantly adjusting and modifying our style of living according to the latest scientific inventions and discoveries. Thus study of Computer Sciences develop culture of a society and nation.

AESTHETIC VALUE

Science is beauty, art, a source of entertainment and a successful means of attaining physical comforts. Can you imagine the joy and bliss of Graham Bell inventor of 'telephone', when his word were clearly heard on the other side by Watson? The words were, "Watson, come here, I want you". When Watson heard these words, he rushed to the room of Graham Bell shouting," "I have clearly heard your message."

The joy and satisfaction they got from their successful invention was similar to the joy got by Archimedes from his discovery that he became totally oblivious of his naked body while coming out of the public bath and ran on the streets shouting, "Eureka, Eureka". One gets extreme joy on one's successful discovery or invention. Even the study of science is a source of great pleasure when one gets answers to his questions about the mysteries of nature.

A child even experiences great joy when he gets answers to his queries like—'Where do stars and moon go away during the day time?" 'Why does a hydrogen gas filled balloon rise up like a ball? "How is light produced in the room on pressing a switch"? etc. The child's joy takes the fork of this interest in studying Computer Sciences. Man derives boundless bliss on the revelation of the mysteries of nature, and the mysteries of greatest 'Artist' and His art. Study of Computer Science help us to utilize our leisure purposefully. In addition to makes our lives happy by providing scientific gadgets for our entertainment in our spare time, cinema, television, radio, newspapers are gifts of Computer Sciences for our entertainment.

Scientific hobbies can well be a source of joy in our leisure time. The useful and gainful hobbies related to Computer Sciences like photography, construction of scientific toys, manufacturing tooth paste, varnishes, inks etc. are not only interesting but are also financially useful.

MORAL VALUE

Some people believe that Science is responsible for lack of faith in God, but in reality the situation is reverse. No doubt that science does not permit blind faith. It also does not admit faith in idol worship nor follows many useless customs and rituals. The pursuit of knowledge of nature of study of science cannot be called contrary to religion and faithlessness. Therefore the study of Computer Sciences and its pursuit not only include all the traits of morality but also develop them.

The qualities of honesty of purpose, truth, justice, punctuality, determination, patience, self-control, self-respect, self-confidence and tolerance are automatically developed in man if he follows scientific methods in his pursuit of knowledge. The habit of lawfulness, the faculty of distinction between right and wrong and respect for other's point of view are some other desirable traits of character developed through the study of Computer Sciences.

The person busy in pursuit of truth and reality imbibes in himself the qualities of morality. In Computer Sciences there is nor place for self-opinionated person and his sentiments or democracies. Here every conclusion depends upon tests and actual observations and not by cheat and deceit. The ideal of "Truth is beauty" is always kept in view.

SOCIAL VALUE

Study of Computer Sciences provides great impetus and opportunities for the development and progress of the society as well as useful experiences of the society as well as useful experiences of the inculcation of social values and virtues in the students. It helps the students to know the material and objects surrounded in their physical and social environment. Hamessing the forces of nature for the welfare and progress of the society is the every essence of any invention and development put forward in the subject Computer Sciences.

Due to the all round progress and development put forward by the study of Computer Sciences the World Society has become now a global society. What we do in our present society is totally dependent upon the progress and development brought out by the study of Computer Sciences. It has given eyes to the society in the form of telescopes, microscopes, cameras and televisions, transport in the shape of fast electric trains and a variety of transport vehicles and wings in the form of supersonic Jets and rockets. The globalization and proximity brought out by the progress in Computer Sciences has necessitated developing social, democratic and humanistic values in the individuals for the welfare and their own adjustment in the society as well as for the broader cause of a globalize society.

TRAINING IN PROBLEM SOLVING ABILITY

Students of Computer Sciences get enough opportunities for being trained in the use of scientific method and scientific approach for the solution of the problems. In general, as we know, the following thought process is involved in solving a problem through scientific method in Computer Sciences.

1. The nature and purpose of the problem.
2. Analysis of the problem.
3. Testing the validity of the various solutions of the problem.
4. Testing of the results through applications in other problems of similar nature.

Acceptance of the result thus obtained as scientific principle and law for the future use. The above thought processes and methods are also needed in solving all problems of daily life. First we try to understand the nature of the problem. Then after thinking of various solutions, we test them and finally accept one solution after examining its validity and correctness. As a result one gets desirable training in problem solving ability through the study of Computer Sciences.

The values and benefits so derived with the study of Computer Sciences in the school classes are thus very much responsible for making its study compulsory in all the ten years of schooling in our country. Utility of a subject in one's personal and social life is enough to justify its place in school curriculum. The study of Computer Sciences, whether we consider it from personal or social angle, has a quite unique importance in our own as well as in life of the nation. Therefore, the decision of providing a compulsory status for the study of sciences in corporation Computer Science is quite justified and valid.

VOCATIONAL VALUE

Study of Computer Science is helpful in opening vast vista of useful professions and vocations for being adopted in the future life. The most pestigious professions and vocations, related to engineering, computer technology, physical and chemical analysis of objects and environmental surrounding, physical and chemical inventions related to progress and development of the society etc. are keenly attached and dependent upon the study of Computer Sciences.

The key of entering into a wide number of useful professions and vocations in our modern society (the list of which we have already given in chapter first of this text under the title "Professions in the area of Computer Sciences"). Very well lies in the study of Computer Sciences. In this way, we can safely claim that study of Computer Sciences have a great "bread and butter value" enabling or preparing the would be citizens for earning their livelihood in their future life.

GLOBALIZATION AND COMPUTER SCIENCES

The term globalization derived from the words 'globe' and 'signifies' the removal of barriers of distances or of other nature for bringing people of the world together in terms of their relationships of events. For the understanding of its meaning let us think over on a few definitions given below:

1. The sociologist, Anthony Giddens, defines globalization as a decoupling of space and time, emphasizing that with instantaneous communi-cations, knowledge and culture can be shared around the world simultaneously.
2. The Dutch academician Rudd Lubbess defines it as process in which geographical distances become of diminishing importance in the establishment and maintenance of cross economic, political and socio-cultural relations.
3. David Held and Anthony McGrew say that globaliza-tion can be conceived as a process (or set of processes) which embodies a transformation in the spatial organization of social relations and transactions, expressed in trans-continental or inter-regional flows and network of activity, interaction, and power.

These definitions point out the following things about the meaning and nature of the term globalization:

1. Globalization in the result of a rapid and efficient system of communication network. It aims towards the sharing of knowledge and culture among the people and communities of the world.
2. Globalization makes possible nearness between the individual and organization of the world community belonging to different regions, countries or continents in terms of their social relationships, interactions and sharing of comforts and power.

In the light of the above meaning and characteristics, the term globalization may be defined as the process of interlinking the individuals and organizations of the world community economically, politically and socio-culturally by barriers of the space and time.

ROLE OF COMPUTER SCIENCE IN THE PROCESS OF GLOBALIZATION

The global society or globalization is something, which is an accepted reality of the modern age. The development of science and technology especially related to the field of Computer Sciences is responsible to a great extent for accelerating the process of globalization.

A few of such inventions and discoveries related to the subject of Computer Science may be named as below:

- Development of printing material and communi-cation through written verbal material.

- Development of transport system with the discoveries and inventions related to travel on land surface, air, sea and space.
- Development of communication network with the inventions and discoveries like telephone, wireless, telegraph, teleprompter, radio, television, video, camera, photography still and movie pictures, satellite communication, mobile telephony, tele-conferencing, video conferencing etc.
- Development of modern sophisticated communi-cation system with the help of computer technology, internet access facilitating, e-mail and audio-visual transmission through web camera and web sites coupled with audio listening and speaking devices.
- The great invention and discoveries mentioned as above in the field of transport and communication services brought out by Computer Sciences have helped in the process of globalization in the ways narrated as below:
  (i) Travelling from one corner of the globe to the other has become too convenient and less time consuming. It has provided needed mobility to the individuals or group as a whole for the interaction with the rest of the world.
  (ii) It is quite easy and speedy as well as to transport commodities from one corner of the globe to the other. That is why, it is no wonder to get benefit of the productions of the commodities grown or manufactured in one part of the globe to the other parts in no time with a reduced cost and labour.
  (iii) We can be in touch with the individuals, organi-zations and events belonging to the farthest corners of the globe with the help of the much development means and tools of communication. The distance has to barriers at all for any type of communication—audio as well as visual.

The facilities available as above in terms of removing barriers of distances have invariably brought together the individuals, groups and nations of the world in the form of a single knitted unit truly in the spirit of "Basudheve Kutumbkam" i.e. "the whole world is my family". As a result the people of the world have a close interaction, inter-dependence and inter-relationship with each other irrespective of their living and working distances.

What happens with an individual, community, region or a country now affects in one way or the other the rest of the world. Poverty of a region is now the concern of the other events and political turmoil. As a result you may find that terrorism has become global, trafficking in drugs or human beings has become global, sexually transmitted and also other types of viral and infectious diseases have become global. One the other hand we now have a tremendous increase in the speed or globalization at the economic as well as socio-cultural exchange fronts. It has resulted in the process of denationalization of market, politics and legal systems for paving the way of the so-called global economy. The emergence of the phenomenon of global trade and commerce has now provided enormous opportunities for an organization or company belonging to a particular part of the global to establish itself in the foreign market. It is easy for her now to adopt first her product or services to the final users linguistic and cultural requirements and then take advantages of the internet revolution for establishing a virtual presence on the international market place with a multilingual corporate website or even resorting to an electronic business, trade and commerce according to the mutual convenience of the business/trade partners. In this way globalization has resulted in intertwining the fates of the individuals, community and nations of the world and this dream has become true only on account of the services provided by the numerous inventions and discoveries made in the field of Computer Sciences.

COMPUTER SCIENCE RESEARCH INSTITUTIONS

Three categories of institutions conduct CS research in India: the major teaching and research institutes devoted to science and technology, government-sponsored laboratories and industry-sponsored laboratories.

- *The Six Major Research and Teaching Institutes Devoted to Science and Technology:* These six institutes are the IITs (of which there are five, with one more coming up in Assam) and IISc, located in Bangalore. These institutions form a select group in the minds of the government as well as the citizens.

The next tier of institutions is made up primarily of the Regional Engineering Colleges (RECs), with one located in each state. Also, there are several other universities where computer science research is being conducted quietly. (One such is the University of Hyderabad; researchers here are very active in (collaborative) AI research, keeping close contacts with overseas colleagues.) But a considerable gap does exist between the six top tier institutions and the next because of high teaching load imposed on the faculty, students being, on average, of a lower quality, and finally poorer infrastructure, namely library and computing facilities.

- *Government-sponsored Institutions:* These institutions are funded by different government ministries and departments.

TIFR and the Institute for Mathematical Sciences (MatScience) perform research which is predominantly of a theoretical nature. These are funded by DAE. Defence-related work takes place in a number of labs around the country, many located in Bangalore and Hyderabad, both in Southern India. A good example is CAIR which can be described as a "think-tank" serving the AI and robotics needs of Indian Ministry of Defence. It is a component of the Defence Research and Development Organization (DRDO).

The Ministry of Planning funds ISI, with its primary location in Calcutta. (It is worth noting that the first indigenous digital computer—fabricated using discrete transistor units—was commissioned by ISI in 1966 in collaboration with Jadavpur University.)

NCST also carries out research in several areas of computer science besides having education and training among its functions. NCST is a successor of the erstwhile National Centre for Software Development and Computing Techniques (NCSDCT) which was a component of TIFR. The Indian Space Research Organization (ISRO), is also involved in computer science work, but most of its work is of an applied nature, in the context of satellites and launch vehicles. ISRO has been building satellites for remote sensing as well as for communication. Its most recent success involved the launch of the Polar Synchronous Launch Vehicle capable of launching 1000-Kg class satellites into sun-synchronous orbits.

National Aerospace Laboratories (NAL), Bhabha Atomic Research Centre (BARC), and Centre for the Development of Advanced Computation (CDAC) have had the development of parallel processing platforms for solving computational science problems as the main focus of their computer science research.

- *Industrial Labs:* Tata Research Development and Design Centre (TRDDC), supported by the Tata group of companies, and the SPIC science foundation (SSF), sponsored by SPIC, a petrochemical corporation, are good examples. While the latter is primarily involved in theoretical computer science research, TRDDC is geared up to "result-oriented research" to meet the needs of Tata Consultancy Services (TCS) and its clients, and more generally, the Tata group of companies. The uniqueness of TRDDC comes from its self-supporting R&D effort. Even though most of the projects are done for TCS, TRDDC also has funds from DST, MoD, and other government organizations.

In addition, there are several labs that are sponsored by many multinationals in India, such as Texas Instruments (which led the way, as early as in 1987), Motorola, and Oracle. But, at this point, these labs are mostly involved in developmental activities defined and subcontracted by their parent organizations.

STUDENTS AND FACULTY AT THE EDUCATIONAL INSTITUTIONS

US and Europe have a very high regard for graduate students trained at the IITs and in IISc. The reasons are easy to find. Admission to the Bachelors' programme (called B.Tech) at the IITs is through a fiercely competitive entrance examination called the Joint Entrance Examination (JEE). It is written by over 100,000 students every year, with less than 1500 selected—based purely on their ranking in the JEE. The curriculum at the IITs is on par with top institutions in developed countries. A laudable feature of the B.Tech programme is that during the final year, students are required to do a project, which in many instances are quite ambitious with students going on to publish their work in conferences and journals. All the academic research institutions have a Masters' programme (called M.Tech), students selected once again after a competitive examination called GATE, perhaps not quite as competitive as JEE. M.Tech's come (more often than not) from a non-IIT background and their preparedness in computer science is also considered to be lacking, but they make up for it through their hard work.

While some of the IITs require computer science background (for example, IIT Bombay does not admit students who are not among the top 7 per cent in computer science GATE), others do not. M.Tech's also do a project, but since the programme itself is only three semesters long and the project is done during the third, there is less time to execute a project of an involved nature. Also, if a student arrives with no computer science background, it does not allow him or her to do a substantial project.

Some institutions have a programme called Master of Science, which is purely research project oriented. The number in this category is quite small and not all academic institutions have an M.S. programme. As part of the Quality Improvement Programme (QIP), an effort to modernize the faculty at teaching institutions, faculty from smaller colleges and universities are encouraged to apply to do their Ph.Ds at IITs and other institutions. For instance, four of the computer science faculty at the Regional Engineering College (REC) in Trichy (out of just about a dozen) are currently doing their Ph.D.'s under this programme. Since most of the faculty at smaller educational institutions offering programmes in CS do not have Ph.Ds, the QIP is a worthy enterprise.

All graduate students are supported by the Ministry of Human Resource Development (MHRD) (even though there is a move, especially for Ph.D. students to be paid from research grants). If one enters the Ph.D. programme after a Bachelors' degree, assistantship is guaranteed for five years; for those joining after a Masters degree, four and a half years. Because of this and the fact that all faculty salaries are on a 12-month basis, there is very little compulsion for an academic researcher to seek external funding for his or her research, except perhaps to support travel and for books and equipment. IISc has the largest contingent of Ph.D. students, having produced 20 Ph.Ds during 94-95 with over 40 in the pipeline.

Each IIT has between 10 and 15 students pursuing their Ph.Ds., a number smaller on average compared to the recent past. I often heard the remark that the number of students interested in a Ph.D degree and of Ph.D. caliber has been decreasing. This does not augur well for the future of Indian computer science. It is hence important to understand the reasons for this trend. We will discuss some of these here. Faculty at the top educational institutions belong to three ranks, Assistant Professor, Associate Professor and Professor. The nomenclature varies in other institutions. While fresh Ph.Ds have joined as Assistant Professors in some of the institutions, most places insist on a few years' experience. Even though Assistant Professorship is tenured, the requirements to move into a higher rank are not very transparent. In fact, IITs don't appear to have the notion of promotions. If one desires a higher rank, he or she must respond to an advertisement for that rank. The lack of transparency as well as norms for such promotions causes, as a junior faculty put it, "the dilemma of whether to focus on 'local developmental work' or 'internationally publishable work'."

With the "graying" of the research-oriented academic institutions, there is a need to infuse fresh blood. But with very few retirements in the offing, the number of openings in established institutions is small. Even if one finds a position, a fresh Assistant Professor should be content with a take-home-pay that could be substantially less than the earnings of a fresh Master's student entering the private sector.

A large proportion of the well-trained IIT and IISc students go abroad, mainly to the US, for their further studies. So India does not reap the benefits of having trained them. Among the IIT students who stay in India after their B.Tech's, a sizable number opt for a career in management, and hence join the MBA programme in one of the four prestigious Indian Institutes of Management (IIM). As a result, the number of IIT students who pursue a career in science or engineering within India is dishearteningly small. Whereas in the pure sciences, the percentage of women in India (both among students and faculty) is much higher than in the US, in engineering disciplines, the situation is the opposite. Being associated with engineering, the computer science research roster in India has a very small number of women. To its credit, IIT Madras has two women faculty in the computer science department, with one serving as its current head. IISc and IIT Bombay have one each in their faculty.

Inbreeding, often associated with stagnation, is a common phenomenon at the top educational institutions, with the ratio—of those with a Ph.D. from the same institution—sometimes approaching one-half. Even though an institution tries not to hire one of its own immediately after his or her Ph.D., most have no hesitation if the person has spent a year or two elsewhere before returning to his or her Ph.D. institution.

Among the educational institutions, according to many computer science researchers around the country, IISc has a greater appreciation for research in pure sciences and this is true for computer science as well. Many of the IIT faculty I talked to feel that training and educating students is their foremost task, in contrast, for example, with IISc, ISI, and TIFR, where research is. There is also a general feeling that the IITs can do a better job if they set their performance thresholds higher. The directors of the IITs have a bigger say in setting the directions of their respective institutions than the heads of the above mentioned research-oriented institutions. Hence, any changes or redirections, giving more emphasis and recognition for research and thereby tapping the available research potential, awaits their directives and blessings.

IMPACT OF COMPUTER SCIENCES ON MODERN COMMUNITIES

Development and progress in the field of Computer Sciences has influenced the life and livings of the modern Communities and Society in so many ways like below:

CONSTRUCTION OF BUILDINGS AND RESIDENTIAL COLONIES

On Account of the availability of a variety of load bearable and non-load bearable material through the development in Computer Sciences, the modern communities look modern in terms of the construction of their buildings in the form of business centers, offices and residential colonies.

Transportation and Communication Systems

Development in Computer Sciences has been able to provide the latest available transportation and communi-cation systems to the modern communities. The distances are no more a barrier for the people living at the farthest distances of the globe.

Modernization of the Systems

The development in the Computer Sciences have modernized the sources of availability of food stuff in the shape of modernization of the method of farming, poultry farming, cattle beading, fisheries, bee keeping etc. It has resulted in multiplying the production of the food stuff as well as reducing the complexities or manual labour. The food stuff cannot be better preserved through the modern techniques available as a result of invention and discoveries in Computer Sciences. Development in Computer Sciences is helping the modern communities to take care of their water resources. It has provided artificial irrigation means as well as availability of drinking water with the construction of big water reservoirs, dams and sophisticated distribution system. It has provided big plants and simple household gadgets for the availability of pure drinking water to the modern communities. It has also provided means to have artificial rains and cultivation of water for providing additional sources of water to the modern communities.

Modern means for the entertainment and leisure time hobbies

Development in Computer Science has provided modern and methods for the entertainment and uplifting of leisure to the modern communities.

Radio, Television Video, Films and Computer services have taken a total command of providing entertainment and leisure time hobbies to the modern communities.

Health care and treatment of diseases

Development in Computer Sciences have helped much in taking care of the health including treatment of illness and diseases of the members of the modern communities. It has provided better knowledge and information for the prevention and care of the diseases as well maintenance of good physical and mental health through its wider network of information technology. The dreaded diseases are now no more so dreaded as happened to be in the past. With the vast discoveries and invention in the field of health and medical sciences as well as tremendous progress in chemical sciences. Modern communities can avail the latest treatment of the diseases and look after of their health.

Development of inter-relationship and dependence

Development of Computer Sciences are responsible for making the modern communities too much inter-related and inter-dependent. It has given birth to the phenomenon of globalization in every aspect—physical, mental, emotional social, cultural and ethical of the behaviour of teach and every person belonging to the modern communities of this globe. What happens to a community of the world, residing at any farthest corner of the world equally affects the working and behaviour of the other segment of the world communities. We will discuss in detail such globalization impact of Computer Sciences soon in this very chapter. With all what has been said above, we should not conclude the developments in Computer Sciences are always bound to cast positive and desirable impact well being and progress of the modern communities. If handled improperly and utilized destructively these can yield bitter and horrifying results. Such negative impact of the development Computer Sciences on modern communities may be summarized as below:

- Too much urbanization of the communities.
- Causing heavy pollution of every sort like air pollution, water pollution, noise pollution, cultural pollution etc.
- Inequitable distribution of wealth and other material comforts in the population.
- Abolishment of the concept and existence of the harming of health and welfare of the people.
- Development of the weapons of destruction and their unmindful application.
- Side effects of the fertilizers, chemicals, pesticides insecticides used in growing foodstuff and killing harmful bio-stuff.
- Neglect of moral values and social responsibilities at the cost of material development and individualism.

Index

I

L

M

O

P

R

S

T

V